History of Computing

The *History of Computing* series publishes high-quality books which address the history of computing, with an emphasis on the 'externalist' view of this history, more accessible to a wider audience. The series examines content and history from four main quadrants: the history of relevant technologies, the history of the core science, the history of relevant business and economic developments, and the history of computing as it pertains to social history and societal developments.

Titles can span a variety of product types, including but not exclusively, themed volumes, biographies, 'profile' books (with brief biographies of a number of key people), expansions of workshop proceedings, general readers, scholarly expositions, titles used as ancillary textbooks, revivals and new editions of previous worthy titles.

These books will appeal, varyingly, to academics and students in computer science, history, mathematics, business and technology studies. Some titles will also directly appeal to professionals and practitioners of different backgrounds.

More information about this series at http://www.springer.com/series/8442

Bernadette Longo

Words and Power

Computers, Language, and U.S. Cold War Values

 Springer

Bernadette Longo (iD)
New Jersey Institute of Technology
Newark, NJ, USA

'

ISSN 2190-6831   ISSN 2190-684X   (electronic)
History of Computing
ISBN 978-3-030-70375-2   ISBN 978-3-030-70373-8   (eBook)
https://doi.org/10.1007/978-3-030-70373-8

This Springer imprint is published by the registered company Springer Nature Switzerland AG
The registered company address is: Gewerbestrasse 11, 6330 Cham, Switzerland

Acknowledgment

When the idea for this book was first conceived in 2019, the word *pandemic* brought to mind images of Spanish flu patients in medical wards after World War I. Now I have been living in isolation for over 9 months because of the COVID-19 pandemic. Many of the plans I had for this book needed to be reconsidered because of travel bans, business closures, and health risks. Life has changed, but one constant has been the story that I wanted to tell in this book.

A number of people have been instrumental in bringing this story to completion: Peggy Kidwell at the National Museum of American History has supported my humanistic approach to technology studies for nearly two decades and continues to give me encouragement. I want to mention her 1998 article "Stalking the Elusive Computer Bug" in the *IEEE Annals of the History of Computing* as a kindred study of the importance of establishing a shared terminology for early computer developers, even though I did not cite it directly in this book.

Archivist Nathan Brewer at the IEEE History Center digitized materials in their collection for me while their workplace was closed due to the pandemic. Those materials were enlightening on the personal relationships that shaped the IRE glossary work in the late 1940s and early 1950s. In a period when I was unable to visit those collections in person, Nathan enabled my work to continue.

While the archive closures continued, David Brock and Dag Spicer at the Computer History Museum, and Erik Rau and Linda Gross at the Hagley Museum also generously digitized materials and sent them to me to inform the story in this book. Max Campbell at IBM Corporate Archives was also helpful in searching materials for me while I was not able to visit the archives in person. It has been heartening to collaborate with these colleagues in a virtual world while our real world has been mostly shut down.

The idea for this book originated in an earlier world when I could travel to archives to work with boxes of materials in person. It grew out of a biography of computer pioneer and social activist Edmund Berkeley that I was working on at the Charles Babbage Institute. Throughout the years that I worked on this project and even when it was doubtful that I would ever bring it to completion, Tom Misa and

Jeff Yost never gave up on that project. The reception of that book encouraged me that there is a place for humanistic and cultural studies in the world of computer history.

Newark, NJ, USA   Bernadette Longo

Contents

Abbreviations

ABC	Atanasoff-Berry Computer
ACE	Automatic Computing Engine
ACM	Association for Computing Machinery
AEC	Atomic Energy Commission
AEC GAC	Atomic Energy Commission General Advisory Committee
AIEE	American Institute of Electrical Engineers
AMD	US National Bureau of Standards Applied Mathematics Division
AMP	US National Bureau of Standards Applied Mathematics Panel
BCD	Binary Coded Decimal
BINAC	Binary Automatic Computer
BRL	Ballistics Research Laboratory
C3S	ACM Curriculum Committee on Computer Science
CBS	Columbia Broadcasting System
CPU	Central Processing Unit
CRC	Computer Research Corporation
EDSAC	Electronic Delay Storage Automatic Computer
EDVAC	Electronic Discrete Variable Automatic Computer
ENIAC	Electronic Numerical Integrator and Computer
ERMA	Electronic Recording Machine, Accounting
IAS	Institute for Advanced Study in Princeton, New Jersey
IBM	International Business Machine Corporation
IFF	Identification, Friend or Foe
INA	US National Bureau of Standards Institute for Numerical Analysis
IRE	Institute of Radio Engineers
IWE	Institute of Wireless Engineers
MANIAC	Mathematical Analyzer Numerical Integrator and Computer
MIDAC	Michigan Digital Automatic Computer
MIT	Massachusetts Institute of Technology

MTAC Committee	National Research Council Committee on the Bibliography of Mathematical Tables and Other Aids to Computation
NBS	US National Bureau of Standards
NCR	National Cash Register Corporation
NIST	National Institute of Standards and Technology
NOTS	Naval Ordnance Testing Station
NPL	National Physical Laboratory, England
NRDC	National Defense Research Council
NSF	National Science Foundation
OCR	Optical Character Recognition
OSRD	Office of Scientific Research and Development
RAYDAC	Raytheon Digital Automatic Computer
RCA	Radio Corporation of America
SAGE	Semi-automatic Ground Environment
SEAC	Standards Eastern Automatic Computer
SSEC	IBM Selective Sequence Electronic Calculator
SWAC	Standards Western Automatic Computer
UCLA	University of California, Los Angeles
UN	United Nations
UNAEC	United Nations Atomic Energy Commission
UNIVAC	Universal Automatic Computer
UNO	United Nations Organization
US	United States
USN	United States Navy
USO	United Service Organizations
USSR	Union of Soviet Socialist Republics

Chapter 1
Introduction

Abstract This introduction provides a rationale for a humanistic study of computer history based on philosophical theories of Michel Foucault and François Lyotard. It also explores questions about how one possible definition was produced and legitimated while other possible definitions were not legitimated, even though they may have been produced. The introduction finally discusses the educational role of a type of dictionary – glossaries – in establishing a professional community around the development and operation of electronic computers.

"The manner in which sense perception is organized, the medium in which it is accomplished, is determined not only by nature but by historical circumstances as well." Walter Benjamin, "The work of art in the age of mechanical reproduction," 1936 [3]

"Good technical writing is so clear that it is invisible. Yet technical writing is the mechanism that controls systems of management and discipline, thereby organizing the operations of modern institutions and the people within them." Bernadette Longo, "Spurious Coin," 2000 [11]

"Scientific knowledge, like language, is intrinsically the common property of a group or else nothing at all. To understand it we shall need to know the special characteristics of the groups that create and use it." Thomas Kuhn, "The Structure of Scientific Revolutions," 1970 [9]

1.1 Why Words Matter

For those of us who carry smart-phone computers in our pockets, it is difficult to imagine a time when there were only a handful of computers in the world. Yet I know a colleague who, as a student, liked to study at a desk inside one of these computers at his university because it was quiet and solitary in there. Yes, he studied at a full-sized desk **inside** the computer.

When computers were room-sized machines, there was no discipline called "computer science." There were mathematicians and electrical engineers and physicists who dreamed of "mechanical brains." And then they built large-scale automatic calculating machinery. That's what these machines were called in the mid-twentieth century. In those early days of computer development, people worked

© Springer Nature Switzerland AG 2021

B. Longo, *Words and Power*, History of Computing,

https://doi.org/10.1007/978-3-030-70373-8_1

in laboratories that were isolated from one another. There was no standardized terminology that those people used to communicate information about their computer
development projects. There were no established communication channels to facilitate information sharing. This is a story of how computer people developed that
body of specialized terminology and established those communication channels as
important building blocks for creating the distinct discipline and profession we now
call computer science.

This is also a story of how these computer people worked within an international
context of hot and cold wars – how those international relationships shaped percep-
tions of their work and the products of that work. At the center of this story are the
people who first imagined large-scale automatic calculating machines and worked
together to create them. Early on, they were motivated by the rapidly growing telephone industry and its demand for complex number calculations that were needed
for expansion of long-distance telephony. Technology development was outstripping human calculating ability.

Computer developers were then motivated by the military imperative to generate
ballistic firing tables more quickly than was possible by human computers working
with pencils, papers, and desktop mechanical calculators. As World War II ground
on, the expansion of military theaters into more geographic areas with specific
atmospheric conditions was threatening the Allies' ability to dominate Axis forces.
Ultimately, the computers that were developed for calculating ballistic firing tables
were put to use to help physicists analyze questions about thermonuclear explosions
and the feasibility of dropping the first atomic bomb, which subsequently led to the
end of World War II and the beginning of the Cold War. As World War II ended and
a new kind of ideological/psychological war began, the computer developers, who
had been working in isolation behind laboratory walls secured by information
restrictions, came together with a new urgency to develop "mechanical brains" that
would help to protect the Free World against the threat of Communism. The world
also faced the threat of international thermonuclear warfare, along with the possibility of harnessing atomic power for generating electricity and prosperity. The urgent
threat and the unfulfilled promise of the Atomic Age would require mathematical
calculating ability that exceeded that of human computers. This new age required
new machines that mimicked human calculations but worked much faster than
humans. Computer people shouldered their responsibilities for developing these
machines and shaping human relations in the Atomic Age.

1.2   What People Tell Us About Computers

Although computer histories are often told in heroic terms, smaller stories of human
relations underpin these tales of hardware and software development. The decisions
that computer people made within their institutional and social contexts shaped the
paths of technology development as they built room-sized digital computers with
thousands of vacuum tubes. The actions of computer developers after World War II
influenced the trajectory of technology development and professionalization

through the Atomic Age and beyond. The actions of these early computer people continue shape the human-computer interactions that we expect from our intelligent machines today.

When computer histories foreground innovations in hardware and software – in what Michael Mahoney (1988) called "'insider' history full of facts and firsts" [14, p. 114] – these stories minimize the social contexts in which people made decisions and took actions that contributed to these innovations. Without these contexts, the progress of technological innovation can seem inevitable rather than localized and tentative. These "insider" accounts do provide firsthand knowledge of computer development from one perspective but are limited "by the current state of knowledge and bound by the professional culture" [14, p. 114]. Authors who lived these histories firsthand might take their particular and localized states of knowledge as "givens … [but] a more critical outside viewer might see [these] as choices" [14, p. 114] among equally possible alternative paths. From an "insider" perspective, choices made by people relating to the development of electronic computers can be seen as inevitable steps in technological progress. From this worldview, they acted within an objective realm of pure and applied science – a realm free of politics and culture.

This path of technology development from large-scale automatic calculating machines to smart phones was not inevitable but instead reflects the politics and cultures of specific locations and times along the way [11, 13]. As Tom Misa (2007) argued, the actions of computer people bring about cultural – as well as technological – changes. This is why Misa advocated that histories of computer development should include the social and institutional influences impacting people who worked on these machines and their programming [17, p. 54–56]. He also foresaw that studying the history of computing in contexts of "broad historical transformations" would necessarily require historians to draw on a "wider set of research methods" than used to write more decontextualized histories of technology development [17, p. 59]. Following Misa's advice, human-centered stories of computer development and biographies of computer people can contribute to developing histories of computing machinery that encompass broad historical transformations, both cultural and technological.

In his overview of the state of computer historiography, James Cortada (2015) found that human-centered stories of computer development "have been slow to appear" despite the maturation of the field [4, p. 27]. He noted, though, that this humanities-based approach to computer history resulted in studies that "emphasize the role of specific individuals in shaping development and use of computing" [4, p. 27]. The study that follows here responds to Cortada's call to investigate how the actions of specific individuals shaped the development and use of computers, as well as the development of computer science as a profession. In particular, this study looks at how the efforts of early computer people to establish a standardized nomenclature for their field helped them to respond to the need for rapid technology development in the face of Cold War national security concerns. This nomenclature allowed for information sharing among people from different laboratories who had worked in isolation during World War II. It also provided a foundation for developing computer literature that was necessary for the growth of computer science as a profession separate from mathematics, electrical engineering, and physics.

1.3   What Technical Language Tells Us About People

As I have argued elsewhere [11, 12], technical language is the mechanism that people employ to turn knowledge into cultural capital or social value. Rather than being a neutral conduit to transport information from one point to another in a positivist sense, technical language mediates the transfer from an applied scientist or computer developer to other developers or end users. Through this mediation, technical language serves an active role in knowledge creation within social contexts. In the case of early computer development, people designing these mechanical and electronic calculating machines initially lacked a common body of specialized terms to describe and communicate information about their work to other people. They relied on analogy and terminology from other fields, such as electrical engineering or psychology, to represent ideas about computing machines. At first, terms were specific to individual laboratories and the people working in them. As computer developers communicated with each other more widely after World War II security clearances relaxed, idiosyncratic terms were standardized through collaboration and contest within institutions.

Language is how we give voice to technical knowledge that participates in systems of institutional power. It is shaped by these societal systems, while simultaneously shaping them. In this current study, computer terminology was initially a contested site of knowledge production as people came together from their isolated workplaces with a common goal of rapid computer development. Whose knowledge would prevail? Who would claim the power to define terms that would become authoritative in a new industry and profession that was shaping social, political, and economic relations on an international scale? Debate about these knowledge production questions took place within military, academic, and industrial institutions. Some knowledge would be legitimated through standardized terminology, such as knowledge about electronic computing machines and programming. Other possible knowledge would be marginalized, such as knowledge about analog and other mechanical calculating machines. In these debates, institutions themselves can be seen as cultural agents influencing discourse and professional development. Vincent Leitch (1992) described how institutions act as cultural agents to legitimate and reward knowledge made through standardized technical language:

> Through various discursive and technical means, institutions constitute and disseminate systems of rules, conventions, and practices that condition the creation, circulation, and use of resources, information, knowledge and belief. Institutions include, therefore, both material forms and mechanisms of production, distribution and consumption and ideological norms and protocols shaping the reception, comprehension, and application of discourse. ... Institutions often enable things to function, inaugurate new modes of knowledge, initiate productive associations, offer assistance and support, provide useful information, create

helpful social ties, simplify large-scale problems, protect the vulnerable, and enrich the community. [10, p. 127–128]

Because institutions are cultural agents that affect discourse practices, recognition of organizations' participation in cultural contexts enables a study that can illuminate assumptions about the inevitable roles of technical language in a specific culture at given historical moments – roles such as information mediator or professional foundation builder.

This study traces the development and standardization of computer terminology in the United States from the 1940s into the 1960s. Its method of inquiry has heeded Thomas Kuhn's (1970) call for historians of science to "display the historical integrity of that science in its own time" [9, p. 3]. In this vein, I have attempted to reconstruct a cultural context for past language practices within a field that would become computer science in order to understand these past practices not as ill-fitting or quaint compared to contemporary understanding, but as legitimate practices within their situated historical contexts. Since technical language deals in knowledge made through pure and applied science, the practice of communicating this knowledge can be seen as a scientific mechanism or apparatus for determining proper valuation and credit for the product, in this case computers. By communicating their knowledge, scientists and technology developers sought to modify the scriptures of their field and, thereby, the concepts that regulate further knowledge production. If a person's or a committee's communication could modify these concepts in ways that could be translated into technological advances, that knowledge was accorded value. This ability to transform knowledge into value is central to the function of technical language.

Translating language into technological advances is not merely a collaborative effort but also involves contests for cultural capital. "Making sense" to the winners of these contests may not agree with the "common sense" of others, whose language and knowledge was delegitimated. Jean-François Lyotard (1988) described this silencing of devalued knowledge as a "wrong" suffered in "a case of conflict between (at least) two parties, that cannot be equitably resolved for lack of a rule of judgment applicable to both arguments" [13, p. xi]. In the case of early computer development, there were no mutually agreed-upon rules for equitable judgment in cases of disputed definitions for what would become the *lingua franca* of a new profession called computer science. In the absence of rules of equitable judgment, decisions about whose discourse would prevail must privilege one group's knowledge production over other possible ways of making knowledge. Unlike a simple idea of collaboration, Lyotard's theory of knowledge production through discourse legitimation holds that power is unevenly distributed among possible ways of knowing. Discourse becomes a site of contests for knowledge legitimation and cultural advantage. Technical language participates in these struggles by assigning value to legitimated knowledge as the currency of a scientific knowledge economy. Devalued knowledge and its associated technical language will not circulate in this economy at full cultural value.

Struggles for value are contained within technical language. For Michel Foucault (1980), discourse holds histories of struggles for knowledge legitimation and the articulated discourse subsumes other discourses that were possible, but not articulated. In arguing for the study of culture through discourse analysis, Foucault described how the legitimated discourse embodies these struggles for legitimation:

> In the two cases – in the case of the erudite as in the case of the disqualified knowledges – with what in fact were these buried, subjugated knowledge really concerned? They were concerned with a *historical knowledge of struggles*. In the specialized areas of erudition as in the disqualified, popular knowledge there lay the memory of hostile encounters which even up to this day have been confined to the margins of knowledge. [7, p. 83]

At the margins of what became legitimated knowledge about computer science, we can find erudite knowledge that was previously legitimate but was subsumed by subsequently legitimated knowledge. Information about analog or relay computers are examples of this type of erudite knowledge that was once state-of-the-art but became outdated by subsequent knowledge about electronic computers. Technical language was the tool that computer developers used to communicate knowledge about these computer designs. Whose language would be acceptable and whose would fall by the wayside? Whose information and ideas would be rewarded with cultural capital and whose would be devalued? These questions are addressed in this study about contests for defining computer terms that would convey cultural value as much as technical information.

Cultural studies of technical language point to the fruitfulness of an investigative approach based on Foucault's (1969) archaeological research methods and augmented by closely related lines of critical theory to illuminate how struggles for knowledge legitimation are influenced by institutional, political, economic, and/or social relationships, pressures, and tensions within cultural contexts that transcend any one affiliated group. This type of study can help to answer questions about why technical language practices work to value some types of knowledge while devaluing other possible knowledges. Such a study can begin by asking Foucault's question, "How is it that one particular statement appeared rather than another?" [5, p. 27]. The statements that did appear in technical texts retell stories of the struggles, contradictions, and tensions within historic relations of knowledge and power. These statements also hold the silence of other statements that were possible, but did not appear in technical texts at the particular time and place under study. By looking at statements that did appear and positing possible statements that did not appear, the genealogical historian can construct what Foucault (1963) called a "systematic history of discourses" [6, p. 14]. The current systematic history (or genealogy) of discourse relating to early electronic computer development asks questions about how one possible definition was produced and legitimated while other possible definitions were not legitimated, even though they may have been produced.

In the tradition of Francis Bacon's (1620) public science, technical language participates in a social system that was established to democratize knowledge. Bacon's full plan was more comprehensive than just what we now know as the "scientific method." It included social institutions, making science the vehicle for carrying out a social project: "It might also be asked … whether I am speaking of natural philosophy only, or whether I mean that the other sciences – logic, ethics politics – should also be carried on by my method. I would answer that I certainly do think that my words have a universal application. … For I am compiling a history and tables of discovery about anger, fear, shame, and the like, and also about political matters … just as much as about hot and cold, or light, or vegetation or the like" [1, p. 3:370]. This social organization for public science that Bacon put forward in the seventeenth century marked a radical break with then-traditional views of scientific practices as being the protected domain of elite and cloistered groups. By bringing science and philosophy out of these cloisters and into the larger world, Bacon rationalized the societal role of the low arts, such as mechanics, chemistry, mining, and metallurgy, based on their benefit to humankind. Because Bacon's project for a public science was so vast, many workers were needed to accumulate a complete body of scientific knowledge. In the seventeenth century, the printing press enabled a systematized educational system that prepared people to participate in that vast public science project. Textbooks, handbooks, and dictionaries became integral communication tools underpinning that educational system for preparing scientists and technicians to participate in a project for the betterment of the public welfare. Three centuries later, computer developers worked within this Baconian public science tradition and the need for a common technical language upon which it relied.

This study will focus on the educational role of a type of dictionary – glossaries – in establishing a professional community around the development and operation of electronic computers. Since the first glossaries were created by monks for self-education, such compilations of word definitions "have become 'guardians of absolute and eternal truth' [2, p. 122] and powerful tools for legitimizing certain types of knowledge" [15, p. 3]. As Menagarishvili (2020) pointed out in her lexicographical study of technical dictionaries, the act of defining terms reflects a position of social power because these definitions become normative and educational [16, p. 15]. She argued that dictionaries of science and technology are "products of capitalism" [16, p. 15] that participate among institutions in a scientific knowledge economy. The development of glossaries of standardized computer terms that is the focus of this current study reinforces the claim that people who exert the power to define terms also exert a power to define a new profession with consequent economic and political implications. The sites where this work takes place reflect struggles for knowledge legitimation in the sense that Foucault (1963, 1969, 1980) and Lyotard (1988) explain as privileging some kinds of (technical) knowledge and silencing other possible ways of making knowledge on the topic [5, p. 76]. In this study, knowledge and definitions made within sanctioned institutional groups necessarily prevailed over knowledge made through more populist processes as computer developers formalized a profession called computer science.

Language as a tool for knowledge-making and communication also functions within national and political systems, such as the fluctuating international alliances at the end of World War II. This study examines how the United States' version of the English language was implicated in international security concerns, as nations grappled with rapid development of atomic weapons that relied on computerized guided missile technologies to address the threat of a World War III in the twentieth century. At the beginning of that century before World War I, mining engineer and journalist Thomas A. Rickard (1908) asserted the importance of a dominant English language for making technical knowledge with political and economic value: "The English language is the common heritage of the people of not one mining district, nor one region, nor one country, nor one continent ... it is the heritage of the race to which Britishers, Americans, Canadians, Australians, and Afrikanders all belong, and also of the various races that they have assimilated in the course of their effort to conquer nature the world over. ... Let us have a mintage that will pass current at full value throughout the English-speaking world" [18, p. 19]. Without a pure mintage, Rickard argued that the value of technical knowledge would be diminished; it could not circulate at full value in a technical knowledge economy. When early computer developers argued about the definitions of computer terms, their contests sought to mint technical knowledge with full cultural value – knowledge that would underpin national security and international relations. Their contests about words underpinned larger global contests.

As Paul Goodman (2010) argued, "technology is a branch of moral philosophy ... It aims at prudent goods for the commonweal" [8, p. 40]. Computer developers in the mid-twentieth-century United States shouldered their responsibility for the commonweal as they saw it from their vantage point. They did their part to develop electronic digital computers that would guide missile weapons systems, as well as calculate payrolls, route telephone calls, and predict elections. This is a story about how these people standardized their language to cooperate in these developments. It is also a story about contests for professional legitimacy and whose knowledge prevailed. Chapter 2 of this story traces the international political context for the work of computer developers as World War II ended, providing details of the deteriorating relationship between the United States and the Soviet Union who were formerly allies during the war. Chapter 3 highlights the importance of cooperation between the United States and England, which relied in large part on a shared language for effective communication to underpin national security, technology development, and public education about science. Chapter 4 describes how computer developers shared information about technology innovations in the early 1940s and through World War II. In this period, information was largely shared among people who had established contacts with leaders in the field of computer development, yet they often found that they had difficulty sharing information because of differences in their terminology developed in isolated laboratories. Chapter 5 describes how computer developers used existing documents to share information about innovations in computer design in the years immediately after World War II. This documentary approach to information sharing was especially important for people working in the computer field that was being established in southern California to support the aircraft industry and guided missile development. Chapter 6 places efforts to standardize computer terminology within a historical context of language standardizing efforts for earlier technologies of electricity and radio. Language standardization efforts from the Institute of Radio Engineers (IRE) and American

Institute of Electrical Engineers (AIEE) began to focus on creating glossaries of terms relating to automatic computing devices in the late 1940s. The glossaries developed in these organizations reflected the priorities of committee members with backgrounds in military, academic, and industry projects. Chapter 7 describes the work of three computer terminology glossary projects: Edmund Berkeley's periodical publications in *Computers and Automation*, IRE committees working on "Definitions of Terms" compilations of electronic computer terminology, and the ACM committee compiling specialized terminology for computer programming as distinguished from computer machine design. These efforts illustrate the importance of institutional support for language standardization efforts. Chapter 8 describes the importance of training people to work in the growing computer field as military and industry projects demanded more workers for their projects. People trained in the specialized computer field prompted universities to consider developing specialized curricula and departments in what would become known as computer science.

References

1. Bacon, Francis. 1620. Novum organum. *The works of Francis Bacon*. 3 volumes. Trans. Basil Montague, ed. Philadelphia: Parry & MacMillan. 1854.
2. Béjoint, Henri. 2010. *The lexicography of English: From origins to present*. New York: Oxford University Press.
3. Benjamin, Walter. 1968. The work of art in the age of mechanical reproduction. Harry Zohn, trans. In *Illuminations*, ed. Hannah Arendt, 217–252. New York: Shocken Books.
4. Cortada, James W. 2015. Studying history as it unfolds, Part 1: Creating the history of information technologies. *IEEE Annals of the History of Computing 37.3*: 20–31.
5. Foucault, Michel. 1969. *Archaeology of knowledge*. Trans. A. M. Sheridan Smith. New York: Barnes & Noble. 1972.
6. ———. 1963. *Birth of the clinic*. Trans. A. M. Sheridan. London: Routledge. 1973.
7. ———. 1980. *Power/knowledge: Selected interviews and other writings 1972–77*. Trans. Colin Gordon et al. and ed. New York: Pantheon Press.
8. Goodman, Paul. 2010. *New reformation: Notes of a neolithic conservative*. Oakland: PM Press.
9. Kuhn, Thomas S. 1970. *The structure of scientific revolutions*. 2nd ed. Chicago: University of Chicago Press.
10. Leitch, Vincent B. 1992. *Cultural criticism, literary theory, poststructuralism*. New York: Columbia University Press.
11. Longo, Bernadette. 2000. *Spurious coin: A history of science, management, and technical writing*. Albany: State University of New York Press.
12. ———. 2018, April 6. Humanizing computer history. Paper presented at the Humanities for STEM Symposium. New York University Center for the Humanities. https://osf.io/y9g5f/. Accessed 17 Nov 2020.
13. Lyotard, Jean-François. 1988. *The differend: Phrases in dispute*. Trans. George Van Den Abbeele. Minneapolis: University of Minnesota Press.
14. Mahoney, Michael S. 1988. 'The history of computing in the history of technology. *IEEE Annals of the History of Computing 10* (2): 113–125.
15. Menagarishvili, Olga. 2012. *Dictionaries of science as participants in the scientific knowledge economy*. University of Minnesota Digital Conservancy., https://hdl.handle.net/11299/138293. Accessed 14 Feb 2021.

16. ———. 2020. Dictionaries of science and technology and issues of power. *Revue de l'Institut des langues et cultures d'Europe, Amérique, Afrique, Asie et Australie* (ILCEA). https://doi.org/10.4000/ilcea.10614. Accessed 16 Nov 2020.
17. Misa, Thomas J. 2007, October–December. Understanding "how computing has changed the world". *IEEE Annals of the History of Computing* 29 (4): 52–63. https://doi.org/10.1109/MAHC.2007.68. Accessed 17 Nov 2020.
18. Rickard, Thomas A. 1908. *A guide to technical writing*. San Francisco: The Mining and Scientific Press.

Chapter 2
From Hot War to Cold Peace

Abstract This chapter traces a chronological shift of the relationship between the United States and Russia as World War II ended and the Cold War began. These political events provide a backdrop for the sense of urgency that computer developers felt as their technological innovations became critical components for US national security based on atomic weapons systems.

"That since wars begin in the minds of men, it is in the minds of men that the defences of peace must be constructed..." United Nations Educational, "Scientific and Cultural Organization Constitution," 16 November 1945 [15]

"Comrade Stalin has called our writers engineers of human souls. What does this mean?"
A. A. Zdhanov, "Speech delivered at Soviet Writers Congress," 1934 [17]

7 May 1945... Nazi General Alfred Jodl signed an agreement, on behalf of the German High Command, unconditionally surrendering all German forces, thereby ending World War II in Europe.

2 August 1945... The World War II allies (the United States, the United Kingdom, and Soviet Union) signed the Potsdam Agreement, establishing military occupation and reconstruction of Germany and the European Theater. The Soviet Union annexed territories in eastern Poland and the Baltic States (Estonia, Latvia, and Lithuania) that they had occupied since 1939 and territories in eastern Finland that they had occupied since 1940, along with parts of East Prussia and Ukraine.

6 August 1945... The United States (US) dropped an atomic bomb on Hiroshima, a Japanese industrial and military center, killing over 70,000 people – nearly 30% of its population – in the immediate blast and firestorm. Three days later, the Soviet Union invaded a weakened Japan. Later that day, the United States dropped a second atomic bomb on the industrial seaport of Nagasaki, killing over 30,000 people. Japanese Emperor Hirohito announced his country's surrender to the allies on August 14, ending World War II in the Pacific theater. He signed the Japanese Instrument of Surrender on 2 September 1945 aboard the US Navy battleship *USS Missouri.*

5 March 1946... US President Harry Truman took the stage at Westminster College in his home state of Missouri as Winston Churchill delivered a speech entitled "The Sinews of Peace," now more commonly known as the "Iron Curtain Speech" [4]. Churchill declared, "[T]he United States stands at this time at the

© Springer Nature Switzerland AG 2021
B. Longo, *Words and Power*, History of Computing,
https://doi.org/10.1007/978-3-030-70373-8_2

pinnacle of world power. It is a solemn moment for the America Democracy. For with primacy in power is also joined an awe-inspiring accountability to the future." Churchill called on the United States to use its postwar supremacy to guard the "safety and welfare, the freedom and progress, of all the homes and families of all the men and women in all the lands" against "two gaunt marauders, war and tyranny." He argued that "if the dangers of war and tyranny are removed, there is no doubt that science and co-operation can bring in the next few years to the world, certainly in the next few decades newly taught in the sharpening school of war, an expansion of material well-being beyond anything that has yet occurred in human experience" [4].

Although Churchill saw that American supremacy in weapons and technology could potentially usher in a new age of peace and material well-being to people around the world, he cautioned that these advancements could only be realized through what he called "the fraternal association of the English-speaking peoples" [4]. This fraternal association built on shared communication and "kindred systems of society" would support "continuance of the intimate relations between our military advisers, leading to common study of potential dangers, the similarity of weapons and manuals of instructions, and to the interchange of officers and cadets at technical colleges." Churchill saw this "special relationship" between the United States and the British Commonwealth as being vital to the success of the fledgling United Nations, whose "prime purpose" was preventing war: "We must make sure that its work is fruitful, that it is a reality and not a sham, that it is a force for action, and not merely a frothing of words, that it is a true temple of peace in which the shields of many nations can some day be hung up, and not merely a cockpit in a Tower of Babel." He argued that a fraternal association of English-speaking peoples could provide a strong foundation for the work of the United Nations: "Before we cast away the solid assurances of national armaments for self-preservation we must be certain that our temple is built, not upon shifting sands or quagmires, but upon a rock" [4].

Churchill cautioned that the task of building this temple of peace was threatened by a clash of politics and culture. He stated, "A shadow has fallen upon the scenes so lately light by the Allied victory. Nobody knows what Soviet Russia and its Communist international organization intends to do in the immediate future, or what are the limits, if any, to their expansive and proselytizing tendencies. … From Stettin in the Baltic to Trieste in the Adriatic an *iron curtain* has descended across the Continent. … [T]his is certainly not the Liberated Europe we fought to build up. Nor is it one which contains the essentials of permanent peace" [4]. Churchill noted that "all the capitals of the ancient states of Central and Eastern Europe" were at that time behind the iron curtain in what he called the "Soviet sphere." He argued that the "Communist parties, which were very small in all these Eastern States of Europe, have been raised to pre-eminence and power far beyond their numbers and are seeking everywhere to obtain totalitarian control." And this Communist threat reached beyond the current Soviet sphere to "a great number of countries, far from the Russian frontiers and throughout the world, [where] Communist fifth columns are established and work in complete unity and absolute obedience to the directions they receive from the Communist center." Although he noted that Communism was in "its infancy" in the United States and the British Commonwealth, Churchill argued that Communism posed "a growing challenge and peril to Christian civilization." He restated Britain's goal of establishing "mutual assistance and collaboration with Russia," but also cautioned that "there is nothing for which they have less respect than for weakness, especially military weakness" [4].

On that afternoon in March 1946, Churchill argued for the United States to join with the British Commonwealth in order to strengthen world security through a fraternal association of English-speaking peoples who could expedite development of weapons and military systems. Through this association, the United States and Britain would work together to build a temple of peace, along with other countries in the United Nations. "Indeed, they must do so or else the temple may not be built, or, being built, it may collapse, and we should all be proved again unteachable and have to go and try to learn again for a third time in a school of war incomparably more rigorous than that from which we have just been released" [4]. In the previous 30 years, Churchill and others in his audience had lived through two World Wars with increasingly lethal weapons. The specter of a third all-encompassing war was a real possibility. But the prospect of a nuclear war would make the next world conflict far more devastating than previous wars. Churchill expressed an urgency for strengthening military security through technology development, lest the "dark ages may return, the Stone Age may return on gleaming wings of science, and what might now shower immeasurable material blessings upon mankind, may even bring about its total destruction. Beware, I say; time may be short. Do not let us take the course of allowing events to drift along until it's too late" [4].

Concerning Soviet expansion of Communist states, Churchill argued, "I do not believe that Soviet Russia desires war. What they desire is the fruits of war and the indefinite expansion of their power and doctrines. But what we have to consider here today while time remains, is the permanent prevention of war and the establishment of conditions of freedom and democracy as rapidly as possible in all countries. … What is needed is a settlement, and the longer this is delayed, the more difficult it will be and the greater our dangers will become" [4]. Here Churchill advocated for the United States and Britain to negotiate a postwar political and territorial settlement among the wartime allies, with the English-speaking associates establishing their position of military and technological strength in order to counter Russia's urge to expand their sphere of political influence and protect what they saw as their national security in Eastern Europe. Six years earlier, when German expansion threatened Russia's western border in Poland, Churchill had expressed a similar opinion on Russia's political goals in a speech called "The Russian Enigma" (1939): "[Russia] is a riddle wrapped in a mystery inside an enigma; but perhaps there is a key. That key is Russian national interest" [3]. Churchill believed that the key to negotiations with Russia was understanding that they operated first from considerations of their national interest, often realized as expansionism in the pursuit of national security. In the aftermath of the World War II, Churchill advocated for diplomacy and negotiation to establish a new world order among the wartime allies instead of relying only on military supremacy – a world order based on the fraternal association of English-speaking countries backed by nuclear weapons. This finer, diplomatic point in Churchill's argument was largely lost in subsequent reactions to his "Iron Curtain Speech."

New York Times political reporter Arthur Krock (1946), for example, noted that Churchill's speech was greeted with "'moderate applause,'" which "registered a higher point of open approbation than the suggestion will receive at this time from those in charge of our foreign policy" [11]. The United Press International (UPI) reported this reaction to Churchill's speech in the US Congress: "Members of Congress today generally agreed with Winston Churchill's remarks yesterday about Russia, but were cool to his alliance proposal, feeling that international differences should be worked out through the United Nations with Russian participation" [16]. Representative May of Kentucky, chairman of the House Military Affairs Committee, agreed that Russia should be given a chance to work through the United Nations, although as reported in the *New York Times* (1946), Rep. McCormack of Massachusetts issued a statement that "Moscow 'has been unwilling to date to cooperate for world peace'" [1]. Some members of Congress supported Churchill's proposal, like Rep. Colmer of Mississippi who declared it to be "realistic." Others found the proposal to be "shocking" and "a return to power politics" that would lead to "a third world war" [1]. The speech and its aftermath marked a turning point in US-USSR relations. As diplomatic historian Fraser Harbutt (1981) concluded, "What is clear ... is that within forty-eight hours of Churchill's visit, the substantive transformation of American policy began" [6, p. 626].

Although both US President Truman and Secretary of State Byrnes had been aware of Churchill's remarks in advance of his speech [5, p. 307], on 8 March the President sought to distance himself from the fraternal association proposal. When he was asked in a news conference whether he endorsed the principles of Churchill's speech, Truman answered, "I didn't know what would be in Mr. Churchill's speech. This is a country of free speech. Mr. Churchill had a perfect right to say what he pleased. I was there as his host in Missouri, because I had told him if he would come over here and give the lecture at that little college, that I would be glad to introduce him." In a follow-up question, Truman was asked about his opinion of the speech now that he had heard it. He answered, "I have no comment" [14]. In a 11 March 1946 editorial, *Time Magazine* reported, "On the Continent the schism between Russia and the West was forcing the great mass of moderate men into two opposing camps, with the extremists in both getting ready for 'when war comes.' As Jimmy Byrnes and [US delegate to the United Nations] Arthur Vandenberg spoke of a stronger U.S. foreign policy ... war talk was also heard in the U.S." [2].

War talk was heard in the Soviet Union (USSR) as well, as reported in a memo from US Ambassador to the USSR George Kennan. On 11 March, *Pravda*, the official newspaper of the Communist Party, printed large portions of Churchill's speech, along with a front page editorial arguing that Churchill proposed a "unity of Western Democracies under hegemony of Anglo American military alliance" [8]. The editorial further argued "that this union would be directed against the USSR, and that its realization would signify breakdown of coalition and UNO, but that it is condemned to utter failure." In a telegram from Kennan to Secretary of State James Byrnes,

Kennan presented his analysis of this unusual move to publicize Churchill's speech so extensively in *Pravda*:

> This method of procedure was chosen after Kremlin had carefully waited to see reaction to Churchill's speech in US and England and indicates Moscow considers echo to Churchill's statements to have been so weak that it is worthwhile to throw Sov influence into scales of international public reaction. Had Churchill's speech found greater support in English and American public opinion and govt circles, Moscow would doubtless have taken a much more serious view of it and drawn other conclusions as to treatment. [8]

Kennan further stated that Moscow was "relieved" that the reaction to Churchill's proposal was so tepid and believed that there was an "excellent possibility that Western Democracies will not succeed in organizing any effective common front on military level against Sov bloc" [8].

Shortly after Churchill's speech was published in *Pravda*, Premier Joseph Stalin gave an interview to *Pravda*, the official newspaper of the Communist Party, in which he voiced his reaction to Churchill's proposal. Calling Churchill a "warmonger," Stalin likened his proposal for a fraternal association of English-speaking nations to Hitler's race theory:

> Hitler began his work of unleashing war by proclaiming a race theory, declaring that only German-speaking people constituted a superior nation. Mr. Churchill sets out to unleash war with a race theory, asserting that only English-speaking nations are superior nations, who are called upon to decide the destinies of the entire world. ... Actually, Mr. Churchill, and his friends in Britain and the United States, present to the non-English speaking nations something in the nature of an ultimatum: "Accept our rule voluntarily, and then all will be well; otherwise war is inevitable." ... It is quite probable, accordingly, that the non-English-speaking nations, which constitute the vast majority of the population of the world, will not agree to submit to a new slavery. [13]

Stalin's bottom line: "There can be no doubt that Mr. Churchill's position is a war position, a call for war on the U.S.S.R." [13].

On 14 March, US Ambassador Kennan sent his analysis of Stalin's remarks to Secretary of State Byrnes, stating that "this interview represents most violent Soviet reaction I can recall to any foreign statement" [9]. He continued, "Kremlin had tactical reasons of high importance and urgency for seizing this speech and presenting it to Soviet public, not for what it was, but for what Kremlin wished it to appear," which was "evidence of strong sentiment in west for new 'intervention' against Soviet Union." This violent reaction between the Soviet Union and United States may have surfaced in reaction to Churchill's proposal for a fraternal association of English-speaking countries, but the uneasy cooperation among wartime allies had been weakening for months before this tipping point.

On 9 February 1946, Joseph Stalin had given a speech to a meeting of voters in Moscow on the occasion of his nomination for election to the Supreme Soviet, where new postwar guidelines for the Communist Party would be determined. In this speech, Stalin claimed that the Soviet system of government was shown to be superior to capitalist systems as a result of the outcomes of the recent war. He claimed, "Now the issue is that the Soviet social system has proved to be more viable and stable than the non-Soviet social system, that the Soviet social system is a better form of organization of society than any non-Soviet social system" [12]. And further, "Now the issue is that the Soviet state system has proved to be a model multinational state, that the Soviet state system is a system of state organization in which the national problem and the problem of the collaboration of nations have found a better solution than in any other multinational state." In Stalin's view, not only would the Soviet system provide a better structure to support multinational cooperation than the fledgling United Nations; it would also support better planning for production of consumer goods and technological development: "I have no doubt that if we give our scientists proper assistance they will be able in the near future not only to overtake but even outstrip the achievements of science beyond the borders of our country" Here Stalin foreshadowed his country's intention to rival the United States in an impending nuclear arms race. Stalin's intentions for a postwar Soviet Union resonated far beyond the walls of the Bolshoi Theater where he spoke on that day in February. "The speech was broadcast on the radio and printed in tens of millions of copies. Shrewd listeners and readers immediately recognized it as a death knell to hopes of a better life, as well as postwar cooperation with Western allies" [18, p. 52]. The speech signaled an increased likelihood of future wars [6].

On 22 February, Ambassador Kennan sent a long telegram to Secretary Byrnes with an "analysis of our international environment," with special emphasis on the Soviet postwar outlook. Kennan noted that Stalin considers that the USSR "lives in antagonistic 'capitalist encirclement' with which in the long run there can be no permanent peaceful coexistence" [7, p. 1]. He found, "At the bottom of Kremin's neurotic view of world affairs is traditional and instinctive Russian sense of insecurity. ... And they have learned to seek security only in patient but deadly struggle for total destruction of rival power, never in compacts and compromises with it" [7, p. 4]. Kennan found that Soviet strategies operated on both official and unofficial levels, with encouragement and support from sympathetic elements within capitalist societies, such as progressives or other groups, whose goals aligned with Soviet interests. These groups could be used for promulgation of Soviet policies on a "subterranean plane" rather than through official channels, to "undermine general political and strategic potential of major western powers" [7, p. 8]. Kennan stated that what he forecast for US-USSR relations was "not a pleasant picture. Problem of how to cope with this force is undoubtedly greatest task our diplomacy has ever faced and probably greatest it will ever have to face." He offered this strategy for coping with what he characterized as an insecure, suspicious, and irrational adversary: "Soviet power ... is neither schematic nor adventunstic [sic]. It does not work by fixed plans. It does not take unnecessary risks. Impervious to logic of reason, and it is highly sensitive to logic of force. For this reason it can easily withdraw – and usually does when strong resistance is encountered at any point. Thus, if the adversary has sufficient force and makes clear his readiness to use it, he rarely has to do so" [7, p. 9]. Kennan's stance toward the Soviets conceded that expansion into Eastern Europe was triggered by their desire to secure Russia from invaders from the west, as this had been their vulnerability in numerous wars. Ideologically, Soviet expansion was based on a desire to prove that a social and economic system built on Communist principles was superior to any capitalist system. Culturally, Kennan found in Russians an ability to create and promulgate alternate truths when this was politically advantageous. These alternative truths could form the basis for insistent political operations on a subterranean level to achieve their economic or military goals. The only way to counter this Communist force was with counter-force.

In a 20 March 1946 memo, Kennan complained of recent articles in the US press encouraging "assurances to assuage Russia's fears" or "closer diplomatic contact" with Stalin. He argued, "Belief that Soviet 'suspicions' are of such a nature that they could be altered or assuaged by personal contacts, rational arguments or official assurances reflects a serious misunderstanding about Soviet realities" [10, p. 1]. He concluded, "I think there can be no more dangerous tendency in American public opinion than one which places on our government an obligation to accomplish the impossible by gestures of good will and conciliation toward a political entity constitutionally incapable of being conciliated. On the other hand, there is no tendency more agreeable to purposes of Moscow diplomacy. Kremlin has no reason to discourage a delusion so useful to its purposes" [10, p. 4]. With this memo, Kennan sought to close the door on goodwill negotiations between the United States and Russia in the face of their moves to annex territories into what was soon to become the Soviet Union. He argued that conciliation was only in the interest of Russia and not in the postwar security interests of the United States.

In less than a year after the Axis countries' surrender to the Allied countries in 1945, relations between the United States and Russia had deteriorated to such an extent that US diplomat George Kennan recommended that the United States adopt an adversarial posture with their wartime ally. Great Britain, the third of the wartime allies, was in a weakened position after suffering greatly from German bombing raids. They needed to align themselves with the United States in order to benefit from the technology development that promised to underpin national security efforts in the face of Russian aggression in Europe and Asia. Kennan's analysis and strategy prevailed in official US circles, with its emphasis on containment and deterrence rather than diplomacy. US postwar foreign policy and national security decisions would then have global consequences. The stage was set for the Cold War.

References

1. Anonymous. 1946. Congress splits on Churchill plea. *New York Times*. March 7.
2. ———. 1946. The nations: A bet on peace. *Time Magazine*. March 11.
3. Churchill, Winston. 1939, October 1. The Russian enigma. The Churchill Society London. http://www.churchill-society-london.org.uk/RusnEnig.html. Accessed 29 Oct 2020.
4. ———. 1946, March 5. The sinews of peace. International Churchill Society. https://winston-churchill.org/resources/speeches/1946-1963-elder-statesman/the-sinews-of-peace/. Accessed 29 Oct 2020.
5. Gaddis, John Lewis. 2000. *The United States and the origins of the Cold War, 1941–1946*. Revised ed. New York: Columbia University Press.
6. Harbutt, Fraser. 1981–1982. American challenge, Soviet response: The beginning of the Cold War, February – May, 1946. *Political Science Quarterly* 96 (4): 623–639.

7. Kennan, George. 1946, February 22. Telegram to James Byrnes. Harry S. Truman Library. https://www.trumanlibrary.gov/library/research-files/telegram-george-kennan-james-byrnes-long-telegram. Accessed 29 Oct 2020.

8. ———. 1946, March 11. Telegram to James Byrnes. Harry S. Truman Library. https://www.trumanlibrary.gov/library/research-files/telegram-george-kennan-james-byrnes?documentid=4&pagenumber=1. Accessed 29 Oct 2020.

9. ———. 1946, March 14. Telegram to James Byrnes. Harry S. Truman Library. https://www.trumanlibrary.gov/library/research-files/telegram-george-kennan-james-byrnes?documentid=5&pagenumber=1. Accessed 29 Oct 2020.

10. ———. 1946, March 20. Telegram to James Byrnes. Harry S. Truman Library. https://www.trumanlibrary.gov/library/research-files/telegram-george-kennan-james-byrnes?documentid=6&pagenumber=1. Accessed 29 Oct 2020.

11. Krock, Arthur. 1946. In the nation: One link Churchill speech may preserve. *New York Times*. March 7.

12. Stalin, J.V. 1946, February 9. Speech delivered at a meeting of voters of the Stalin Electoral District, Moscow. Wilson Center Digital Archive. http://digitalarchive.wilsoncenter.org/document/116179. Accessed 29 Oct 2020.

13. ———. 1946, March. Interview to Pravda correspondent concerning Mr. Winston Churchill's speech at Fulton. Marxist Internet Archive. https://www.marxists.org/reference/archive/stalin/works/1946/03/x01.htm. Accessed 29 Oct 2020.

14. Truman, Harry S. 1946, March 8. The president's news conference. Harry S. Truman Library. https://www.trumanlibrary.gov/library/public-papers/53/presidents-news-conference. Accessed 29 Oct 2020.

15. United Nations Educational, Scientific and Cultural Organization. 1945. UNESCO Constitution. UNESCO Legal Instruments. http://portal.unesco.org/en/ev.php-URL_ID=15244&URL_DO=DO_TOPIC&URL_SECTION=201.html. Accessed 29 Oct 2020.

16. United Press International (UPI). 1946. Full use of UNO is urged. *New York Times*. March 7.

17. Zdhanov, A.A. 1934. Soviet literature – The richest in ideas, the most advanced literature. Speech given at Soviet Writers Congress. https://www.marxists.org/subject/art/lit_crit/soviet-writercongress/zdhanov.htm. Accessed 27 Feb 2021.

18. Zubok, Vladislav M. 2007. *A failed empire: The Soviet Union in the Cold War from Stalin to Gorbachev*. Chapel Hill: University of North Carolina Press.

Chapter 3
Who Will Control Atomic Power?

Abstract This chapter highlights the importance of cooperation between the United States and England in the development of radar, which was instrumental in equipping the Allies to prevail in World War II. It also sets out US President Truman's belief that this international cooperation among military, academic, and industry agencies was as important of a wartime battleground as the front lines of the war itself. This cooperation relied in large part on a shared language, and this idea that effective communication could underpin national security was discussed in relation to technology development and public education for decision-making about computer innovations.

> *"Unless Russia is faced with an iron fist and strong language another war is in the making. Only one language do they understand—'How many [military] divisions have you?'"* US President Harry Truman, *"Unsent letter to Secretary of State Byrnes,"* 5 January 1945 [38]

> *"My Fellow Citizens of the World: We are here to make a choice between the quick and the dead."* Bernard Baruch, *"Speech to the United Nations Atomic Energy Commission,"* 14 June 1946 [7]

As World War II ended, the Allies (the United States, Britain, and Russia) had prevailed over the fascist threat of the Axis powers (Germany, Italy, and Japan) in battles waged with new military technologies, as much as with troops and conventional weapons. For example, radar systems were developed and manufactured in both Allied and Axis countries to detect and track enemy military assets on land and sea. As France fell to the Nazis and war came closer to the shores of England in 1940, British scientists were on the verge of making a breakthrough in radar technology that promised to change wartime power dynamics. The British government, however, realized that they lacked manufacturing capacity, so Prime Minister Winston Churchill agreed to share information on this strategic technology in exchange for the United States (US) manufacturing and financial resources. A team of top British scientists and engineers, headed by Chairman of the British Aeronautic Research Committee Sir Henry Tizard, traveled to the United States in August 1940. They met with engineers and scientists at General Electric, Westinghouse, Radio Corporation of America (RCA), Sperry, and Bell Labs/Western Electric in order to share their secret findings relating to development of an advanced microwave radar called the cavity magnetron.

© Springer Nature Switzerland AG 2021
B. Longo, *Words and Power*, History of Computing,
https://doi.org/10.1007/978-3-030-70373-8_3

In September 1940, the Tizard Mission also traveled to Washington, DC, to meet with members of the recently formed National Defense Research Council (NDRC), headed by former Dean of Engineering at Massachusetts Institute of Technology (MIT) Vannevar Bush. The NDRC "sought to apply civilian scientific ideas in military operations. NDRC's Section D-1, known as the Microwave Committee, consisted of representatives from industry and was charged with investigating radio detection and countermeasures" [14, p. 3]. The Tizard Mission also met with representatives of the US Navy and Army to disclose that they were able to detect clear, pulsed echoes from aircraft with their cavity magnetron. Based on the promise of these research findings, the NDRC worked with the British government to establish a research and development Radiation Laboratory at MIT, with manufactured components to be provided by industrial partners. By November 1940, the cavity magnetron was in mass production; by early in 1941, portable airborne radar devices had been fitted to US and British aircraft and the course of World War II changed [25].

Development of this wartime technology demonstrated that government agencies, private industry, and universities could work together to streamline rapid technology development for military dominance and national security; each member of the partnership profited. For example, by the end of World War II, Bell Labs/Western Electric had supplied 70 different types of radar to the US government, which totaled half of the government's radar purchases [27]. The MIT Radiation Lab had employed almost 4000 people, created over 100 different radar systems, and produced $1.5 billion of radar equipment. After the war, the NDRC voted to continue funding the MIT RadLab for research into communication technologies, optics, and other areas. These projects were overseen by a committee of members from the Army, Navy, and Air Force. "The remarkable success of this wartime effort depended not only on the goodwill between the U.S. and Britain, but also on an innovative partnership that was taking shape between academia, industry, and the government; and the new cooperation that was evolving between physicists, engineers, and other scientists from different academic backgrounds. These fledgling bonds would transform scientific research and how it would be carried out in the future" [14, p. 1].

3.1 The Battle of the Laboratories

President Truman credited the importance of military-industrial-academic partnerships for wartime victory in a 6 August 1945 press release announcing that the United States had dropped an atomic bomb that day on the Japanese city of Hiroshima. He equated the work of scientists and engineers at national laboratories in this effort to the work of wartime combat troops: "The battle of the laboratories held fateful risks for us as well as the battles of the air, land and sea, and we have now won the battle of the laboratories as we have won the other battles" [36]. He noted that the model of information sharing between Britain and the United States that started with the Tizard Mission had been extended to the Manhattan Project for developing atomic weapons: "The United States had available the large number of scientists of distinction in the many needed areas of knowledge. It had the tremendous industrial and financial resources necessary for the project ... We now have two great plants and many lesser works devoted to the production of atomic power. Employment during peak construction numbered 125,000 .... We have spent two billion dollars on the greatest scientific gamble in history – and won" [36]. Truman described the creation of a wartime partnership that would carry the United States and its allies into the postwar world:

> But the greatest marvel is not the size of the enterprise, its secrecy, nor its cost, but the achievement of scientific brains in putting together infinitely complex pieces of knowledge held by many men in different fields of science into a workable plan. And hardly less marvellous [sic] has been the capacity of industry to design, and of labor to operate, the machines and methods to do things never done before so that the brain child of many minds came forth in physical shape and performed as it was supposed to do. Both science and industry worked under the direction of the United States Army, which achieved a unique success in managing so diverse a problem in the advancement of knowledge in an amazingly short time. It is doubtful if such another combination could be got together in the world. What has been done is the greatest achievement of organized science in history [36].

Days before the President issued this press release, the Allies had signed the Potsdam Agreement to negotiate what territories each of the Allied countries would occupy in Europe after the war.[1] The United States and Britain had shared information and efforts to develop the atomic bomb that they now hoped would lead to the surrender of the Japanese forces, thereby ending the worldwide war. Although the United States and Britain had shared information on atomic bomb development, Russia had largely been left out of these discussions. In his diary note for 24 July 1945, Truman's Assistant Press Secretary Eben A. Ayers wrote, "At the plenary session on July 24, Truman walked over to Stalin and (in the words of [Truman's personal aide Admiral William D.] Leahy) 'told him quietly that we had developed a powerful weapon more potent than anything yet seen in war. The President said later that Stalin's reply indicated no special interest and that the Generalissimo did not seem to have any conception of what Truman was talking about." Ayers' diary entry continued with this encounter from President Truman's perspective: "The President told me ... that he told Stalin during the Potsdam conference that the U.S. had perfected a powerful new weapon. He said he did NOT tell Stalin that it was an atomic bomb or weapon. He said Stalin did not seem particularly impressed but he smiled and said that was fine" [6]. In a footnote to his collection of Truman's private papers, historian Robert H. Ferrell (1980) clarified that Stalin had, indeed, understood the import of Truman's statement: "...when [Stalin] got back to his quarters, [Soviet Foreign Minister] Molotov was heard to say to him, 'We'll have to talk it over with [Soviet nuclear physicist] Kurchatov and get him to speed things up. ... At Potsdam, the President obviously did not know that Russian spies had already penetrated the [US] bomb project and that Stalin would have the bomb

---

[1] The Potsdam Conference was held in Occupied Germany from 17 July to 2 August 1945.

'secret' with a few weeks of Alamogordo" [13, p. 54].[2] On the verge of total victory over the Axis powers, President Truman credited the US wartime military-industrial-academic partnership with a pivotal role in achieving this victory and preserving the way-of-life in the Free World. It is not surprising that this successful partnership model from the global hot war was then transferred to meet Cold War security challenges.

At the Los Alamos National Laboratory where the atomic bomb was developed, summer 1945 saw an abrupt exodus of lab personnel who hoped to resume their prewar lives away from New Mexico. "The postwar period was a time of transition and rapid change. At Los Alamos, the long months of intense effort had climaxed in victory, followed by a crashing letdown. ... The status of the Laboratory itself was faltering; there was a lack of national policy to determine the use and control of atomic energy" [21, p. 125]. Before Robert Oppenheimer left his post as director of the Los Alamos Lab, he developed a plan for splitting atomic energy research activities at Los Alamos from the subsequent engineering and production activities, which were formally established at the nearby Sandia National Laboratory. Jerrold Zacharias was brought in from the MIT Radiation Lab to head what came to be known as "Z-Division" operations at Sandia Lab. "The emphasis on 'readiness' as an increasingly important part of postwar defense strategy had sanctioned the decision to establish the engineering and production facility" at the Sandia Lab [21, p. 207]. On 21 August 1945, Oppenheimer announced that the mission of Z-Division would "include responsibility for the assembly of a stockpile of the existing Fat Man model [of atomic bomb], including development and surveillance tests, and the development and testing of new models" [21, p. 127]. The determination of who would control the future of Z-Division was contested among proponents of military, industrial, governmental, and academic interests.

3.2   The Battle for Control of Atomic Power

Behind debates in the United States about who would control the engineering and production of atomic weapons was a realization that the US monopoly of the atomic bomb was temporary. In the US State Department on 7 January 1946, Secretary James Byrnes named a Committee on Atomic Energy, headed by Undersecretary Dean Acheson, to develop a "proposal for the establishment of a commission to consider the problems arising as to the control of atomic energy and other weapons of possible mass destruction" [1]. A Board of Consultants, chaired by Tennessee Valley Authority[3] head David Lilienthal, was named to come up with this proposal.

---

[2] The first test detonation of the US nuclear device, code named Trinity, took place at the US Air Force Alamogordo Bombing and Gunnery Range in New Mexico on 16 July 1945.

[3] The Tennessee Valley Authority (TVA) was created in 1933 as part of President Franklin Roosevelt's New Deal. The purpose of the TVA was twofold: (1) improving the quality of life in the region through economic development and (2) bringing electricity to the region by building

Other members of this board were management organization specialist and former president of the United Service Organizations (USO) Chester Barnard, Manhattan Project director and physicist J. Robert Oppenheimer, Monsanto chemist and Manhattan Project contributor Charles Thomas, and General Electric engineer Harry Winne. This committee was formed with the anticipation of a "favorable action by the United Nations Organization" on the proposal that they would develop for the control of atomic energy and weapons [1]. Less than 2 weeks after Secretary Byrnes named this US Committee on Atomic Energy, the United Nations established its Atomic Energy Commission (UNAEC) with six permanent member states (United States, Britain, France, Soviet Union, China, Canada) and six rotating member states.

On 16 March 1946, the US Atomic Energy Committee delivered what has become known as the Acheson-Lilienthal Report to Secretary Byrnes, with the following two conclusions: "a) that only if the dangerous aspects of atomic energy are taken out of national hands and placed in international hands is there any reasonable prospect of devising safeguards against the use of atomic energy for bombs, and (b) only if the international agency was engaged in development and operation could it possibly discharge adequately its functions as a safeguarder of the world's future" [1]. This report "called for the creation of the Atomic Development Authority to oversee the mining and use of fissile materials, the operation of all nuclear facilities that could produce weaponry, and the right to dispense licenses to those countries wishing to pursue peaceful nuclear research" [2]. It "asserted that a complete protection against national nuclear military ambitions could not be assured even if all nations undertook to outlaw atomic weapons and accepted to submit all their peaceful nuclear activities to international safeguards ... [The Acheson-Lilienthal Report] therefore proposed that no facility, easily transformable for weapons production, should be left in national hands" [23, p. 59]. The Atomic Development Agency would be overseen by the UNAEC. The plan relied on US-Soviet cooperation and did not specify any penalties for a nation who violated the spirit of this collaborative effort. It recognized that the United States would no longer have a monopoly on atomic weapons, but did not specify when the United States would destroy its nuclear arsenal. In the 6 weeks it took for the committee to prepare its proposal, tensions between the United States and the Soviet Union had increased. By the time Byrnes received the report, US Ambassador Kennan had filed his "long telegram" warning the State Department that the Soviet Union was no longer an ally but was instead a national security threat [28]. This was no time to trust that the Soviets would collaborate on the development of atomic weapons without verifying that they acted in good faith.

Before Acheson and Lilienthal could deliver their proposal to the United Nations, President Truman appointed industrialist Bernard Baruch as the US ambassador to the UN. Baruch presented a modified version of the Acheson-Lilienthal proposal to

---

dams on the Tennessee River. "Against the backdrop of World War II, TVA launched one of the largest hydropower construction programs ever undertaken in the United States" [35]. After World War II, there was interest in harnessing atomic energy for generating steam and electricity.

the UNAEC on 14 June 1946. In the Baruch Plan, after the Atomic Development Agency was formed, no more atomic bombs would be built and existing bombs would be destroyed, thus reducing and ultimately eliminating all nuclear weapons. This plan also included penalties, such as facility inspections, for violations of the agreement that included illegally owning atomic bombs. In his concluding remarks, Baruch stated, "All of us are consecrated to making an end of gloom and hopelessness" [7]. Soviet Ambassador to the UN Andrei Gromyko rejected this plan. On 19 June, Gromyko put forward his own plan for collaboration on nuclear development and international exchange of scientific information. His plan called for nations to "prohibit the production and employment of weapons based on the use of atomic energy," as well as the destruction of all existing weapons within 3 months of signing the agreement. Violations of this agreement would be considered "a most serious crime against humanity." Signatories had 6 months to pass laws establishing "severe penalties" for violating the agreement [24]. "This was tantamount to an American unilateral disarmament without any counterpart or international control to verify the respect of the convention" [23, p. 60]. Baruch rejected this plan on behalf of the US government on 5 July; 4 days earlier the United States had carried out Operation Crossroads, its first postwar atomic bomb tests to determine bomb damage to naval vessels off the Bikini Islands. When Truman and Baruch forced their plan to a vote in the UNAEC on 30 December 1946, it was approved to send to the UN Security Council for further debate on a 10–0–2 vote with the Soviet Union and Poland abstaining. The Baruch plan was never taken up for a vote in the Security Council and "the world came to live with the continued insecurity and danger of an atomic arms race" [22, p. 73]. Six days before that UNAEC vote in December, the first Soviet nuclear reactor had reached criticality;[4] the Soviets were on the brink of developing their own atomic weapons. In the United States, concerns with military readiness and the nuclear weapons stockpile moved to the forefront of national awareness.

National security concerns regarding the future of nuclear power and atomic weapons were central to debates about who would control US atomic development: military or civilian agencies. In May 1946, the military made an initial move to control Sandia Lab engineering and production operations with a civil service and military workforce to "handle the assembly, stockpile, surveillance, and field test operations" [21, p. 141]. Earlier that year, however, President Truman had voiced his preference for civilian control of atomic development. After debates between interested parties in the military and federal government, the Atomic Energy Act was signed into law in Congress on 1 August 1946 to give primary responsibility for wartime and peaceful development of atomic energy to the government on behalf of the civilian population. The Atomic Energy Commission created in that act would be headed by civilians, with oversight carried out through committees with military

---

[4]Definition of criticality according to the Glossary of the US Nuclear Regulatory Commission: "The normal operating condition of a reactor, in which nuclear fuel sustains a fission chain reaction. A reactor achieves criticality (and is said to be critical) when each fission event releases a sufficient number of neutrons to sustain an ongoing series of reactions" [5].

leadership [21, p. 214]. Successful coordination of this critical effort would rely on establishing effective communication channels to share and protect sensitive information.

The Atomic Energy Act of 1946 began by acknowledging the impact of atomic energy on weapons of war, but stated that the "effect of the use of atomic energy for civilian purposes upon the social, economic, and political structures of today cannot now be determined" [39]. In order to establish oversight for the yet-to-be-envisioned changes brought about by the development of atomic energy, the Act established the Atomic Energy Commission with the "paramount objective of assuring the common defense and security, the development and utilization of atomic energy shall, so far as practicable, be directed toward improving the public welfare, increasing the standard of living, strengthening free competition in private enterprise, and promoting world peace" [39]. In order to carry out these existential goals, the Act enumerated research programs that would be funded by private enterprise as well as public agencies to "encourage maximum scientific progress" [39]. The Act also stipulated that communication channels be established to facilitate these research goals in the service of national security. It established a "program for the control of scientific and technical information which will permit the dissemination of such information to encourage scientific progress, and for the sharing on a reciprocal basis of information concerning the practical industrial application of atomic energy as soon as effective and enforceable safeguards against its use for destructive purposes can be devised" [38, p. 4–5; 39]. This legislation recognized the important role that people sharing technical information through established inter-agency channels would play for ensuring rapid development of control systems for atomic weapons and nuclear power for economic welfare.

The Atomic Energy Act set up goals, policies, and an organizational structure for carrying out atomic development for national security and public welfare. At midnight on 31 December 1946, members of the Atomic Energy Commission (AEC) assumed the responsibility for achieving the goals set out in that legislation. Throughout 1946, General Leslie Groves[5] advocated for an expanded role for national laboratories to expedite research, development, and production of nuclear weapons. In the model of the Los Alamos Laboratory that Groves had overseen through the Manhattan Project, he believed that these lab operations should be government funded with university management [20, p. 9]. In order to determine the state of military readiness of the Los Alamos and Sandia Labs, AEC Chairman Lilienthal and the rest of the commissioners flew to New Mexico to tour the labs on 16 November 1946. After the tours, Lilienthal commented that he had "learned quite a lot" about "what had *not* been done in the way of planning, coordination, and

---

[5] Groves had served as director of the Manhattan Project. In 1946 he was appointed to the Military Liaison Committee of the Atomic Energy Commission (AEC); this committee was the liaison between the AEC and the US Department of Defense. In February 1947, Groves was appointed chief of the Armed Forces Special Weapons Project to oversee military uses of nuclear weapons [21, p. 216]. In 1948, he left the military to become vice president at Sperry Corporation, a major wartime supplier of analog computer-controlled bomb sights and airborne radar systems.

the like" [20, p. 10; italics in original]. Misgivings about military readiness in the wake of breakdowns in dialogue with the Soviets were deepened after a subsequent lab tour by AEC Commissioner Robert Bacher[6] and a "more depressing" [20, p. 10] report to the AEC in January 1947. After discussing Bacher's report, members of the AEC General Advisory Committee (GAC) "agreed that Los Alamos should be revitalized and weapons research accelerated, particularly in view of the failure of various disarmament plans in United Nations negotiations" [20] and continued advances in nuclear development taking place in the Soviet Union.

3.3   Information Sharing for National Readiness

In April 1947, AEC GAC Chairman Oppenheimer and members of the GAC Weapons Subcommittee flew to New Mexico to tour the Los Alamos and Sandia Labs. At Los Alamos, Lab Director Norris Bradbury discussed development of new weapons and the need to test stockpiled weapons. At Sandia, they evaluated production capacity and found assembly operations housed in a military surplus quonset hut. "There, Sandia technicians sorted weapon components from the wartime project, tested new ones, and transferred them to the ordnance section at Kirtland [Air Force Base] where high-explosive charges would be added when available. Completed weapons were to be stored in igloos located in an arroyo south of the runways" [20, p. 10]. Sandia personnel operated largely on their own, with little oversight from the Los Alamos Lab. Their engineers produced mock-ups of existing stockpiled weapons. Sandia's military liaison trained officers in assembly, handling and testing of these weapons, as well as documenting these procedures in technical manuals to standardize operations. Despite the good work and enthusiasm among the Sandia personnel, operations there in April 1947 were "a long way from production-line status" [20, p. 11].

After reading the report from the GAC tour, AEC Chairman Lilienthal considered that the "result of these inspections was a shock. The substantial stockpile of atom bombs we and the top military assumed was there, in readiness, did not exist. Furthermore, the production facilities that might enable us to produce quantities of atomic weapons and weapons so engineered that they would not continue to require a Ph.D. in physics to handle them in the field, likewise did not exist. No quantity production of weapons was possible under the existing handicraft setup" [20, p. 11]. When Lilienthal briefed President Truman on the findings of this report in mid-April, the President was "also shocked" [20, p. 11]. Truman later described his reaction this way: "In this, their first report, I was advised that there were serious weaknesses in the operation from the standpoint of national defense and security. The number of bombs was disappointing, and those we had were not assembled" [38, p. 296]. In the face of continued Soviet research into weapons-grade plutonium

---

[6]Robert Bacher was a nuclear physicist and one of the leaders of the Manhattan Project [21].

development, as well as their aggression in Greece and Turkey, this news about the precarious state of US military readiness threatened to weaken President Truman's pledge, known now as the Truman Doctrine [37], to back democratic governments around the world who sought to deter Soviet expansion.[7] This move to exert US global power relied on maintaining nuclear weapon superiority, which at that point largely relied on military surplus facilities and word-of-mouth instructions for assembling weapons at the Sandia Lab.

In November 1947, the AEC GAC sent Weapons Subcommittee member John Manley[8] to Sandia Lab to reassess the state of operations there. In his subsequent report, Manley found that staff turnover at the lab presented the most serious obstacle to ongoing operations that were necessary for robust military readiness. "In his opinion, the result of having 'different people with different concepts introducing different perturbations that might last beyond a person's tenure would be a lack of standardization of components and manuals and the eventual retardation of development programs'" [20, p. 13]. Without an organizational mechanism for establishing standard procedures for engineering, production, and handling of weapons systems, Manley's report to the AEC found that weapons development would be hindered. Against a backdrop of Truman's stated intention for the United States to counter Soviet expansion, this lack of communication channels at Sandia Lab to ensure that standardized information would persist, even with rapid personnel turnover, threatened US national security.

The establishment of communication channels for sharing technical information was a topic of debate between people who considered this to be a security threat and those who considered this to be essential for scientific and technical progress. President Truman considered information sharing, as had taken place between the United States and Britain in World War II, to be essential for rapid the technology development on which postwar national security relied. Debates in the United Nations about international control of nuclear information included consideration of whether information on weapons development would be shared, as well as information about peaceful uses of nuclear power. Once these debates foundered at the end of 1946, the United States, Britain, and Canada "adopted a uniform system for handling the information jointly developed [about atomic research and development]. In January 1948 the three governments had agreed upon a *modus vivendi* providing for co-operation involving exchange of scientific and technical information" [38, p. 303]. In December 1947, when the AEC communicated the findings of the Manley report to President Truman, GAC Chairman Oppenheimer strongly argued for the importance of open communication for scientific communication:

---

[7] See brief background on the Truman Doctrine [13, p. 105–106]: "On March 12, 1947, the President went before Congress and asked for $400 million for military and economic aid to Greece and Turkey, and broadly promised assistance to nations threatened by world communism." This turn from isolation to world leadership would guide US foreign policy for the next 40 years.

[8] John H. Manley was a physicist who worked on the Manhattan Project and was one of Robert Oppenheimer's chief aids [21].

We have been forced to recognize, in studying the possible implementation of technical policy, how adverse the effect of secrecy, and of the inevitable misunderstanding and error which accompany it, have been on progress, and thus on the common defense and security. ... Even in the fields of technology, in industrial applications, in military problems, the fruits of secrecy are misapprehension, ignorance, and apathy. It will be a continuing problem for the Government of the United States to re-evaluate the risks of unwise disclosure, and weigh them against the undoubted dangers of maintaining secrecy at the cost of error and stagnation. Only by such re-evaluation can the development of atomic energy make its maximum contribution to the securing of the peace, and to the perpetuation and growth of the values of our civilization [38, p. 301].

Although President Truman was "uncompromisingly opposed to sharing or yielding atomic military secrets to any other government" [38, p. 301], circumstances at Sandia Lab where people were responsible for weapons production and deployment called for establishing communication channels for sharing technical information. These channels would be necessary for training personnel in standardized procedures and coordinating efforts among civilian, industrial, and military partners.

Immediately after Manley's report, "the AEC made a concerted effort to improve the ordnance facility at Sandia Base and build up the nuclear stockpile" [20, p. 14; 20, p. 251]. Paul Larsen from the Johns Hopkins Applied Physics Lab[9] was named director of the Sandia Lab; shortly thereafter the lab transferred in two technical writers and one technical illustrator to work on operations manuals for weapons testing equipment [30, p. 16]. Sandia's national security mission was the weaponization of atomic research and development, "the design of fuzing and firing systems to detonate a weapon at a particular time and altitude, assuring optimum destruction of a special target" [21, p. 252]. In 1947, industrial contractors were identified to carry out essential aspects of the lab's mission: Union Carbide (Oak Ridge, Tennessee) and Mason and Hanger (Burlington, Iowa) were brought on to test and assemble weapons components [20, p. 15]. The success of this expanded mission relied on exacting operations that required collaboration among workers from industrial, military, and university backgrounds. This type of multidisciplinary operation relied on standardized information and communication channels. Effective communication in this environment required a shared vocabulary of technical terms for findings that might have been developed in disparate industrial or university research labs. Secrecy or misunderstanding in this environment could hinder weapons development at best. At worst, it could threaten national security and the position of the United States as the global champion of democracy.

---

[9] In Paul J. Larsen's earlier career, he had "worked on the first transatlantic radio broadcasting station for the Marconi Wireless Company and managed research laboratories for Radio Corporation of America" (RCA). He also worked at Bell Telephone Laboratories. [21, p. 252].

3.4   A Common Tongue

The role of a common language in national security had been appreciated since the US and British collaboration on radar development during World War II. Churchill explicitly acknowledged the strategic advantage of shared language in a September 1943 speech he gave on the occasion of receiving an honorary degree from Harvard University. The title of the speech, "The Gift of a Common Tongue," summed up his message on the strength of "Anglo-American amity and unity": "The great Bismark … is said to have observed towards the close of his life that the most potent factor in human society at the end of the nineteenth century was the fact that the British and American peoples spoke the same language" [10]. The "priceless heritage" of a common tongue "enabled [the US and Britain] to wage war together with an intimacy and harmony never before achieved among allies" [10]. This foundation of a shared language that Churchill celebrated later underpinned the collaboration that President Truman described in his 6 August 1945 speech as "the battle of the laboratories" [36]. What Truman described as "the achievement of scientific brains in putting together infinitely complex pieces of knowledge held by many men in different fields of science into a workable plan" [36] first relied on a common facility in the English language among the international group of scientists. But more than a colloquial understanding of the English language, the people who were responsible for rapid technology development for national security needed a common vocabulary of technical terms.

In an isolated setting such as the Los Alamos Laboratory in the high desert of Northern New Mexico, people working together could develop the necessary shared technical terminology to carry out their research and development missions. After the war, however, when the mission expanded to include industrial and civilian collaborators coming from disparate settings with their own discourse communities,[10] a common set of technical terms could not be assumed across different locations. During the war, research and development projects had been carried out in isolated industrial and university laboratories working with separated military units under security mandates for secrecy. When these scientists and engineers sought to collaborate on projects after the war, they often found that they were working at cross purposes, in part because they lacked a shared understanding of technical terms for concepts that were rapidly changing. This communication impediment slowed the technology development that US civilian and military leaders – such as Robert Oppenheimer, Vannevar Bush, and James Conant – believed was the foundation of military readiness in the Cold War just as it had been in World War II.

The question of how to improve communication for technical development was open to debate. In his September 1943 address at Harvard, Churchill put forward the

---

[10]According to linguist John Swales, discourse communities have six characteristics: (a) communality of interest; (b) mechanisms for intercommunication among members; (c) feedback mechanisms; (d) discoursal expectations, such as appropriate topics and genres; (e) specialized terminology; and (f) critical mass of members with content expertise [34, p. 212–213].

idea of Basic English as an answer to streamlining communication for international cooperation. Crediting the Harvard Commission on English Language Studies as being on the forefront of Basic English development, Churchill explained his vision for the role of a common language in international relations: "It would certainly be a grand convenience for us all to be able to move freely about the world – as we shall be able to do more freely than ever before as the science of the world develops – and be able to find everywhere a medium, albeit primitive, of intercourse and understanding. Might it not also be an advantage to many races, and an aid to the building-up of our new structure for preserving peace?" [10]. Churchill argued that the basis for rapid scientific advancement rested on a shared language of Basic English.

Basic English was a plan for establishing a simplified English language through the use of a limited vocabulary of 850 words with simplified grammar rules. This idea was introduced in 1930 by English linguist Charles K. Ogden who thought that Basic English would facilitate the clear statement of ideas with English as the international *lingua franca*. Ogden identified social problems that resulted from imprecise and unclear use of language:

> (i) we often use words with confused and ambiguous meanings, and from this ambiguity a number of accidents can result; (ii) many of these accidents would be avoided if we fixed with absolute precision the meaning of the terms we used; (iii) this method has proved fruitful in the exact sciences … and in military life; and (iv) a science of language that could extend these criteria also into ordinary language would make social life, individual relationships, and ethical problems less ambiguous and more precise [33].

If imprecise language could cause social problems, Ogden set out to facilitate international peace through a linguistic system for more a more exact language: "It is the business of all internationally-minded persons to make Basic English part of the system of education in every country, so that there may be more communication, less chance of war, and less learning of languages -- which after all, for most of us, is a very unnecessary waste of time" [32, Part I]. Acknowledging that specialized scientific terminology was beyond the scope of the 850-word vocabulary, Ogden called for an international committee of scientists to agree on these specialized terms: "The great need now is for Committees to be formed by those responsible for the organizations of science in different countries, so that workers in every branch may be in no doubt to which words are international" [32, Part II]. Ogden's language reform plan for a Basic English had some influence on linguistic philosophers, especially those like mechanical engineer Willard C. Brinton who sought to develop pictographic vocabularies for communicating ideas and meaning [9]. Brinton, who was named president of the Harvard Engineering Society in 1932, was especially interested in communicating mathematical information through visual representations and Basic English.

When Churchill suggested that Basic English could become the *lingua franca* of a modern international community, he expressed the hope that peace could be achieved on a basis of shared communication after fascism was defeated. In April 1944, he sent a letter to President Roosevelt encouraging him to pursue this approach for underpinning international relations with Basic English. Roosevelt referred this matter to Secretary of State Cordell Hull, who was working on the *Charter of the*

United Nations. Hull advised Roosevelt that "before we go very far we should take steps to ascertain the views of competent Government specialists and private linguistics experts" [29, p. 154]. Roosevelt, who did not want to "pour ice water" on Churchill's idea, asked Hull to find a "sympathetic" Congressional committee to review the idea [29, p. 154]. Secretary Hull, however, was not the only person who was lukewarm about the prospects of Basic English for postwar international relations. In the March 1944 *Harper's Magazine*, linguist Rudolf Flesch expressed his doubts about the utility of Basic English for the robust deliberations upon which world peace could be built.

In the early 1940s, writing researcher Rudolf Flesch began to formulate an argument for adopting a scientific approach to functional writing. His approach to a simplified writing focused more on sentence structure and word form than on restricting vocabulary. In countering the efficacy of Basic English, Flesch questioned "whether an international language is desirable at all" [15, p. 340]. Even if this international language was desirable, Flesch further questioned whether English was the most efficient language upon which to base this shared language, since English is not as simple a language as Chinese, for example. Instead of restricting vocabulary, Flesch suggested that language simplicity was "mainly a question of sentence structure and concreteness of expression" [15, p. 341]. Flesch concluded that "Basic is still a thousand times better than the academic or bureaucratic jargon we have to wade through every day" [15, p. 343], but he worked to devise a mathematically based approach to communicating information – even complex technical information – in a format that could be readily understood even by people who were unfamiliar with the topic.

As a doctoral student in the Readability Laboratory of the American Association of Adult Education at Columbia University, Flesch began to formulate an argument for adopting a scientific approach to functional writing. He fashioned an early readability formula from the "staggering amount of word counts and sentence measurements" generated from this body of scientific research and applied it to "English for grown-ups" [16, p. 194]. In addition to gleaning from the fields of educational research and psychology, Flesch compared his "scientific rhetoric" [18] to Aristotle's teachings, and explained that he had been "dealing with simple language as a researcher, librarian, teacher, editor, and writer" [17, p. xii]. He ultimately came up with "a statistical formula for measuring readability" [17, p. xii] in his 1944 dissertation, which was published under the title *Marks of a Readable Style*. Readers quickly bought 700 copies of this initial work [4, p. 24]. By 1945, Flesch was the editor of trade bulletins in the US Office of Price Administration National Office, "translating price regulations into sports-article English" aimed at a seventh-grade reader [17, p. 194–195]. This translation work was important because of the "information overload" generated during the New Deal and World War II. Vannevar Bush, for example, described the growth of information at the Office of Scientific Research and Development during the war: "So many new government agencies had sprung up, demanding so much interagency coordination, that memos in triplicate were flooding the government. Even military operations spawned massive amounts of paperwork ... Incredibly, a federal government that had entered the war with just

$650,000 worth of printing and reproducing equipment owned $50 million worth within a year. The Office of Price Administration alone produced more paper than the entire government had before the war" [40, p. 269]. More robust and standardized communication channels were needed to streamline and manage this information overload, especially when national security was at stake.

Flesch's work not only reflected a belief in science; it participated in a cultural project to uphold democratic decision-making by working to educate the general citizenry in technological issues through a plain style of popularized science writing. As Paul Edwards (1996) argued, culture and politics are necessarily intertwined: "...the idea of 'culture' does allow us to understand *representation* as an arena of political action. The 'politics of culture' refers to the embedding of structures of power and interests in shared representations: concepts, media, and conventional structures of thought" [12, p. 151, italics in original]. Edwards defined the term politics as "the contest among social groups for power recognition, and the satisfaction of interests. The contest is acted out in many arenas and with varying degrees of visibility" [12, p. 148]. Flesch's scientific approach to language and his advocacy of a plain style of technical writing was necessarily embedded in the politics of his time. This political purpose for popular science writing reflected a national concern with truth, propaganda, democracy, and national security that permeated US society in the post-World War II years. In part, this concern manifested itself in debates about proper relationships among government agencies, research operations, private corporations, universities, the press, and the general citizenry. For example, as World War II was winding down, Vannevar Bush grappled with tensions between a federally centralized model of technology development – like the Manhattan Project at the Los Alamos Laboratory – and the democratic tradition of an inspired inventor working in a private lab, like Thomas Edison. Bush had participated with the British Tizard Mission to develop microwave radar in 1940 and was named by President Roosevelt to head the newly formed Office of Scientific Research and Development (OSRD) in 1941. Reviewing his wartime work to centralize scientific research through the OSRD, Bush "considered the central moral achievement of the war the nation's reconciliation of the conflict between free men in a democratic society and the short-term benefits of tight control and command over a nation's resources" [40, p. 226]. The question of who would control postwar technology development was central in determining what kind of nation we would become in the last half of the twentieth century.

Technology development under a totalitarian, Communist government could potentially be more efficient than in a democracy, because decision-making was more streamlined. In a totalitarian regime, a few people could make decisions that affected large groups of people; in a democracy, these decisions were subject to popular review and participation. If the United States was to successfully compete with the Soviet Union in the arena of technology development and national security, streamlining popular participation in these decision-making processes would help to achieve this national security goal. One component of this project was educating publics about scientific and technical topics. In his Foreword to Flesch's 1949 book *The Art of Readable Writing*, Associated Press Executive Editor Alan J. Gould credited Flesch's work with journalists as "playing an important part in lifting writing habits" in an "era of great crisis in human history. These are times in which it is supremely vital to convey ideas and report the news so that basic truths may be *better* understood by *more* people" [19, p. ix; italics in original]. Through his work with Flesch, Gould concluded that "in a confused world – we have a better chance of reducing the total content of confusion" [19, p. ix]. Efficient functional communication would not only help to strengthen an informed citizenry; it would also help to establish robust communication channels to facilitate collaboration among people in military, industrial, and academic sectors of society. An educated citizenry would be better prepared to understand and act on the rapidly changing social, technological, and political situations that scientists and engineers were introducing.

One such educational piece was authored by long-time Bush friend and colleague, Harvard President James Conant. Conant had participated in the Manhattan Project as "Chairman of the National Defense Research Committee in overseeing the successful development of weapons systems, including the atomic bomb, during World War II" and led "the Nation's atomic energy program after the war as Chairman of the Committee on Atomic Energy of the Joint Research and Development Board and as a member of the General Advisory Committee to the Atomic Energy Commission" [3]. In *Science and Common Sense: A World Famous Scientist and Educator Explains How Science Works* (1951), Conant contrasted scientific exploration in the Soviet Union and United States and then voiced this conclusion on the relationship between science and the well-being of the US capitalist state:

> In the technological competition between business firms, the most progressive company has the most to gain by the advance of science. So the United States as a nation can benefit more than any other country by the continued vigor of scientific investigation. … Therefore, whatever any other nation may do, whatever the tension of the times, we must continue to foster science; and that means fostering freedom of inquiry, of discussion, and of publication [11, p. 353].

By advocating freedom of inquiry, discussion, and publication, Conant relied on a science-literate citizenry and on the clear writing of science popularizers. Foreign journalist Edward Hunter (1956) used more lurid phrasing to emphasize the importance of an informed citizenry in fighting the Cold War: "Truth is the most important serum and integrity the most devastating weapon that can be used against the totalitarian concept. Facts can demolish the entire fake communist paradise. Nothing should be allowed to interfere with the task of getting those facts across to the people who need and can use them" [26, p. 310]. In a cold war based on psychology and propaganda, words were weapons, and understanding was defense. Functional communication based on mathematical principles could provide the linguistic tools for military defense.

Another educational piece was authored by Edmund Berkeley, who had collaborated with Flesch to create a readability laboratory at Prudential Insurance in 1947 when Berkeley was the Chief Research Consultant there. Flesch described the purpose of his scientific rhetoric to Berkeley as applying "symbolic logic for the systematic simplification of complex exposition" [18]. Berkeley was a Harvard-trained mathematician who had focused his career on the applications of symbolic logic in predicting insurance risk at Prudential and in early computer development through his company Berkeley Enterprises. After seeing the Complex Number Calculator that George Stibitz was developing at Bell Labs in late fall of 1939, Berkeley realized that this device, built with telephone relay switches, could help people think. "If people could work with digital computers like the Complex Number Calculator to apply symbolic logic to complex, ill-defined social problems, then there was a possibility that people could make better decisions about war and finances and other things that affected society at large" [31, p. 12]. During World War II, Berkeley went on leave from Prudential to go on active duty as a lieutenant with the Naval Reserve. In late summer of 1945, he was assigned to the Harvard Computation Lab to report to Commander Howard Aiken, Officer-In-Charge of the Bureau of Ordnance Computing Project, and then developing the Mark II computer in collaboration with IBM. The Mark II was one of the first machines to use the binary coded decimal (BCD) coding and floating-point arithmetic that Stibitz had introduced in calculating machines at Bell Labs. While Berkeley worked on the early stages of design on the Mark II, he reported that he "applied symbolic logic to save about $4000 of relays in the design" [31, p. 31]. This machine was built and tested at the Harvard lab during 1946 and 1947; it was installed and running at Dahlgren Naval Proving Ground by February 1948.

By that time, Berkeley had returned to Prudential where he advocated for the integration of electronic computers into insurance company operations. He was also finishing a book about computers, *Giant Brains or Machines That Think* (1949), aimed at educating average Americans about these important new calculating devices. Knowing that his readers would not be familiar with computers, Berkeley applied Flesch's readability concepts and avoided using technical terms. But when technical terms were necessary, such as *memory*, Berkeley defined the term in the text: "The *memory* of a mechanical brain consists of physical equipment in which information can be stored" [8, p. 27]. He was sufficiently concerned about the role of words in "the problem of explanation and understanding" [8, p. ix] that he included an appendix on "Words and Ideas," where he discussed the process of going from explanation to understanding of new technical terms. In the preface to this book, Berkeley described the importance of this new topic of automatic calculating machines to the average reader: Computers "are powerful instruments for obtaining new knowledge. They apply in science, business, government, and other activities. ... Along with the release of atomic energy, they are one of the great achievements of the present century. No one can afford to be unaware of their significance" [8, p. vii]. As computers became more instrumental for guiding missiles in atomic weapon systems being developed for military readiness, creating a shared understanding of technical terms among an educated US public became as strategically important as the weapons themselves.

References

1. Acheson, Dean, and David Lilienthal. 1946, March 17. *Report on the international control of atomic energy*. Atomic Heritage Foundation. https://www.atomicheritage.org/key-documents/acheson-lilienthal-report. Accessed 29 Oct 2020.
2. Anonymous. n.d. *The Acheson-Lilienthal & Baruch plans, 1946*. U.S. Department of State Archive. https://2001-2009.state.gov/r/pa/ho/time/cwr/88100.htm. Accessed 29 Oct 2020.
3. ———. n.d. *Profile of James B. Conant*. Atomic Heritage Foundation. https://www.atomicheritage.org/profile/james-b-conant. Accessed 29 Oct 2020.
4. ———. 1947, April 12. Apostle of "plain talk." *Business Week*: 22–25. Edmund C. Berkeley Papers [CBI50] Charles Babbage Institute, University of Minnesota, Minneapolis.
5. ———. 2020, June 26. *Definition of criticality*. US Nuclear Regulatory Commission. https://www.nrc.gov/reading-rm/basic-ref/glossary/criticality.html. Accessed 30 Oct 2020.
6. Ayers, Eben A. 1945, June 1. *Diary entries*. Harry S. Truman Library. https://www.trumanlibrary.gov/library/research-files/diary-entries?documentid=NA&pagenumber=5. Accessed 30 Oct 2020.
7. Baruch, Bernard. 1946, June 14. *Speech presented to the United Nations Atomic Energy Commission*. Atomicarchive.com. https://www.atomicarchive.com/resources/documents/deterrence/baruch-plan.html. Accessed 29 October 2020.
8. Berkeley, Edmund C. 1949. *Giant brains or machines that think*. New York: Wiley.
9. Brinton, Willard C. 1919. *Graphic methods for presenting facts*. New York: The Engineering Magazine Company.
10. Churchill, Winston S. 1943, September 6. *The gift of a common tongue*. International Churchill Society. https://winstonchurchill.org/resources/speeches/1941-1945-war-leader/the-price-of-greatness-is-responsibility/. Accessed 29 Oct 2020.
11. Conant, James B. 1951. *Science and common sense*. New Haven: Yale University Press.
12. Edwards, Paul N. 1996. *The closed world: Computers and the politics of discourse in cold war America*. Cambridge, MA: MIT Press.
13. Ferrell, Robert H., ed. 1980. *Off the record: The private papers of Harry S. Truman*. New York: Harper & Row.
14. Fleischer, Dorothy A. 1991. The MIT radiation laboratory – RLE's microwave heritage. *RLE Currents* 4 (2): 1–11.
15. Flesch, Rudolf. 1944, March. How basic is basic English? *Harpers Magazine*: pp. 339–343.
16. ———. 1945. The science of making sense. *The American Mercury* 60 (254): 194–197.
17. ———. 1946. *The art of plain talk*. New York: Harper & Brothers.
18. ———. 1947, May 29. *Letter to Edmund Berkeley*. Edmund C. Berkeley Papers [CBI50] Charles Babbage Institute, University of Minnesota, Minneapolis.
19. ———. 1949. *The art of readable writing*. New York: Harper & Brothers.
20. Furman, Necah Stewart. 1988. *Sandia National Laboratories: A product of postwar readiness, 1945–1950*. Albuquerque: Sandia National Laboratories.
21. ———. 1990. *Sandia National Laboratories: The postwar decade*. Albuquerque: University of New Mexico Press.
22. Gerber, Larry G. 1982. The Baruch plan and the origins of the Cold War. *Diplomatic History* 6 (1): 69–95.
23. Goldschmidt, Bertrand. 1986, Spring. A forerunner of the NPT? The Soviet proposals of 1947: A retrospective look at attempts to control the spread of nuclear weapons. *IAEA Bulletin* 28 (1): 58–64.
24. Gromyko, Andrei. 1946, June 19. Address by the Soviet representative to the United National Atomic Energy Commission. In US Department of State. 1960. *Documents on disarmament, 1945–1956*. Washington, DC: US Department of State.
25. Hind, Angela. 2007. *Briefcase that changed the world*. BBC News. http://news.bbc.co.uk/2/hi/science/nature/6331897.stm. Accessed 29 Oct 2020.

26. Hunter, Edward. 1956. *Brainwashing: The story of men who defied it*. New York: Farrar, Straus and Cudahy.
27. Iardella, Albert B., ed. 1964. *Western electric and the bell system: A survey of service*. New York: Western Electric Company.
28. Kennan, George. 1946, February 22. *Telegram to James Byrnes*. Harry S. Truman Library. https://www.trumanlibrary.gov/library/research-files/telegram-george-kennan-james-byrnes-long-telegram. Accessed 31 Oct 2020.
29. Kimball, Warren F., ed. 1984. *Churchill and Roosevelt, volume three: The complete correspondence*. Princeton: Princeton University Press.
30. Larsen, P.J. 1948, February 18. *Memo to N.E.* Bradbury: Sandia National Laboratories Z Division Status Report.
31. Longo, Bernadette. 2015. *Edmund Berkeley and the social responsibility of computer professionals*. San Rafael: Morgan & Claypool Press – ACM.
32. Ogden, Charles K. 1930. *Basic English: A general introduction with rules and grammar*. Basic English Institute. http://ogden.basic-english.org/. Accessed 29 Oct 2020.
33. Ogden, Charles K., and I.A. Richards. 1923. *The meaning of meaning*. Orlando: Harcourt Brace Jovanovich, Publishers. 1989.
34. Swales, John. 1988. Discourse communities, genres, and English as an international language. *World Englishes* 7 (2): 211–220.
35. Tennessee Valley Authority. n.d. *Our history*. Tennessee Valley Authority. https://www.tva.com/about-tva/our-history. Accessed 31 October 2020.
36. Truman, Harry S. 1945, August 6. *Press release by the White House*. Harry S. Truman Library. https://www.trumanlibrary.gov/library/research-files/press-release-white-house?documentid=NA&pagenumber=1. Accessed 29 Oct 2020.
37. ———. 1947, March 12. *Address before a joint session of Congress*. Yale Law School Lillian Goldman Law Library. https://avalon.law.yale.edu/20th_century/trudoc.asp. Accessed 29 Oct 2020.
38. ———. 1956. *Memoirs volume two: Years of trial and hope*. Garden City: Doubleday & Company.
39. United States Congress. *Atomic Energy Act of 1946*. Atomicarchive.com. https://www.atomicarchive.com/resources/documents/deterrence/atomic-energy-act.html. Accessed 29 October 2020.
40. Zachary, G. Pascal. 1999. *Endless frontier: Vannevar Bush, engineer of the American century*. Cambridge, MA: MIT Press.

Chapter 4
Sharing Information (or Not) for Computer Development

Abstract This chapter describes how computer developers shared information about technology innovations in the early 1940s and through World War II. During this period, much information about computer development was isolated in university laboratories where people worked under national security restrictions. In the absence of formal communication channels for sharing information, computer developers relied on personal relationships and face-to-face meetings to learn about new designs and approaches to automatic machine calculation. In this period, information was largely shared among people who had established contacts with leaders in the field of computer development, yet they often found that they had difficulty sharing information because of differences in terminology they developed in isolated laboratories.

"By collecting the small core of people who were involved with computers and exposing them to an equally small core of people who were interested, these conferences played a vital role in advancing the state of the art." Henry Tropp, "The Effervescent Years," 1974 [28]

"There is currently such a shortage of trained mathematicians required to operate the modern computing machine that these machines are not working full time. With the number of machines being built or projected it is probable that within ten years, two thousand persons will be required in this work ... this is a substantial fraction of all professional mathematicians in the country." Richard Clippinger, "Mathematical Requirements for the Personnel of a Computing Laboratory," 1950 [12]

If technology development after World War II could help to make the United States more secure, then an informed citizenry within this democratic country could help to direct the development of technology in an efficient manner. At the functional level, efficient communication was needed so that the people developing these new technologies could work together effectively across disciplinary and societal boundaries. Flesch's readability formula emerged as a mathematical hope for improving communication skills among workers in business and government. Books and articles aimed at general readers helped to inform people about the importance of developments in science and technology, as well as to inspire younger readers to go into these careers. But technology developers also needed a common vocabulary to share among themselves the research findings, engineering plans, and

© Springer Nature Switzerland AG 2021
B. Longo, *Words and Power*, History of Computing,
https://doi.org/10.1007/978-3-030-70373-8_4

deployment goals coming from different labs and agencies. Postwar computer developers worked to develop communication structures to support knowledge sharing among people who might unknowingly be working on related projects.

Mathematicians and people who had worked on military projects during World War II helped to establish these communication structures. Mina Rees (1980), director of the mathematical section of the Office of Naval Research, emphasized the importance of the US military in laying a foundation for postwar cooperation for knowledge sharing and technology development: "Although automatically sequenced electronic computers were not available before the end of the war, the needs of the war played a decisive role in their initial development and the military services continued their interest and provided much of the funding for the post-war developments" [26, p. 611]. She recalled the central role that military contracts with university laboratories played in enabling early development of electronic computers and supporting the continuation of this development after the war:

> Before the end of the war, there was an awakening realization among mathematicians that a new focus in numerical analysis would be needed as the [automatically sequenced electronic computer] machines became more important in scientific work. … some of the men and women who had wartime experience did develop an interest in this emerging field. As the speed and capacity of machines increased after the war's end, the scope of mathematical problems that would require attention if the machines were to be properly used expanded significantly and, partly under the stimulation of the Office of Naval Research, these problems aroused the interest of increasing numbers of mathematicians." [26, p. 610-611]

During the war, mathematicians had worked together on research projects under the auspices of groups such as the Applied Mathematics Panel of the National Defense Research Committee (NDRC), which was established in 1942 and headed by Warren Weaver. Weaver had previously headed the NDRC Fire Control Section "whose most important assignment was to develop an anti-aircraft director that would serve as an essential component in the system that was needed to protect Britain from German bombing" [26, p. 609]. In addition to Weaver as chair, Panel members included Richard Courant (New York University), Griffith C. Evans (University of California, Berkeley), Thornton C. Fry (Bell Telephone Laboratories), Lawrence M. Graves (University of Chicago), Marston Morse (Institute for Advanced Study in Princeton), Oswald Veblen (Institute for Advanced Study in Princeton), and Samuel S. Wilks (Princeton University), with mathematician Mina Rees as the technical aide to the Panel [25, p. 609]. This small group made funding decisions to support mathematicians who were involved with military work, such as the Electronic Numerical Integrator and Computer (ENIAC) built at the University of Pennsylvania Moore School of Engineering. The Applied Mathematics Panel was disbanded in 1946, yet there was concern that postwar support be continued for the military projects that this group had previously funded. Electronic computer development was high on the list of projects to be funded in support of work such as the linear programming groundwork done by George Dantzig as head of the combat analysis branch of the Air Force Headquarters Statistical Control during the war. After the war he was requested by the Office of the Air Controller "to mechanize this planning, since it seemed likely that electronic computers with very large capacity and great speed would soon become available" [26, p. 618]. Military operations' problems like the one Dantzig worked on through linear programming ultimately relied on the development of electronic computing machines for the large number of calculations this mathematical modelling approach required. Few people in 1946 understood Dantzig's ideas about solving these complex optimization problems. Few people understood the principles underpinning the design and operation of large-scale electronic computers. Yet even with their small numbers, computer developers found it difficult to stay abreast of the advances in their rapidly changing field because they did not yet have robust channels for sharing information.

4.1   Bell Laboratories' Complex Number Calculator Demonstration

In the early 1940s, one of the most effective structures for computer developers to share information was through face-to-face meetings. George Stibitz convened one such group at Dartmouth College in 1940 to demonstrate the Complex Number Calculator from Bell Telephone Laboratories. Stibitz, who Mina Rees (1980) later called "one of the most powerful of the early digital computer designers" [26, p. 610], was a research mathematician at Bell who in the mid-1930s was working on circuit problems. He was specifically working on switching network problems that required many complex number calculations: "These computations were so laborious that they had to be done by a group of about ten women using pencil and paper along with the crude mechanical calculators of the day" [28, p. 71]. Stibitz realized that he might be able to complete complex number calculations needed for long-distance telephony by combining the concepts of binary arithmetic with mechanical computation using telephone relay switches. At home, he assembled a rudimentary calculator on his kitchen table, using relay switches he borrowed from work. When he showed this "Model K" (for kitchen table) binary calculator to his colleagues at the lab, they found it amusing but did not take it seriously. Undaunted, Stibitz continued to work on this relay-based computer with Bell Labs switching engineer Samuel Williams. By 1938, Bell management realized that their "computational staff was in an overload situation and felt that a Stibitz-designed relay machine could help alleviate the overload problem" [17, p. 22]. By early 1940 they had an operational Complex Number Calculator ready to demonstrate to their peers.

Stibitz publicly demonstrated the Complex Number Calculator and its remote operations at a meeting of the American Mathematical Society and the Mathematical Association of America held at Dartmouth College in September 1940. The joint conference was attended by 460 participants; Stibitz gave a paper in the first session of the Mathematical Association's gathering entitled "Calculating with Telephone Equipment" [2]. Stibitz and Williams also demonstrated the calculator in operation to a group that included a number of prominent mathematicians, such as John von Neumann from the Institute of Advanced Study in Princeton, Massachusetts Institute of Technology Professor Norbert Wiener, and Harvard Professor George D. Birkhoff.

The demonstration was also attended by John Mauchly, who was then teaching physics at Ursinus College near Philadelphia, and Edmund Berkeley, an actuary at Prudential Insurance in New York City and former mathematics student of Prof. Birkhoff. During this demonstration, mathematicians at Dartmouth College in New Hampshire sent messages via long-distance telephone lines to the Complex Number Calculator at Bell Labs in New York City, over 250 miles away. The human operators at Dartmouth entered problems into remote terminals, their information was sent over telephone lines to the central processing unit (CPU) in New York where their problems were solved, and the results were returned in seconds to the human operators at Dartmouth. This demonstration of computing via telephone equipment introduced possibilities of using a computer with binary code to speed up routine complex number calculations for long-distance telephony. It also introduced the idea of remote terminal telecommunications using a shared CPU to those people attending the meeting.

Through his paper and demonstration, Stibitz shared the work he had been doing at Bell Labs that would not otherwise be accessible to people outside the lab who were thinking about applications of binary mathematics to communications or information theory. The mathematicians who attended the conference and demonstration learned new information about how mathematical theory could be translated into a mechanical device for completing complex number calculations for telephone communication and other applications. For example, from the information he learned at this in-person demonstration of innovative computer design, Edmund Berkeley saw the possibility that this type of relay calculator with binary programming could carry out symbolic logic operations related to decision-making about large groups of people, such as calculating risk. He realized that this automatic calculator design could be applied to "questions he worked with in the insurance industry—questions in natural language using a series of yes/no answers structured through the application of symbolic logic. He began to explore how this relay calculator brain, combined with symbolic logic, could be applied to actuarial calculations of risk at Prudential Insurance" [24, p. 13] and other insurance companies, as well. When Berkeley returned to his office at Prudential, he began to work out a plan for integrating this Complex Number Calculator into Prudential operations, which then relied on a punched card compiling system designed in 1895 by Prudential actuary John K. Gore. Berkeley's proposals were not adopted by Prudential management, primarily due to the expense of moving their large data processing operations away from their proprietary punched card system.

4.2   From the Complex Number Calculator to ENIAC

John Mauchly was another person whose life – and the course of computer development – was changed by seeing the Complex Number Calculator demonstrated in the fall of 1940. At the time of that demonstration, Mauchly was head of the Physics Department at Ursinus College in Pennsylvania, where he had been pursuing an analog computer design for handling large amounts of statistical weather data. After reading publications by Wallace J. Eckert from Columbia University's IBM-sponsored computational laboratory, however, Mauchly became interested in the possibility of using a punched card computer design for analyzing weather data as an alternative to the analog computer he had been designing. In December 1940, Mauchly presented a paper to the American Association for the Advancement of Science "on his search for statistically verifiable patterns in precipitation" [27, p. 74] after building "an analog computer to do harmonic analysis of weather data" [29, p. 1109]. John Atanasoff from Iowa State University attended Mauchly's paper presentation and introduced himself upon learning of their mutual interest in computing machines. After some conversation, Atanasoff invited Mauchly to visit him at Iowa State to see the electronic Atanasoff-Berry Computer (ABC) he was building there using vacuum tubes. Mauchly accepted his offer and traveled to Ames, Iowa, for 4 days in June 1941. During this visit, Mauchly discussed the design of the electronic computer with Atanasoff and his assistant Clifford Berry and read the 35-page document they had written in preparation for a patent application.[1] Although the development of the ABC machine was interrupted by World War II when Atanasoff moved to the Naval Ordnance Laboratory in Washington, DC, his meeting with Mauchly did have significant consequences for computer development. Herman Goldstine (1972) later stated, "During the visit the two men apparently went into Atanasoff's ideas in considerable detail. The discussion greatly influenced Mauchly" [13, p. 125–126]. Martin Campbell-Kelly and William Aspray (1996) also credited this meeting between Mauchly and Atanasoff as bearing fruit in later computer designs: "The extent to which Mauchly drew on Atanasoff's ideas remains unknown. … At the very least we can infer that Mauchly saw the potential significance of the ABC and that this may have led him to propose a similar, electronic solution to the [Army Ballistics Research Laboratory's] computing problems" later at the University of Pennsylvania Moore School of Engineering [10, p. 85].[2]

After visiting Atanasoff at Iowa State University in the summer of 1941, Mauchly took a course on Defense Training in Electronics offered by the United States Department of War through the Moore School of Engineering. It was there that he met Presper Eckert, a graduate electronic engineering student at the Moore School who was the laboratory assistant for the summer course. Before returning to his position at Ursinus College, Mauchly was offered a position as an instructor at the Moore School, which he accepted for the opportunity to work with better

---

[1] Atanasoff and Iowa State University did not complete their patent application for the ABC computer. Mauchly's visit became the basis for a patent dispute when Mauchly did apply for a patent for the ENIAC computer design [19].

[2] In 1971, John Atanasoff was called to testify about his design of the Atanasoff-Berry Computer and his 1941 meeting with John Mauchly in the Honeywell vs. Sperry Rand patent dispute. US District Court Judge Eric Larson found "the testimony of Atanasoff with respect to the knowledge and information derived by Mauchly to be credible" [20], thus affirming that Atanasoff originated the design for an electronic computer that was subsequently used in the design of the ENIAC at the Moore School.

computing resources [28, p. 75]. He also found an enthusiastic collaborator in Eckert for his ideas about building an electronic computer. When these two met, Eckert was working on a delay-line storage device from the Radiation Laboratory at Massachusetts Institute of Technology (MIT) [10, p. 85]. Mauchly was "sketching in his laboratory notebook various emendations to Atanasoff's ideas. By August 1942 [Mauchly] had advanced in his thinking enough to write a brief memorandum summarizing his ideas" [13, p. 148]. Although this first memo proposing the building of an electronic computer was not taken up by anyone at the Moore School, it did spark interest in Herman Goldstine, who was the Army representative to the Ballistics Research Laboratory at the Moore School. He saw that this improved computer design could speed up the calculations needed to compile ballistics firing tables for the many locations where World War II was being fought, a workload that was overwhelming the ranks of human computers then doing that job. With his support and position, Goldstine was able to persuade leadership at the Army and the National Defense Research Council to approve resources to build what would become the ENIAC based on Mauchly's design proposal.

In recalling this period of great activity at the Moore School, Goldstine (1972) wrote, "During this period very many visitors came to the Moore School and left to spread the word about the new world of the computer" [13, p. 121], both the Electronic Numerical Integrator and Computer (ENIAC) and the subsequent Electronic Discrete Variable Automatic Computer (EDVAC) models. These visitors included John von Neumann, James W. Alexander, and Oswald Veblen from the Institute for Advanced Study in Princeton; Mina Rees who was the executive assistant to Warren Weaver, director of the Applied Mathematics Panel of the National Defense Research Council (NDRC) and who became the head of the Mathematics Branch of the Office of Naval Research in 1946; Vladimir K. Zworykin and Jan Rajchman from Radio Corporation of America (RCA) where they were interested in developing "special tubes for memory purposes" [13, p. 213] in digital computers; Stanley P. Frankel and Nicholas Metropolis from the Theoretical Physics Division at the Los Alamos National Laboratory who were interested in running a turbulence problem on the ENIAC relating to the development of the atomic bomb; and Jay Forrester from the Servomechanism Laboratory at MIT, where he would later lead the development of the Whirlwind computer for the Semi-Automatic Ground Environment (SAGE) air defense system. [See 13, p. 211–224.] When he visited the Moore School, Forrester was developing an analog computer to simulate an airplane's performance under contract with the Navy Office of Research and Inventions. What he learned from his visit to the Moore School changed his mind about his basic analog design and influenced him to work instead with an EDVAC-type electronic, binary computer which became the direction for his development of the Whirlwind machine at MIT [13, p. 212–213].

During the war years, the group of mathematicians, physicists, and electrical engineers who were interested in developing digital computers was small enough that they mostly knew each other first- or second-hand. Because there was not yet a discipline or profession specifically called *computer science*, there were not yet professional journals, college curricula, or professional associations focused only on this branch of learning. People who were interested in developing digital computers for specific purposes relied mostly on visits to university laboratories, where military funding provided personnel and equipment for building these devices. They also relied on written correspondence among developers, as well as reports developers wrote for internal operations in their labs, in situations where these reports were not kept secret under a security classification. Computer historian Henry Tropp (1974) noted that the "visitor's log book at Harvard [Computation Laboratory] during the Mark I era reads like a *who's who* in computation and technology. Stibitz visited Harvard as did Mauchly, Jay Forrester, Louis Ridenour, and John von Neumann. Maurice Wilkes and L. J. Comrie visited from England, Couffignal came from France, van der Pohl came from Holland, and Swoboda came from Czechoslovakia. There were even members of a Russian delegation who visited before the Cold War era" [28, p. 79]. By 1945, however, the number of people working at disparate locations and the need for rapid calculations for artillery firing charts and weapons development provided a new urgency around computer development. Haphazard meetings among developers were fortified with more intentional opportunities for learning and sharing information.

4.3   The Beginning of a Professional Association to Share Information

In October 1945, R. C. Archibald was chair of the National Research Council's Committee on the Bibliography of Mathematical Tables and Other Aids to Computation (MTAC Committee) and editor of that group's publication *Mathematical Tables and Other Aids to Computation*. As chair of the MTAC Committee, Archibald had set up subcommittees for "every aspect of computation that he could conceive" [16, p. 2], designating these subcommittees with alphabetical letters from A to Z. Subcommittee Z was organized for computing machinery. It was chaired by L. J. Comrie, the "developer in 1930 of mathematical tables for the British Nautical Almanac Office using punched-card bookkeeping machines and who, in that decade, established the first commercial calculating service in Great Britain" [23]. The subcommittee included these additional seven members:

- Samuel Caldwell, who worked with his dissertation advisor Vannevar Bush at MIT to develop the Differential Analyzer analog computer there. After earning this degree, he joined the faculty in the MIT Electrical Engineering Department, where he served as a faculty supervisor for development of the Whirlwind computer [25, p. 51].
- Howard Aiken, who "designed the world's first large-scale digital computer, the Mark I, for the International Business Machine Corporation" (IBM) delivered to the US Navy in 1944, was director of Harvard's Computation Laboratory from 1946 to 1961 [3]. The Mark I was an electromagnetic, relay computer.

- Derrick H. Lehmer was a mathematician interested "in mechanizing the solution of linear congruence relations" [21]. During WWII, he worked at the Ballistics Research Lab at the Moore School to develop the ENIAC for the Aberdeen Army Proving Ground. From 1951 to 1953, he worked on the Standards Western Automatic Computer (SWAC) electronic computer with Harry Huskey.
- J. C. P. Miller was an English mathematician working in number theory and geometry at the University of Cambridge. He was an early member of the Computer Laboratory there, where development of the Electronic Delay Storage Automatic Computer (EDSAC) began in 1946.
- George Stibitz was the developer of the Complex Numerical Calculator at Bell Telephone Laboratories. "During World War II, Stibitz took a leave of absence from Bell Telephone Laboratories and joined Division 7 (Gun-Fire Control) of the National Defense Research Committee (NDRC), later the Office of Scientific Research and Development (OSRD), as a technical aide" [22].
- Irven A. Travis was an electrical engineering professor at the University of Pennsylvania who worked on analog, mechanical, and electronic computing projects at the Moore School with John Brainerd during the 1930s and 1940s [8]. He was the chief of fire control research for the Navy Bureau of Ordnance during WWII. In 1949 he joined Burroughs Corporation where he led computer development projects.
- John R. Womersley was appointed as the first superintendent of the Mathematics Division of the National Physical Laboratory (NPL) in England in 1944, where he began work on the Automatic Computing Engine (ACE) electronic computer. At the NPL, he hired Alan Turing to design and Donald Davies to work on the ACE project [11].

In his influential MTAC Committee roles, Archibald would have known about the work being done on computing devices in the USA and England, especially on the Mark I at Harvard, the Complex Numerical Calculator at Bell Labs, the Differential Analyzer at MIT, and the ENIAC at the Moore School [16, p. 3–4]. At the end of World War II, he decided to organize a conference at MIT for people working on computing devices to "familiarize each member of the group with present potentialities in the field and to make known probably [sic] future developments" [16, p. 4]. In convening this conference, Archibald was intentionally creating a formal opportunity for 84 computer developers to share information about their devices to ensure that technology development for high-speed computation would not falter in the postwar years. He was also attempting to create a professional association for people involved with computing, both human computers and mechanical/electronic computer operators [16].

The meeting was set to take place at MIT on 29–31 October 1945, "'entirely without publicity and attendance by invitation only'" [13, p. 219–220]. Archibald and conference chair Comrie invited "those active in connection with mechanical computation on both sides of the Atlantic" [14, p. 285–286] from universities, private businesses, and government/military agencies.[3] Seeing an opportunity to showcase the work being done at MIT, Vannevar Bush planned to present "the first public demonstration of its new Differential Analyzer" [4] on the opening day of the conference before the formal program began. At the time of this conference, Bush had been the president of the Carnegie Institution for Science in Washington, DC, for 6 years after leaving his teaching and research position at MIT. In 1940, he had been instrumental in persuading President Roosevelt to create the Office of Scientific Research and Development (OSRD), which initiated the Manhattan Project to develop an atomic bomb under Bush's leadership. Almost 4 months before the 1945 conference called by Archibald and Comrie, Bush had sent his recommendations for postwar support for science research and technology development to President Roosevelt in his report *Science: The Endless Frontier.*

The 1945 MIT Subcommittee Z conference was "the first public discussion of electronic computation after the end of the war" [16, p. 4]. Presentations during the 2 days of formal program covered many different computer design concepts: analog, relay, punched card, mechanical, and electronic. The nearly 100 people who took part in this conference had an opportunity to see some equipment in action, review illustrations, and reports of newer electronic designs being used in the ENIAC and EDVAC machines at the Moore School and consider how the traditions of human computing would be impacted by the development of high-speed calculating devices. After the conference, Archibald (1946) reported, "The Conference was most notably successful, and one heard on every side expressions of the hope that such a Conference might become an annual event" [4]. "Yet this meeting was the only time that the war's human computers and computer developers gathered as equals" [14, p. 287]. After this conference, computer developers continued to work largely in isolation, except for the leaders in the field, like Howard Aiken, John von Neumann, and others who operated within networks of shared information. For people outside those networks, sharing information continued to be difficult. And yet, continued rapid technology development depended on sharing knowledge and understanding computer research, as well as the mathematical and physical principles which underpinned this research. Wartime experience with computers had jump-started development of this new technology. But the need for military readiness had not waned in the years following the official end to World War II and the dawn of the Cold War. In describing this transition, Rear Admiral C. Turner Joy (1947) commented that "scientific advances achieved during the war represent an exploitation of the pure science developed during peace. One of the merits of the

---

[3] Universities represented were Harvard, Brown, University of Pennsylvania, MIT, University of Michigan, University of Vermont, Princeton University, and the Institute for Advanced Study in Princeton. Private businesses represented were Bell Laboratories, General Electric, National Cash Register Corporation (NCR), International Business Machines (IBM), Eastman Kodak, Foxboro Instrument Company, and United Aircraft Corporation of Stamford, Connecticut. Governments and military organizations represented were Aberdeen Army Proving Ground, Office of Research and Inventions, Carnegie Institution of Science, National Research Council Committee in the USA and England, Ballistic Research Laboratory, Naval Research Laboratory, Bureau of Ships, Hydrographic Office of the US Navy, and the Bureau of Ordnance.

field of computation and computing devices is that it should contribute ultimately to replenishment of the pure theory from which further technological and engineering advances can result" [18, p. 5]. During the war, the Admiral found that the collaboration between the Navy and the Harvard Computation Lab to develop the Mark I computer, in partnership with IBM, had "served as a training ground for the design, operation, and maintenance of large-scale computers. ... The training of the scientists and engineers in this kind of work has been a great achievement" [18, p. 5]. If this training and development was to continue to meet the national security threats of the Cold War, communication needed to be improved between developers in university labs, private companies, and military and government agencies.

4.4   How to Share Classified Information?

By 1946, the Moore School was receiving so many visitors that their traffic threatened to disrupt work on the next generation of electronic computers – the Electronic Discrete Variable Automatic Computer (EDVAC), which unlike the ENIAC was a binary, stored-program computer. In February 1946, the ENIAC had been publicly dedicated at the Moore School, but the EDVAC was still a classified military project at that time. "In the spring of 1946, many organizations were clamoring to learn more about electronic computation, but there was little information to be found. The field had no journals, no technical magazines" [15, p. 12]. There was no professional field called *computer science* with professional associations or educational standards. Reports, specifications, and manuals relating to machines that were either in operation or in development at laboratories, businesses, or military installations were not widely circulated because they were either proprietary or classified. People who wanted to learn more about these machines had to develop personal contacts and rely on correspondence or in-person visits to share knowledge about state-of-the-art computing technologies. By June 1945, Herman Goldstine, who was the Army liaison to the ENIAC and EDVAC projects, wrote a memo to the Dean of the Moore School informing him that "no further clearances would be granted to visit the ENIAC" [13, p. 216, n. 12]. And yet Goldstine and his Army executive officer of the Moore School Ballistics Research Laboratory (BRL) Paul Gillon were "eager for information on these machines to reach the scientific community as soon as possible, since we realized the great significance these devices would have. We therefore did all in our power to lower the classification of the projects" [13, p. 216]. People in the private business community were also eager to learn more about the design and potentials of these new technologies, as well as the possibilities for military contracts and industrial development.

As the US transitioned from wartime to peacetime operations, Moore School Dean Harold Pender "recognized the duty of the school to ensure that the knowledge of stored-program computing was effectively transmitted to the outside world" [10, p. 98]. He worked with Moore School Director of Research Irven Travis and Professor Carl Chambers to organize an 8-week summer course on the topic, with funding from the Army's Ordnance Department and the Navy's Office of Naval Research. The course was titled Theory and Techniques for Design of Electronic Digital Computers, more commonly now known as the Moore School Lectures. Participation in the course was by invitation and 28 students participated in the lectures, discussions, and demonstrations involving the ENIAC and EDVAC from 8 July to 31 August 1946. These students represented universities, private businesses, and government/military agencies: MIT, Manchester University (England), Cambridge University (England), General Electric, Bell Telephone Company, Reeves Instrument Company, National Bureau of Standards, the US War Department Office of the Chief of Ordnance, Naval Ordnance Laboratory, Frankford Arsenal, Wright Field's Armament Laboratory, Naval Research Laboratory, Aberdeen Proving Ground, US Navy Department, US Army Security Agency, and Navy Department of Research and Inventions. Fifteen of the 28 students were aligned with government or military agencies. Three additional visitors, including Jay Forrester, came from the MIT Servomechanism Laboratory for some of the course.

The course included 48 lectures, largely on circuit design and preparing problems for machine computation, presented by some of the most accomplished computer developers in 1946:

- C. Bradford Sheppard, Kite Sharpless, J. Chuan Chu, and Irven Travis from the Ballistics Research Laboratory at the Moore School.
- John Mauchly and Presper Eckert from Electronic Control Company at the time of the lectures, formerly with the Moore School.
- Herman Goldstine from the Institute for Advanced Study in Princeton University, formerly Army representative to the Ballistics Research Laboratory at the Moore School.
- Arthur Burks from the Institute for Advanced Study in Princeton University, formerly with the Moore School.
- Derrick H. Lehmer from the University of California, Berkeley, formerly with the Moore School.
- Sam Williams from Bell Telephone Laboratories, consultant to the Moore School.
- Howard Aiken from Harvard University Computation Laboratory, developer of the Mark I and Mark II in partnership with IBM.
- Perry Crawford, Jr. from the US Navy Office of Research and Inventions.
- John Curtiss, from the National Bureau of Standards.
- Douglas Hartree from Manchester University, developer of the Meccano differential analyzer.
- Calvin Mooers from the Naval Ordnance Laboratory.
- Hans Rademacher from the University of Pennsylvania Department of Mathematics.
- Jan Rajchman from Radio Corporation of America (RCA) working with the Institute for Advanced Study in Princeton.
- George Stibitz, a private consultant to government and industry, developer of the Complex Number Calculator at Bell Laboratories and member of Division 7

(Gun-Fire Control) of the National Defense Research Committee (NDRC) during World War II.
- John von Neumann from the Institute for Advanced Study in Princeton, author[4]
  of *First Draft of a Report on the EDVAC* in June 1945.

The community of people involved with mechanical and electronic computing at
the end of WWII was small, but the rapid development of high-speed electronic
computing, memory storage, and internal programming would require many more
mathematicians and electrical engineers to meet the growing demand for machinery
and programming. This urgency was compounded by national security needs both
for development of atomic weapons and their guided missile delivery systems, as
well as air defense systems to alert the US military of incoming enemy airplanes
that might repeat the destruction of military assets like the Japanese attack on Pearl
Harbor. As the Russians ramped up their development of an atomic bomb, this
urgency became more acute.

John von Neumann was in the forefront of arguing for the need for high-speed
computing capability to meet the needs of problems requiring three or four dimensions, such as problems involving fluids or turbulence over time [31, p. 249]. Von
Neumann had worked with such problems as a consultant to the Manhattan Project
at the Los Alamos National Lab while they were developing the atomic bombs that
would be dropped on Hiroshima and Nagasaki to finally end the war with Japan
after the Germans had surrendered. He approached the BRL at the Moore School to
run the computations he needed on the ENIAC, and this was the first problem run
on that computer in 1945. In the summer of 1945, Warren Weaver, who was head of
the Applied Mathematics Panel of the NDRC, asked von Neumann to write a report
on computing machines, including the ENIAC and the EDVAC. There was discussion about lowering the security classification of this work from "Classified," which
these two projects had been designated, to "Restricted" to make the report available
to more interested parties [13, p. 215–216]. On 15 May 1946, von Neumann gave a
talk on "Principles of Large-Scale Computing Machines" to a meeting of the
Mathematical Computing Advisory Panel of the US Navy Office of Research and
Inventions in Washington, DC, during which he put forward the need for high-speed
computation capabilities, which was not yet a settled question at that time among
potential military funders. By the end of June, a 101-page report written by von
Neumann and entitled *First Draft of a Report on the EDVAC* was available for 24
people working on the EDVAC at the Moore School [6, p. 58]. This influential
report dealt with "the structure of a *very high speed automatic digital computing
system* and in particular with its *logical control*" [30, sec. 1.1; italics in original].
The document was quickly "'leaked' to the scientific community" [13, p. 216], thus
educating some "insiders" in the US and England about the ground-breaking

---

[4] Although von Neumann's name was listed as the sole author of the *First Draft of a Report on the
EDVAC* that was distributed outside the Moore School laboratory, the report represented work
done by John Mauchly, Presper Eckert, and other members of the team working on the EDVAC in
that laboratory.

concepts of machines and design logic that were explained in the classified report. During the Moore School Lectures later that summer, "a security clearance was obtained toward the end of the course" so the people who had been invited to this gathering could be "shown slides of the EDVAC block diagrams. The students took away no materials other than their personal notes" [10, p. 99].

4.5   Sharing Information Through Personal Relationships

One of the people who received a copy of von Neumann's report was Douglas Hartree from the University of Manchester in England, who had been working during the war "with the [Meccano] differential analyser on various military problems under the auspices of the Ministry of Supply" [13, p. 107]. In this post, he became aware of computers being developed in the US, and in 1945 "arrangements were made for him to pay an official visit" [13, p. 107] to computer labs at Harvard University where the Mark I was in operation and the Moore School at the University of Pennsylvania where the ENIAC had just begun operation. During these in-person visits, Hartree learned about the logic, design, production, and operation of these two different computers, one operating with relay switches and punched cards and the other operating with vacuum tubes and electronics. When he returned to England, Hartree shared what he had learned with Maurice Wilkes, who was the director of the Mathematical Laboratory at Cambridge University. Wilkes had recently written an article putting forward the idea that "certain electronic techniques used in radar could be applied" to building a digital calculator. When Hartree met with Wilkes, he especially "describe[d] the great scale … on which the American effort had been conducted" to give Wilkes an understanding of the resources that were required to realize his idea at Cambridge's Mathematical Lab. Without Hartree's first-hand knowledge that he had just gained from his visit to the US, Wilkes had underestimated the complexity and cost of implementing his ideas in fact.

Wilkes also received a visit from mathematician Leslie Comrie, who had just returned from a trip to the US in May 1946 with a copy of von Neumann's *First Draft of a Report on the EDVAC* which described a simpler design for an electronic computer than had been realized in the ENIAC. Wilkes later recalled, "Rumours of this had reached me, but I did not know anything of their detailed conclusions" [33, p. 108]. In the middle of May 1946, Comrie brought a copy of von Neumann's report to Wilkes in Cambridge for him to read. Wilkes later described the urgency of his encounter with this document in his *Memoirs of a Computer Pioneer* (1985): "Comrie, who was spending the night at St. John's College, obligingly let me keep it until next morning. … I sat up late into the night reading the report. In it, clearly laid out, were the principles on which the development of the modern digital computer was to be based" [33, p. 108]. In the morning, Wilkes returned the report to Comrie, relying on his notes and memory to carry forward what he had learned in it because he was not able to make a copy of the report. Without Comrie's generosity in sharing information he had just received on his in-person visit to the

United States, Wilkes would not have known that his ideas for adapting electronics to computing were feasible and were being proven across the Atlantic Ocean.

After reading the von Neumann report, Wilkes (1985) recalled that "I was much better informed than I had been earlier in the year about the state of the computing art in the United States, but I was hardly in a position to plan a program of work. While I was thinking the matter over, I suddenly received a telegram from Dean Pender of the Moore School inviting me to attend a course on electronic computers that was to take place in Philadelphia during the period 8 July to 31 August. This threw me into a state of some excitement" [33, p. 116]. By participating in the Moore School Lectures in the summer of 1946, Wilkes would have the opportunity to see the ENIAC in person to learn more about its operation and the feasibility of building an electronic computer in his lab at Cambridge. Before traveling to the US, Wilkes "ran into Hartree at a function in the Cavendish Laboratory. He had just returned from a second visit to the United States, this time of two months' duration. The specific purpose of this visit was to discuss non-military uses of the ENIAC" [33, p. 116]. Wilkes (1985) recalled, "He gave me much up-to-date information about computer developments in the United States and he also gave me a number of introductions to the leading people" [33, p. 117]. These "leading people" included Howard Aiken at Harvard University and Samuel Caldwell at MIT. Hartree had also suggested that Wilkes contact Herman Goldstine to arrange for a visit to the Institute for Advanced Study in Princeton, which he did. On the train from Philadelphia during a side trip to Washington, DC, Wilkes ran into John Mauchly, and they "had a discussion about the future of computers" [33, p. 123]. Mauchly suggested that Wilkes take lodging in Philadelphia next door to the apartment where he lived. At this time, communications about computer development was very much based on personal relationships.

4.6 Sharing Information at Conferences

Although Archibald had intended that the MTAC Subcommittee Z conference become an annual event for sharing information on human and machine computing, Subcommittee Z had disbanded before October 1946. No more conferences were held to bring human computers who worked with mechanical desk calculators together with people who were designing automatic computers to replace them. In January 1947, a Symposium on Large-Scale Calculating Machinery was convened at the Harvard Computation Lab, co-sponsored by the Department of the Navy, to bring computer developers together and to demonstrate the Mark I and II computers built in collaboration with the Navy and IBM. The symposium was attended by more than 300 people, which was about six times more than the organizers had anticipated. This opportunity for sharing information was especially important for the non-elite computer people who were not otherwise "in the loop" with Howard Aiken, Grace Hopper, John von Neumann, and their peers. The symposium provided a venue for all participants to discuss current computer developments across organizational and social boundaries. Harvard Lab director Howard Aiken (1947) emphasized the importance of this information sharing in his opening remarks:

> A great variety of new techniques has been introduced into the design of calculating machinery … There has been inadequate publication of results, and inadequate transmittal of results from one group working in the field to another. Consequently, we have often found that we were working on problems that had already been solved by others. We have found that we were beginning researches that were nearing completion in other laboratories. Those are precisely the reasons why this symposium seems so necessary at this time [1, p. 7].

This concern with the impact of poor communication among computer developers was also emphasized by Mina Rees, who chaired the Mathematical Methods section at the symposium. She later (1987) summed up the situation in 1947 in this way: "Around the country there was clear evidence of an increasing desire to stay in touch with the rapidly changing technological scene and to establish improved means of communication among the many persons who were professionally interested in the new machines" [2, p. 831]. In the minds of people in the forefront of postwar computer development that was happening in different economic sectors, establishing communication channels to "stay in touch" had important national security and quality-of-life implications. If computer developers relied primarily on personal relationships and periodic, un-coordinated symposia to "stay in touch," military readiness would be weakened, and the USA could face national security risks from the Soviet Union as technology developers there narrowed the gap in weapon systems.

The Harvard symposium was one of the few opportunities for people from universities and industry to meet for information sharing. In his introduction to the reprint of the symposium proceedings, William Aspray (1985) noted that although in 1947 "most research was being conducted in university laboratories with government funds, academic researchers were beginning to recognize that university laboratories could do no more than build prototypes, and that any future growth of computing would have to occur in industry" [5, p. xv]. Symposium participants from private businesses were at the forefront of building partnerships with universities and military agencies to ensure that postwar technology development would meet Cold War security needs. According to Aspray (1985), "private industries represented at the meeting can be separated into three categories: those interested in developing computer systems … those interested in developing components for systems … and those wanting to use computers in their other commercial activities" [5, p. xix]. The 22 firms listed in these categories were looking for business opportunities, but they were also looking for people in university laboratories to hire away for their projects. The pool of adequately trained people was not large, however, and Aiken argued that universities – and Harvard in particular – should develop curricula for training people to work in the nascent computer industry. Responding to Alan Waterman (Chief of the Office of Naval Research Scientific Planning Division) in the symposium's closing session, Aiken stated, "We must remember that our universities are primarily institutions for the building of men and not for the building of machines, and we must offer courses of instruction in this field" [32, p. 302].

In responding to Samuel Caldwell's presentation at the symposium, Professor Charles C. Bramble (Post Graduate School, US Naval Academy and Dahlgren Proving Ground) also voiced his concern that the shortage of people trained to develop and run computers would impede weapons systems development: "These present machines are expanding the field and spreading the horizon in such a way that one of the most pressing problems for those who are close to the practical side of the computation business is whether the development of the machines and the production of new machines is going to outrun the number of people who are able to operate them. I view the situation in the near future with some alarm" [9, p. 283]. Bramble, who had been involved with weapons development and testing at Dahlgren during and after World War II, foresaw that delays in computer development could mean delays in weapons system development. He stated that "unless some definite steps are taken, the computation business and the running of the machines will certainly suffer very serious growing pains" [9, p. 283]. He called for more training in numerical analysis and the applied skills of computer operation, but the requirements for this type of training were lacking. Developing a curriculum for training workers in what was becoming a computer industry would also require a standard vocabulary of technical terms that did not yet exist in 1947.

In his paper entitled "New Vistas in Mathematics," Alan T. Waterman, chief scientist at the Office of Naval Research, emphasized the importance of maintaining rapid technology development in the US after World War:

> Scientists during the war years were engaged in developing new weapons and devices in industrial, university, and government laboratories, both under contract to the armed services and in collaboration with them in the Office of Scientific Research and Development. The knowledge stored up by research before the war was converted into the tools needed for victory. Very little actual research was done. The price we paid was the loss of knowledge which research would have created if the war had not taken scientists from research and students from their studies. This is a far more serious loss for the national welfare than the depletion of any stock pile of critical material [32, p. 300].

Waterman had worked at the Office of Scientific Research and Development during the war. In his estimation, the loss of research capacity coming out of World War II posed an impediment to the breakthroughs that could protect the US victory as it entered a new, psychological, and ideological cold war. In opening remarks at the symposium, Rear Admiral C. Turner Joy (Commanding Officer of the Dahlgren Naval Proving Ground representing the Bureau of Ordnance) provided more details about his vision for the use of large-scale computing machinery in weapons system development: "With the availability of the Mark I and Mark II computers, it is expected that the Bureau of Ordnance and the Proving Ground will be able adequately to handle all problems in ballistics, including those of guided missiles and of aerodynamics in the supersonic field. The backlog of necessary computations is large" [18, p. 5]. This backlog of knowledge about guided missile development was an impediment to developing the next generation of delivery systems for nuclear weapons. Computers would be instrumental in these weapons guidance systems that promised to be the foundation upon which US national security would be built.

Rapid technology development and personnel training were needed to build that secure foundation; both relied on streamlined communication channels.

In his remarks at the Harvard symposium, Samuel Caldwell (MIT Associate Professor of Electrical Engineering) directly addressed the need for establishing open communication channels to support computer development:

> [A] majority of us who are working on the development of new computing engines are looking forward to the time when we can establish and re-establish among us many of the channels of communication which in the past have served to inform, to stimulate, and to regulate our efforts by the avoidance of needless duplication. ... [I]t is hardly appropriate to say that we wish to "re-establish channels of communication," except in a general sense, for there were no well-established channels of communication in the specific field of large-scale digital computers before the war. Of course, this was due to the fact that there was no well-established field of large-scale digital computer development and design before the war [9, p. 277].

While noting that existing communication channels were not robust enough for rapid computer development, Caldwell forecast that the need for these channels would increase as the nascent computer field grew to meet postwar demands with an enlarged group of institutional entities in collaboration:

> Although a substantial nucleus of knowledge in this field existed before the war ... we must, nevertheless, recognize the tremendous impetus given to the work by the needs of war. ... Unlike many of our wartime scientific activities, however, this [computer] one did not suffer a sharp contraction at war's end. On the contrary, the spectacular success of the wartime program led to still further enlargement of effort. Much of this postwar program is still government supported, but there has arisen a growing and aggressive support from industry and institutions [9, p. 277].

The environment for computer development had grown more complicated after World War II, and the need for innovative computer technologies as part of new weapons systems grew more acute as relations between the US and Soviet Union deteriorated. Caldwell said he found that "many of the group gathered here have expressed their uneasiness over the fact that they do not know what their fellow workers are doing and what results they are achieving—particularly in the intervals between these meetings. ... [T]he need for better communication in the field of machine development has had less attention and is in more urgent need of it" [9, p. 278–279].

Caldwell identified two impediments to establishing an open information sharing system: private industry's patent concerns and the military's concerns for classifying information sensitive to national security. He called for establishing a new professional association to support systematic communication among computer developers, as distinguished from mathematics, physics, or electrical engineering: "It is this communication system that I have described as consisting of two elements: an organization to make us more immediately and more continuously aware of a common purpose and thus furnish the incentive for communication; and a medium for such communication" [9, p. 282]. Mina Rees (1987) remembered that when Caldwell "called for the establishment of a new association to provide for better communication among those interested in the new machinery, it struck a responsive note" [27, p. 831]. After the symposium, Edmund Berkeley took the initiative to develop a proposal for this new professional association for computer people. In September 1947, the Association for Computing Machinery (ACM)[5] was formed during a meeting of 57 people at Columbia University in New York City. The purpose of the ACM was to "advance the science, design, construction, and application of the new machinery for computing, reasoning, and other handling of information. Anyone interested in this purpose may become a member" [7]. John Curtiss from the National Bureau of Standards became the first ACM president and Edmund Berkeley from Prudential Insurance became the first secretary. The wide distribution of information initiated by Edmund Berkeley and supported by the ACM represented a tangible solution to the communication problem facing computer developers at the end of World War II [23, p. 65]. It also began to lay a foundation for establishing computer science as a profession in its own right, separate from mathematics, electrical engineering, and physics.

References

1. Aiken, Howard H. 1948/1985. Representing the computation laboratory. In *Proceedings of a symposium on large-scale digital calculating machinery*, 7. Cambridge, MA: MIT Press.
2. Anonymous. 1940. The twenty-third summer meeting of the mathematical association. *The American Mathematical Monthly* 47 (9): 589–594. http://www.jstor.org/stable/2304107. Accessed 2 Nov 2020.
3. ———. 1973, March 16. Former professor Howard Aiken dies; Invented large-scale computer. *The Harvard Crimson*. https://www.thecrimson.com/article/1973/3/16/former-professor-howard-aiken-dies-invented/. Accessed 2 Nov 2020.
4. Archibald, R. C. 1946, April. Conference on advanced computation techniques. *Mathematical Tables and Other Aids to Computation* 2 (14): 65–68.
5. Aspray, William. 1948/1985. Introduction. In *Proceedings of a symposium on large-scale digital calculating machinery*, ix–xx. Cambridge, MA: MIT Press.
6. Bashe, Charles, et al. 1985. *IBM's early computers*. Cambridge, MA: MIT Press.
7. Berkeley, Edmund. 1947, June 25. *Notice on organization of an "Eastern Association for Computing Machinery." Edmund C.* Berkeley Papers (CBI 50), Charles Babbage Institute, University of Minnesota, Minneapolis.
8. Brainerd, John G. July 1976. Genesis of the ENIAC. *Technology and Culture* 17 (3): 482–488.
9. Caldwell, Samuel H. 1948/1985. Publication, classification, and patents. In *Proceedings of a symposium on large-scale digital calculating machinery*, 277–283. Cambridge, MA: MIT Press.
10. Campbell-Kelly, Martin, and William Aspray. 1996. *Computer: A history of the information machine*. New York: Basic Books.
11. Carpenter, Brian E., and Robert W. Doran. 2014, April–June. John Womersley: Applied mathematician and pioneer of modern computing. *IEEE Annals of the History of Computing* 36: 60–70. https://doi.org/10.1109/MAHC.2014.25. Accessed 2 Nov 2020.

---

[5] This new association was originally named the Eastern Association for Computing Machinery, but the work "Eastern" was dropped by December 1947 as membership rapidly grew in numbers and geography.

12. Clippinger, Richard. 1950. Mathematical requirements for the personnel of a computing laboratory. *American Mathematical Society* 57: 439. Qtd. in Tropp, Henry. February 1974: 70.
13. Goldstine, Herman H. 1972. *The computer from Pascal to von Neumann*. Princeton: Princeton University Press.
14. Grier, David A. 2005. *When computers were human*. Princeton: Princeton University Press.
15. ———. 2006, January . George Stibitz's values and R. C. Archibald's slide rule. *Computer* 39: 11–13. https://doi.org/10.1109/MC.2006.19. Accessed 2 Nov 2020.
16. ———. 2009. Failed societies of computing: Committee Z and the professionalization of programming. In *IEEE conference on the history of technical societies*, 1–6. Philadelphia, PA. https://doi.org/10.1109/HTS.2009.5337870. Accessed 2 Nov 2020.
17. Irvine, M. M. 2001, July–September. Early digital computers at bell telephone laboratories. *IEEE Annals of the History of Computing* 23 (3): 22–42.
18. Joy, C. Turner. 1948/1985. Representing the Bureau of Ordnance. In *Proceedings of a symposium on large-scale digital calculating machinery*, 4–6. Cambridge, MA: MIT Press.
19. JVA Initiative Committee. 2011. *John Mauchly visits Ames*. Iowa State University Department of Computer Science. http://jva.cs.iastate.edu/mauchlyinames.php. Accessed 2 Nov 2020.
20. ———. 2011. *Patent/court case: Honeywell vs. Sperry Rand*. http://jva.cs.iastate.edu/courtcase.php. Iowa State University Department of Computer Science. Accessed 1 Nov 2020.
21. Lee, J.A.N. 1995. *Derek Henry Lehmer. In Computer pioneers*. Los Alamitos: IEEE Computer Society Press. https://history.computer.org/pioneers/lehmer.html. Accessed 2 Nov 2020.
22. ———. 1995. George Robert Stibitz. In *Computer pioneers*. Los Alamitos: IEEE Computer Society Press. https://history.computer.org/pioneers/stibitz.html. Accessed 2 Nov 2020.
23. ———. 1995. Leslie John Comrie. In *Computer pioneers*. Los Alamitos, CA: IEEE Computer Society Press. https://history.computer.org/pioneers/comrie.html. Accessed 2 Nov 2020.
24. Longo, Bernadette. 2015. *Edmund Berkeley and the social responsibility of computer professionals*. San Rafael: Morgan & Claypool Press – ACM.
25. Morse, Philip M. 1956, September 16. *Machine methods of computation and numerical analysis: Quarterly progress report no. 21 and Project Whirlwind summary report no. 47*. https://archivesspace.mit.edu/repositories/2/archival_objects/277015. Accessed 2 Nov 2020.
26. Rees, Mina. 1980, October. The mathematical sciences and World War II. *The American Mathematical Monthly* 87 (8): 607–621.
27. ———. 1987. The computing program at the Office of Naval Research, 1946-1953. *Communications of the ACM* 30 (10): 831–848.
28. Tropp, Henry. 1974, February. The effervescent years: A retrospective. *IEEE Spectrum* 11 (2): 70–79.
29. ———. 2003. Mauchly, John H. In *Encyclopedia of computer science*, 1109–1110. Chichester: Wiley.
30. von Neumann, John. 1946/1993. First draft of a report on the EDVAC. *IEEE Annals of the History of Computing* 15 (4): 27–43.
31. ———. 1989. The principles of large-scale computing machines. *IEEE Annals of the History of Computing* 10 (4): 243–256.
32. Waterman, Alan T. 148/185. New vistas in mathematics. In *Proceedings of a symposium on large-scale digital calculating machinery*, 298–302. Cambridge, MA: MIT Press.
33. Wilkes, Maurice V. 1985. *Memoirs of a computer pioneer*. Cambridge, MA: MIT Press.

Chapter 5
Defining Relationships Among Computers, People, and Information

Abstract This chapter describes how computer developers used existing documents, such as operation manuals and design proposals, to share information about innovations in computer design in the years immediately after World War II, before there were textbooks or formal curricula in a professional field of computer science. This documentary approach to information sharing was especially important for people working in the computer field that was being established in southern California to support the aircraft industry and guided missile development. Foundational documents are detailed: a 1945 report on relay computers written by George Stibitz for the US Army, John von Neumann's 1946 "First Draft of a Report on the EDVAC," Claude Shannon's 1948 Bell Labs report entitled "A Mathematical Theory of Communication" and Warren Weaver's 1949 elaboration on this work, and Edmund Berkeley's 1949 *Giant Brains or Machines that Think*, which is often considered to be the first book on computers for popular audiences.

> "*Essentially,* a mechanical brain *is a machine that handles information, transfers information automatically from one part of the machine to another … No human being is needed.*" Edmund Berkeley, "Giant Brains," 1949 [5]

> "*The large digital computers are not quite the 'brains' they have been called (unless perhaps they are the brains of giant imbeciles), nor are some of the analogies to the human nervous system, so glibly announced by dabblers in the field, quite valid.*" George Stibitz and Jules Larrivee, "Mathematics and Computers," 1957 [33]

> "*An engineering communication theory is just like a very proper and discreet girl accepting your telegram. She pays no attention to the meaning, whether it be sad, or joyous, or embarrassing. But she must be prepared to deal with all that come to her desk.*" Warren Weaver, "Recent Contributions to a Mathematical Theory of Communication," 1949 [37]

In January 1947 when the Symposium on Large-Scale Calculating Machinery was held at Harvard University, the Mark II computer was being finalized there under contract with the US Navy. This machine used electromagnetic relays instead of the electromechanical counters of the earlier Mark I machine, allowing much faster calculations with the newer model. The only other computers in operation at that time were the Electronic Numerical Integrator and Computer (ENIAC) at the University of Pennsylvania Moore School of Engineering, which was put to work

© Springer Nature Switzerland AG 2021
B. Longo, *Words and Power*, History of Computing,
https://doi.org/10.1007/978-3-030-70373-8_5

for the Army in December 1945, and the Complex Number Calculator relay machine which had been operational at Bell Telephone since 1940. Other machines were under development in the United States in early 1947:

- The Electronic Discrete Variable Automatic Computer (EDVAC) binary, stored-program computer at the Moore School
- The IBM Selective Sequence Electronic Calculator (SSEC) electromechanical computer near IBM corporate headquarters in New York City
- The von Neumann electronic, stored-program computer at the Institute for Advanced Study (IAS) in Princeton
- The Whirlwind high-speed stored-program computer at the Massachusetts Institute of Technology
- The Universal Automatic Computer (UNIVAC) electronic stored-program computer at the Electronic Control Company founded by Presper Eckert and John Mauchly in Philadelphia

The universe of high-speed calculating devices was small in 1947. People working on these machines were emerging from their sequestered laboratories where their work had been cloaked under military security clearances during World War II. They found themselves in new circumstances, though, in which they sought to share information about their work with other people rather than keep it secret. For national security reasons, they now wanted to facilitate rapid development of knowledge about computers and their operations. In order to make this happen, they first needed to establish inter-agency communication channels and a shared technical vocabulary. In-person visits and symposia were venues for starting to establish this shared knowledge. But for people who were not computer insiders, the path to learning about computers and electronics depended largely on texts.

The career path of Harry Huskey and the development of the Standards Western Automatic Computer (SWAC) illustrate how an education in computer development often happened through serendipity [20, p. 10]. Upon earning his doctorate in mathematics from the Ohio State University in 1943, Huskey took a position as an instructor at the University of Pennsylvania. While there, he took additional part-time jobs to supplement his income. When an opening on an electrical engineering project at the Moore School came up, he applied and was hired. After receiving his security clearance, Huskey was told he would be working on the ENIAC project. He first worked with the punch card input/output component and later wrote the manuals for the machine. In 1946, Huskey left the University of Pennsylvania and was looking for another permanent teaching position when he received a telegram from Douglas Hartree who was working with Alan Turing at the National Physical Laboratory (NPL) in England to design the electronic Automatic Computing Engine (ACE) stored-program computer. In remembering this offer, Huskey stated, "[My wife and I] didn't know what the NPL was, but we accepted it. ... I think we didn't know about the computer projects" [21, p. 15].

When he joined the NPL project, Huskey worked with numerical analyst Jim Wilkinson to design a mercury delay line memory for the ACE. Huskey had some familiarity with memory storage development from his work at the Moore School: "We had a person working on CRT storage – Williams tube stuff – still trying to decide whether the mercury lines or CRTs or whatever. In England, the first month I was there, they sent me around to visit all these places. And so here was [Freddie] Williams with his Williams tube. Here was [Maurice] Wilkes with his mercury delay lines. And that's all we visited at that point" [21, p. 17]. During his work on the ACE computer, Huskey taught himself electronics: "MIT published a book on digital circuitry and that had answers to most of the questions I had" [21, p. 25]. In the absence of a profession dealing with computers separate from mathematics or electrical engineering, it was up to Huskey to find his own combination of hands-on experience and book learning to prepare himself to meet the demands of innovation in computing technology.

Huskey was working on the ACE project at NPL during 1947 when he "heard a rumor" that the US National Bureau of Standards (NBS) was "going to set up an operation at UCLA" [21, p. 24] to design a computer. His unique combination of experience and education prepared him for the computer development project the NBS had planned for the Institute for Numerical Analysis (INA) at the University of California, Los Angeles (UCLA).[1] He got an offer to head the INA and build an electronic computer there to support applied mathematical approaches for "the examination of new, and the reexamination of old problems in mathematics with a view toward devising the numerical techniques most suitable for their solution on high-speed automatic computers" [8]. This computer was also intended "principally to solve aircraft problems originating with the Air Force and its contractors" [2, p. 2]. The Standards Western Automatic Computer (SWAC) Huskey and his team built at the INA would be the western US counterpart to the Standards Eastern Automatic Computer (SEAC) being built by Samuel Alexander and his team at the NBS in Washington, DC, to support their data processing work there. The INA was one of four satellite labs under the National Applied Mathematics Laboratories of the NBS, established in 1946 through a collaboration with the Office of Naval Research, headed by Mina Rees. The goal of this collaboration was to create a national high-speed computation facility that would "provide computing service to other government agencies and ... play an active part in the further development of computing machinery" [20, p. C1]. John Curtiss was named to oversee these mathematics laboratories.

5.1 Learning Through Personal Relationships and Machine Manuals

When Huskey sought to hire engineers to build this new INA computer with him, he didn't post advertisements, but instead relied on "word of mouth" to attract applicants for the three positions he wanted to fill [21, p. 30]. He hired Ed Lacey to work

---

[1] In 1948, the NBS had planned to "purchase two very large 'Hurricane' computers under development by Raytheon Corporation. One of these computers was to be installed in Washington, the other at the Bureau of Standards' Institute for Numerical Analysis ... Production of the Raytheon computers was proceeding quite slowly, and the Bureau of Standards decided to build its own interim computers, one in the East and one in the West" [28].

on the arithmetic unit, Benny Ambrosio to work on the memory unit, and Dave Rutland to work on the control circuitry [21, p. 30]. Lacey had been working on "antisubmarine sonar systems at the Naval Electronics Laboratory in San Diego." Ambrosio, "an engineer at IBM for many years … had worked on its early vacuum-tube multiplier and other computer-related projects" [30, p. 64]. Huskey also enlisted the help of Bill Gunning at RAND Corporation[2] in Southern California for the complex task of developing Williams tube memory for parallel processing. Rutland, who in 1948 was "one of only a few engineers who had digital circuit design experience in Southern California" [30, p. 63], heard of this job opening from an engineer he worked with in the Aerophysics Laboratory at North American Aviation in Los Angeles where they were developing a long-range missile under contract with the US Air Force. Rutland had been designing digital circuits for missile guidance systems there [30, p. 63]. He and his INA colleagues were now going to build "the first computer in the western United States"; they wanted it to be "the fastest computer in the world" [30, p. 64].

Lacey and Ambrosio were already at work designing their units when Rutland joined the team. Rutland later recalled that he asked Huskey "whether he had any specific way in which [the control unit] should be designed. He said that he did not, and I would have to use my imagination" [30, p. 65]. Although Rutland had a master's degree in electrical engineering from the California Institute of Technology (Cal Tech), he had not had "a single computer course, having learned what a binary number was last year, told yesterday what a digital computer was, and suddenly ordered to design a unique control section for a large general-purpose automatic computer" [30, p. 65]. Rutland didn't have the insider connections that would enable him to call up colleagues at different laboratories or visit their projects in person. He didn't have experience with digital computers and formal education wasn't available outside of one-off symposia or conferences like the Moore School lectures in the summer of 1946. Where could a novice computer developer go to learn about building a control unit for a new, untested device?

Rutland described his situation this way:

> I decided to do some research. But was there anything to research? Computers were so new that I was afraid I would have to start with only a pencil and a blank sheet of paper. … I immediately asked Huskey if he had any reports or books on computers, and my request paid off. … I was happily surprised when Huskey handed me a large volume filled with descriptions of every type of circuit that could possibly be useful in the design of an electronic computer. All the special circuits – with names like flip-flop, gate, adder, multiplier, and so on – were listed. It was a true encyclopedia of computing circuits and had been assembled by the ENIAC engineers at the Moore School of the University of Pennsylvania. Huskey himself was responsible for many of these reports. In 1946, he had assembled a

---

[2] "Project RAND began at Douglas Aircraft in 1946. In 1948 The Rand Corporation, a private nonprofit research corporation, was formed. The arrangement with the Air Force is formalized in Air Force Regulation 20-9: to assist the Air Force in improving its efficiency and effectiveness; Project RAND represents a continuing investment by the Air Force in objective research and analysis" [36].

five-volume *Report on the ENIAC*, which served as a maintenance and service manual. [30, p. 65][3]

Although Rutland had to design new, untested circuits for the SWAC, the *Report on the ENIAC* information provided a "head start" for choosing circuits to test so that he would not have to rely solely on a trial-and-error approach. He depended on a document written by his supervisor Harry Huskey to give him basic knowledge of his new design assignment. Without that document, Rutland would have spent much more time designing the SWAC control unit in isolation from knowledge gained from experiences on other projects at other laboratories.

The *Report on the ENIAC* was a seminal document for establishing a common understanding of electronic computer design. Issued in June 1946, this 787-page document was published in five bound volumes: Operating Manual, Maintenance Manual, and Technical Description Part I (two volumes) and Part II. Technical Description Part I was "intended for those who wish to have a general understanding of how the ENIAC works, without concerning themselves with the details of the circuits" [7, Preface]. Basic definitions were included with descriptions of the components of this innovative design for an electronic computing machine. For example, the Introduction of Part I began by describing the ENIAC and its functions:

> The Electronic Numerical Integrator and Computer (ENIAC) is a high-speed electronic computing machine which operates on discrete variables. It is capable of performing the arithmetic operations of addition, subtraction, multiplication, division, and square rooting on numbers (with sign indication) expressed in decimal form. The ENIAC, furthermore, remembers numbers which it reads from punched cards, or which are stored on the switches of its so called function tables, or which are formed in the process of computation, and makes them available as needed. [7, Section 1.1.1]

Here the author assumed that the reader would not be familiar with the basic functioning of an electronic computer. Therefore, the document needed to include information that would first orient the reader to the purpose of the machine itself before going into the technical details of its operation. The author also needed to define the technical terms that people working with the machine had developed.

After orienting the reader to the machine overall, the term *unit* is next defined as "one or more panels and associated devices (such as the portable function tables, for example) containing the equipment for carrying out certain specific related operations" [7, Section 1.1.2]. The machine's 40 units are described along with a schematic of their installation. Technical terms are defined along with explanations of the function of the units. For example, the term *addition time* of 200 microseconds is defined as the "time unit in which the operation time for various parts of the ENIAC is reckoned ... An addition time is so named because it is the time required to complete an addition" [7, Section 1.1.1]. This type of term was specific to the ENIAC, so people working in the future with other computer designs would have to

---

[3]The *Report on the ENIAC* included an Operating Manual written by Harry Huskey and Arthur Burks; a Maintenance Manual written by Huskey, C. Chu, J. A. Cummings, J. H. Davis, T. K. Sharpless, and R. F. Shaw; and a Technical Manual written by Adele Goldstine.

understand this ENIAC-specific term and decide how it applied to a different machine designs. Chances are good that this concept would get a new name at another location for the unit of time needed to complete an operation on a different type of computer. This nonstandard language would create difficulties in collaborating across design teams. Other terms relating to the *addition time*, like *pulse* and *gate*, would have an existing definition from earlier electrical theory relating to voltage changes; the ENIAC team had more specific definitions for these terms: "The term *pulse* is used to refer to a voltage change (either positive or negative) from some reference level and the restoration to the reference level which takes place in a short time, between 2 and 5 microseconds. The term *gate* also refers to a voltage change and the restoration to the reference level but differs from a pulse in duration. In the ENIAC a gate lasts for at least 10 micro-seconds" [7, Section 1.1.2]. Again, the specificity of these pulse and gate times to the ENIAC operation might have caused some confusion for people who understood those terms as more general electrical terms.

The *Report on the ENIAC* provided specific details on the design and operation of this electronic computer – the first one of its kind. Because it was a one-of-a-kind machine, the terminology used in this report was specific to this particular machine and the people who worked with it both at the Moore School and the Army's Aberdeen Proving Ground. When Rutland referred to this report as he started to learn about digital circuitry for the SWAC project at the INA three years after the *Report on the ENIAC* was first issued, he would have used the vocabulary he picked up from this report for the original SWAC design. So the Moore School terminology would prove useful to the people starting to work on the SWAC project, but new terminology would need to be developed at the INA as they developed new devices, such as computer memory. Terminology developed by people at one laboratory might not readily transfer to people working with other computer designs in other locations.

In recalling the state of information sharing among computer project sites, Rutland cited Julian Bigelow's description of the state of information flow at the Institute for Advanced Study in Princeton (IAS) in the late 1940s: "Several people have asked questions about … how much we knew about – and possibly gained from – developments taking place at other places, such as project Whirlwind at MIT and the ex-Moore School team in Philadelphia. The answer is that we had no communication contact except rumors" [30, p. 66]. Although the IAS was located relatively close to both the Moore School in Philadelphia and MIT in the Boston area, their source of information depended on John von Neumann's insider connections with people in other laboratories to share information about new developments in digital computing. At the INA in Los Angeles, Rutland and his colleagues depended on Huskey's connections but were aided by their affiliation with the NBS in Washington, DC, and work on the SEAC project there.

In addition to the *Report on the ENIAC,* Rutland had knowledge of work on the Whirlwind aircraft defense computer project at MIT and work on the Mark III at Harvard that he gained through his participation in the Second Symposium on Large-Scale Digital Calculating Machinery at Harvard University in December

1949. Huskey took Rutland, Lacey, and Ambrosio to this symposium in order to educate his team on new developments in computing going on in the eastern United States. In the opening remarks to that symposium, Navy Rear Admiral F. I. Entwistle emphasized the importance of the work on the relay computers at the Harvard Computation Lab to the war effort and to postwar national security:

> As we in the Bureau of Ordnance look back on the computing problems with which we were faced prior to the First World War, we find that large-scale computations arose chiefly in connection with the problems of ballistics … In those days, one computer (and by computer I mean a man with a slide rule, log book, and a set of Engel's *Ballistic Tables*) handled all such computations. It probably took the impetus, the acceleration, and the foreboding of World War II to permit conception of the machine that was originated here and is known as Mark I.
>
> … The availability of accurate tables in time of war is very important indeed. When the recent war came along with its bombings, rocket firings, and use of heavier guns for antiaircraft and bombardment, we found our range tables insufficient. In fact, we were about 500 range tables behind. In the course of some years, that figure was decreased to 350; but still it was a problem of one man, one slide rule, and tables. … even with 500 men we would still be at least a year behind.
>
> World War II … showed us that we can no longer afford to fight wars of that magnitude. Many of us in the armed services have come to realize that our job is not to fight wars but to prevent them. If we had realized this in the period from 1925 to 1930, we might have dissuaded the Japanese in 1939 from exerting the effort that was subsequently shown. By keeping us prepared to carry through a war, these machines may help us to prevent wars.
>
> … The fact that we can collaborate and coordinate our efforts with a university such as Harvard, and can arrange for the services of the laboratory here for our mutual benefit, should assure us of the continuation of our so-called democracy. [10]

In these opening remarks, Entwistle set out the history and rationale for rapid development of machine computation to underpin US national security after World War II: national security would depend on collaborations between military and civilian sectors to provide the military strength that would deter other nations from risking war with the United States. Entwistle raised the possibility that this type of military strength could have influenced Japan to reconsider its expansionist forays during the 1930s, especially its effort to establish dominance over Indochina despite US objections in 1940. A year earlier, Japan had been driven out of Manchuria by Russian military forces led by Georgy Zhukov, thus thwarting Japanese plans for expansion in China near Russia's border. In 1940, Japan signed the Tripartite Pact with Germany and Italy to agree that each country would mutually respond to aggression on any of the signatory states. In 1941, the United States and Britain imposed an oil embargo on Japan, thus threatening that country's military readiness. In order to overcome that embargo, Japan had plans to seize the Dutch East Indies to control their rich oil reserves. That Dutch colony was vulnerable because the Netherlands had fallen under German control a year earlier; the Dutch East Indies was protected only by US naval forces that had been staged at Pearl Harbor in Hawaii to deter Japanese aggression [14]. Admiral Entwistle speculated that if the United States had posed a significant threat to Japan in 1939, they would not have dared to take on US military forces through a surprise air raid that nearly destroyed US naval forces at Pearl Harbor in December 1941. At this computer symposium 4 years after the end of WWII, Entwistle's focus was on analyzing how the United States got into that war, how it could have been prevented, and how to apply these lessons to prevent future wars. National security relied on military readiness, which relied on developing air defense systems that would rely on high-speed machine computing.

While at this Harvard symposium, the INA team not only participated along with more than 700 people interested in computer development; they also saw the Harvard Mark III in operation and visited both the Whirlwind team at MIT and the SEAC team in Washington, DC. Rutland credited "the exchange of ideas between us and the engineers in these groups" as helping their team with the design of the SWAC [30, p. 66]. When the team returned to Southern California, however, contacts with people about their computer development activities in the eastern United States were rare.

In the late 1940s, computer development work in the western United States was largely done in isolation from developments on the other side of the continent. Other than personal relationships and written documents, information sharing was sporadic. For example, in an IBM Research forum on computer applications that was held in 1946 at their headquarters in New York City, no one from California attended. In an IBM Educational Research forum in 1947, two educators attended from public schools in Pasadena and Glendale, California. In a scientific computation forum held at IBM headquarters in 1948, seven people from California participated and four presented papers: one each from the INA, Telecomputing Corporation, aircraft manufacturer Northrop Corporation, and aircraft manufacturer Convair. Three additional attendees came from North American Aviation, Douglas Aircraft, and the Naval Ordnance Testing Station (NOTS) at China Lake. Three IBM scientific computation forums from 1949 to 1951 were attended by people working in California at NOTS China Lake, Cal Tech, RAND Corporation, Northrop, INA, Douglas Aircraft, North American Aviation, and Telecomputing Corporation [17, p. 246–247]. Even with this increase in transcontinental participation at the IBM meetings, information sharing across this geographical divide was rare and mostly depended on written documents.

5.2   Defining Human-Computer Relationships

One of these foundational documents was the "Relay Computers" report written by George Stibitz for the National Defense Research Committee (NDRC) Applied Mathematics Panel in February 1945. This report, originally distributed under a restricted security classification, was intended to "acquaint those who have computing problems with the potentialities and limitations of relay computers" [32, p. 1]. Knowing that this topic was largely unfamiliar to his readers, Stibitz first needed to define how he would use the terms *calculator*, *computer*, and *computing system*:

By "calculator" or "calculating machine", we shall mean a device (mechanical, electrical, or what not) capable of accepting two numbers, A and B, and of forming some or any of the combinations A+B, A-B, AxB, A/B. By "computer", we shall mean a machine capable of carrying out automatically a succession of operations of this kind and of storing the necessary intermediate results. A "computing system" will suggest a more elaborate device, probably consisting of several computers. Human agents will be referred to as "operators" to distinguish them from "computers" (machines). [32, p. 2]

When Stibitz wrote this report in early 1945, his Complex Number Calculator relay computer was in operation at Bell Telephone and the Navy's Mark I computer had recently been dedicated at Harvard's Computation Lab, where it was built in a collaboration between Howard Aiken's team, the US Navy, and IBM. Even people on the NBS Applied Mathematics Panel were not necessarily familiar with the technical details of these machines; some would still have thought of *computers* as people whose job was to make mathematical calculations.[4] Thus, Stibitz needed to also define the difference between computing machines and human computers in his report, redefining human computers as *operators* and *computers* as machines. The state of common language regarding computing devices in 1945 was such that the term *computer* itself was contested.

Stibitz saw that the rapid development of high-speed calculating machinery necessitated an agreed-upon vocabulary for information sharing that would facilitate collaboration on this wartime effort. In the absence of this common vocabulary, he needed to define the terms he was using in the report so that the readers on the Applied Mathematics Panel would understand his recommendations regarding relay computer design and operation. He included definitions for foundational concepts such as *computing*, which he defined as "the business of giving numerical values to expressions of the form $y = f(x_1, x_2, \ldots, x_n)$, where the f and the parenthesis taken together imply that a rule has been given which explains how to assign a numerical value to y when numerical values are assigned to $x_1, x_2, \ldots, x_n$. The rule f may require the person doing the computation to add, multiply, or divide the numbers x" [32, p. 8]. Although Stibitz defined the term *computing* for the relay machine that is the subject of his report, he continued to refer the action to a human computer, which was the standard understanding of this term in 1945 when fewer than three mechanical computers were operational in the United States.

Relays were also used as the basis for understanding the term *code* in Stibitz's report. He again began by comparing human to machine computation: "In ordinary hand computations, it is necessary to have a system of notation which will permit the person doing the computing to write down numbers and to read them back again" [32, p. 15]. One such system of notation was with Arabic numbers from 0 to 9, but although this system was understandable to human computers, it was not translatable to the relay computer. For machine calculation, "these numbers may … be represented by the configuration of positions of a set of relay contacts, by the configuration of currents … in a set of wires, by holes … in a set of positions on a punched tape, by a set of electrical impulses in a single wire, etc." [32, p. 14]. Stibitz

---

[4] See David Grier's discussion of human computers [16].

defined *code* as "a scheme for representing any number" from 0 to 9 [32, p. 14]. The code for any number could change as the computation moved through "various parts of a computing system," from the human operator using Arabic numerals to the computer in which those numerals were represented by the positions of "three relays in an ordered set of five relays … called a '3 out of 5' code, and the relays themselves may be called 'elements' of the code" [32, p. 14]. Binary notation was used to represent the open (0) or closed (1) state of the relays; thus each Arabic numeral was represented by five digits of zeroes or ones. Each five-digit combination was defined as a *character* of the *code* and "a set of characters defines a <u>code</u>" [32, p. 14].

In addition to representing numerals, Stibitz explained that code could "include a scheme whereby a certain configuration of relays or currents or holes or pulses represents (and causes) an operation by the calculator. Thus, matters can be arranged so that a certain configuration of holes in a control tape <u>transfer</u> a number from one set of relays to another, etc." [32, p. 14]. Here Stibitz describes rudimentary programming of the relay computer to perform an operation automatically by transferring the result of one operation to another part of the machine, where this information may be *translated* into another code through a process that Stibitz called *conversion*, such as from punched tape to relay representation. The term *programming* was not used to describe this automatic machine operation of *translation* and *conversion*.

Another "Computational Process" that Stibitz discussed in this report was the term *decisions*:

> The operator or the computing machine may frequently encounter 'implicit' steps, where a choice must be made among one or more subsequent computing routines … The resulting choice will be called a 'decision'. … Frequently, steps in a computation which at first glance seem to demand judgment on the part of the operator are actually very rough mental calculations, and can be mechanized without the use of other than familiar numerical operations. … In other cases, judgment is based on the recollection of many similar computations, and hence is actually a mental computation requiring a great quantity of stored information of a crude sort. Mechanisms do not readily store information of this kind, and hence such judgment is difficult to deal with in a computing machine. It must be remembered, however, that human computers also have difficulty in these cases, and it is only after a great deal of specialized work that an operator can successfully use the method. [32, p. 11]

Here Stibitz argues that the relay computer could store "crude" information, but was not well equipped for storing and retrieving more complex information. Thus, the operator of the relay computer would be called upon to intervene in the computation when more complex computational judgment was needed. Stibitz urges his reader not to hold this limitation against the machine, however, pointing out that people also have difficulty with more complex calculations until they have mastered them through repetition. Stibitz is arguing for the utility of the relay computer as an aid to human computation. But he is also pointing out that the relay computer has very limited memory capacity.

When it came to storing information, the terminology used for the relay computer was *relay registering*, which Stibitz described as "A Form of Number Storage:" "Hence, if a number is to be used (or to be used again) in a computation, it should be recorded in a form accessible to the calculator without human aid. The most easily accessible form of storage depends upon the use of so-called 'locking' relay circuits. … A set of relays arranged to store a number or operational symbol in this manner is called a <u>relay register</u>, or a <u>register</u> for short" [32, p. 16]. In this early relay design, the idea of storing complex information in computer memory and being able to retrieve it was not yet feasible. Instead, the human-computer system relied on human memory for operations that required anything but "crude" judgment. The relay computer was not yet able to fully function automatically but was part of a human-computer partnership. Humans were the components of this system with memories that stored complex information.

In explaining design concepts for the relay computer, Stibitz extended the analogy between computers and humans to help his readers understand how these new automatic calculating machines would function. He stated that he found it "convenient" to "follow a general pattern reminiscent of that of the human nervous system, in the sense that the calculator is arranged to have a number of levels of 'nerve centers', with differing orders of intelligence, ranging from a kind of simple reflex at the bottom of the scale up to an overall control which integrates and guides the entire operation." [32, p. 30]. He found "close analogies between the functions of parts of a relay computer and sensory perception, memory, motor responses, and other functions of the nervous system" [32, p. 30]. In designing for "convenience in thinking about the operation of the computer," Stibitz argued for "economy of equipment" and "transparent logic:" "It follows that the number of nerve centers and their arrangement into levels of intelligence in any design will depend not only upon the complexity of the operations to be performed, but also upon the habits of thought of the designer" [32, p. 30]. Here again the boundaries between human and computer are blurred in Stibitz's explanation of the design and operation of the relay computer. Not only did this computer rely on intervention from human operators in its functioning, the machine itself embodied the "habits of thought" and the logic of its human designer. In his description, the machine also mimicked the autonomic and voluntary human nervous system in its design, rudimentary programming, and function. In using the analogy "a computer is like a human," Stibitz employed analogy as an effective linguistic device to help his readers understand the functioning of this new machine in terms of something they already knew about: the human body.

5.3 Language Structure for Understanding the Unknown

An *analogy* can be defined as "a comparison between two objects, or systems of objects, that highlights respects in which they are thought to be similar." *Analogical reasoning,* which is "any type of thinking that relies upon an analogy" is "fundamental to human thought" [4] in cognitive psychology terms. In a 1955 address to the American Psychological Association, Robert Oppenheimer specifically stated that analogy was the basis for understanding new phenomena in sciences such as physics or psychology: "Whether or not we talk of discovery or of invention, analogy is inevitable in human thought, because we come to new things in science with the equipment we have … We cannot, coming to something new, deal with it except on the basis of the familiar … We cannot learn to be surprised or astonished at something unless we have an idea of how it ought to be: and that view is most certainly an analogy" [25, p. 358]. Calling analogy "an indispensable and inevitable tool for scientific progress," Oppenheimer defined analogy in science with structural terms that could be applied to Stibitz's analogy of "a computer is like a human:" "I mean a special kind of similarity which is the similarity of structure, the similarity of form, a similarity of constellation between two sets of structures, two sets of particulars, that are manifestly very different but have structural parallels" [25, p. 356]. In describing the design and operation of a computer built with telephone relay switches to readers who were not familiar with this device, along with those who had some familiarity with it, Stibitz defined the machine itself as being human-like in its problem-solving intelligence. Not only did this analogy draw on the readers' understanding of their own problem-solving intelligence, it would draw on their familiarity with human-created intelligent beings such as Frankenstein's monster in Mary Shelley's 1818 book *Frankenstein, or, The Modern Prometheus*, or the robots in Karel Capek's 1921 play "Rossum's Universal Robots" (RUR). The readers of Stibitz's report could also understand the relay computer as an iteration of these human-created intelligent beings, as well as a structural simulacrum of their own nervous system.

Cognitive scientist Douglas Hofstadter has called analogy "the lifeblood, so to speak, of human thinking," which he described as "the transfer of tightly packed mental chunks from the dormant area of long-term memory into the active area of short-term memory, and on their being unpacked on arrival, then scrutinized. Both transfer and perception are crucial" [19, p. 536]. In Hofstadter's explanation, what is stored in long-term memory are "large-scale memory chunk[s]" that are stored in "nodes." Each memory chunk "can be retrieved as a relatively discrete and separable whole." Once a memory chunk is retrieved, it is transferred to "short-term memory (often called 'working memory'), where it is available for scrutiny" [19, p. 525]. These memory chunks can also be thought of as *schema*, which have been defined in cognitive psychology as "a 'pre-existing assumption about the way the world is organized.' When new information becomes available, a person tries to fit the new information into the pattern which he has used in the past to interpret information about the same situation. If the new information does not fit very well, something has to give" [3, p. 1248]. In these cases of ill-fitting new information, either the new information is adapted to the old schema or the old schema is adapted to the new information – or a little of both happens. In Stibitz's case, he was fitting new information about a mechanical calculator that had some aspects of automatic problem-solving function into an old schema of problem-solving intelligence taking place in a human brain controlled by a human nervous system. His explanation simplified the biology of the nervous system to accommodate the limitations of the mechanical calculator. But in the absence of lived experiences with automatic machine calculators on the part of his readers, relying on shared knowledge of human biology was an effective way to communicate new information about these devices.

Computer designers in the 1940s relied on schema about how the world works, based on their lived experiences, and stored in their long-term memories. When they tackled problems in automatic computer design, they formulated those problems based on their schema. In analyzing the role of schema in scientists' problem formation, philosopher of science Thomas Nickles turned to the implicit cognitive psychology in Thomas Kuhn's explanation of how scientific knowledge is made to argue that "scientists locate new problems in a learned similarity metric defined by old, paradigmatic problems and solutions. ... [T]he problem-schema typically possesses generative power that guides the problem-solving practice" [24, p. S247]. In applying the problem-schema to a new problem, the scientist will reduce the new problem to one or a few problems for which the solution is already known. This reductionist role of the problem-schema functions "in a *rhetorical* rather than a logical manner, since the reduction depends on 'the' similarity relation (resemblance, analogy, metaphor, etc.) rather than upon strict logical derivability. ... In this sense rhetoric becomes at least as important as logic (as traditionally conceived) to a theory of inquiry" [24, p. S247]. In the case of mathematician Stibitz explaining the relay calculator, he used both rhetorical and logical approaches in his report to the members of the Applied Mathematics Panel. His technical design details were expressed mathematically; his overall concept for the purpose and operation of the machine to meet human needs was expressed rhetorically through the use of "the computer is like a human" analogy.

Although the mathematicians on the Applied Mathematics Panel (AMP)in 1945 had "an awakening realization" that numerical analysis was becoming more important to wartime efforts, Mina Rees recalled that it "would be false to give the impression that there was widespread concern among the country's leading mathematicians about what ... would happen in computer development" [27, p. 610]. In educating mathematicians on the AMP about relay computers, Stibitz was laying the groundwork for expanding the field of what would become computer science in the next two decades. This foundation was extended by the Moore School lectures in the summer of 1946, where John von Neumann's *First Draft of a Report on the EDVAC* was shared with the 28 participants in that 6-week course.

5.4   The Ground-Breaking Draft of Machine Logic

John von Neumann's *First Draft of a Report on the EDVAC* was completed for internal use at the Moore School under a restricted security classification in June 1945. Although this 101-page draft report was written by von Neumann and was ultimately circulated with his name as sole author, Herman Goldstine pointed out that the engineering concepts in the report were a compilation of ideas discussed by the Moore School team: John Mauchly, Presper Eckert, Arthur Burks, and Goldstine. Von Neumann's contribution to the report was in articulating the logic of the machine in addition to the engineering design considerations. In explaining why von Neumann's name was the only one appearing on the report, Goldstine stated,

"The reason for this was that the document was intended by von Neumann as a working paper for use in clarifying and coordinating the thinking of the group and was not intended as a publication" [15, p. 196].

The *First Draft of a Report on the EDVAC* addressed the "structure of a *very high speed automatic digital computing system* and … its *logical control*" [35, Section 1.1, italics in original] that was being developed as the second generation of electronic computer after the ENIAC, even though that earlier computer was still in development and wasn't dedicated until February 1946. The report began by defining the term *automatic computing system* as "a (usually highly composite) device, which can carry out instructions to perform calculations of a considerable order of complexity" [35, Section 1.2]. In providing an overview of the computer's operation, von Neumann specified that "instructions which govern this operation must be given to the device in absolutely exhaustive detail. They include all numerical information which is required to solve the problem under consideration." After reviewing different media for providing instructions to the computer (punched cards, teletype tape, steel tape or wire, motion picture film, plugboards), von Neumann concluded, "All these procedures require the use of some code to express the logical and the algebraic problem under consideration, as well as the necessary numerical material. … Once these instructions are given to the device, it must be able to carry them out completely and without any need for further human intervention" [35, Section 1.2], unlike the relay computer described in the Stibitz report.

In order for the EDVAC to compute without human intervention, von Neumann specified that it needed three primary units: the *central arithmetical part (CA)* to control mathematical functioning, the *central control (CC)* as the *elastic* and *all purpose* "logical control organ" to route instructions, and "a considerable" *memory (M)* for computing problems without human intervention. This design called for 1K 44-bit words of liquid mercury delay line memory. Together, von Neumann explained, these three parts "correspond to the associative neurons in the human nervous system. It remains to discuss the equivalent of the *sensory* or *afferent* and the *motor* or *efferent* neurons. These are the *input* and *output* organs of the device…" [35, Section 2.6, italics in original].[5] He extended this analogy – "an automatic computer's organs are like a human nervous system" – throughout the description of the EDVAC design, noting where differences in signal timing could differ between information processing using vacuum tubes and using human nerve axons and synapses. The vacuum tube design had the potential to process information in a serial mode of operation at faster speeds than the human nervous system, in von Neumann's estimation.

The "considerable" memory requirement for the EDVAC was estimated in terms of the *capacity* of the memory: "It is the number of stimuli which this organ can

---

[5] About von Neumann referring to computer components as "organs," David Rutland stated, "Much to the amusement of the engineers, he referred to the different sections of a computer as 'organs' and likened the computer circuits to be analogous to the workings of neurons. Modern research in physiology has shown that each neuron in the brain is many thousands of times more complicated than simple vacuum tube computer circuits" [29, p. 67].

remember, or more precisely, the number of occasions for which it can remember whether or not a stimulus was present. The presence or absence of a stimulus ... can be used to express the value 1 or 0 for a binary digit ... Hence the capacity of a memory is the number of binary digits ... it can retain." The capacity *unit of memory* was thus defined as "the ability to retain the value of one binary digit" [35, Section 12.2], and von Neumann calculated that it would take 32 memory units to store a standard real number. He further calculated that a high-speed computing device like the EDVAC would need "a memory M with a capacity of about a quarter million units!" [35, Section 12.5]. This would make the memory of the machine "the main bottleneck" and the most challenging aspect of the design. He concluded that "the decisive part of the device, determining more than any other part its feasibility, dimensions and cost, is the memory" [35, Section 12.5]. After considering the icon-oscope as a memory device, von Neumann recommended that mercury delay line memory was still superior for the EDVAC design.

In order to allow the fully automatic EDVAC to carry out sequential problem-solving operations, orders stored in the memory needed to be given to the arithmetic and control units in the form of *code* and *code words,* anticipating a stored-program computer. There were four classes of orders in von Neumann's design: (a) orders for the control unit to carry out one of ten specific operations; (b) orders for the control unit to transfer a number from one place to another in the machine; (c) orders for the control unit to transfer its connection from one place to another in memory to receive the next order; and (d) orders for controlling the input and output device(s) [35, Section 14.1]. With these classifications, von Neumann could develop a math-ematically logical *code* for instructing the control unit to carry out orders. The EDVAC design described by von Neumann thus incorporated both a rhetorical explanation by using an analogy between the machine and humans and a logical explanation through the mathematical description of the machine design and opera-tion. The stored-program design articulated in this report was initially shared with 24 people working at the Moore School and, after the security classification was lowered, with the 28 participants in the Moore School lectures in the summer of 1946.

Although the design set out by von Neumann in this report was not ultimately carried out in the EDVAC completed in 1949, Herman Goldstine asserted that the *First Draft of a Report on the EDVAC* was "the most important document ever writ-ten on computing and computers. ... Von Neumann was the first person, as far as I am concerned, who understood explicitly that a computer essentially performed logical functions, and that the electrical aspects were ancillary" [15, p. 191–192]. Von Neumann based his modeling of the logical control of computing operations on earlier work by Warren S. McCulloch and Walter Pitts from the Department of Psychiatry at the University of Illinois College of Medicine [15, p. 196]. In their 1943 article "A Logical Calculus of the Ideas Immanent in Nervous Activity," McCulloch and Pitts stated, "Because of the 'all-or-none' character of nervous activity, neural events and the relations among them can be treated by means of propositional logic" [23, p. 115]. The "all-or-none" character of nervous activity also could correspond to the on-or-off states of relay switches and the zero-or-one states of binary notation. To further facilitate connections between propositional logic, binary notation, and natural language, McCulloch and Pitt based their mathematical analysis of information sent through neural networks on Rudolf Carnap's *Logical Syntax* (1937) language structure. According to Carnap, syntax "consists in formal theories of linguistic symbols" in which "no reference is made in it to either the meaning of the symbols (e.g., the words) or to the sense of the expressions (e.g., the sentences), but simply and solely to the kinds and order of the symbols from which the expressions are constructed" [22]. In Carnap's logical positivist scheme, language could be represented by arbitrary symbols; syntax was determined by rules of relations among symbols that could be analyzed and predicted through application of mathematical probability and symbolic logic. Once this connection between information and human biology was explained mathematically, von Neumann saw how a machine could be built with logical control of information flow. In order to accomplish this transfer from the structure of human to machine language, however, meaning had to be stripped from the information.

5.5   A Mathematical Model of Meaningless Machine Communication

This approach to representing information mathematically was later extended by Claude Shannon in his 1948 paper "A Mathematical Theory of Communication," published in the *Bell Systems Technical Journal*. While working on cryptography at Bell Labs during WWII, Shannon had also been working on a theory for representing communication through mechanical means, such as telegraph, radio, telephone, or television. He found that the "fundamental problem in communication is that of reproducing at one point either exactly or approximately a message selected at another point. Frequently the messages have meaning; that is they refer to or are correlated with certain physical or conceptual entities. These semantic aspects of communication are irrelevant to the engineering problem" [32, p. 379]. In this model, the term *information* is untethered from semantic meaning and is instead defined as "a measure of one's freedom of choice when one selects a message"; the amount of information in a message is "measured by the logarithm of the number of available choices" [36, p. 4]. Using binary mathematical notation, Shannon measured information in units of *binary digits*, or *bits*, which was a term introduced by Bell Labs mathematician John W. Tukey in 1947.

The works of Carnap, McCulloch and Pitt, and Shannon all employed the "computer is like human" analogy to translate information about the human nervous system into mathematical statements. In describing communication in mathematical terms in order to improve mechanical communication devices, Shannon presented this model of communication [31, p. 381] (Fig. 5.1).

Here Shannon used machine terms, such as *transmitter* and *signal*, to describe human communication. These are terms for operational concepts that are similar to

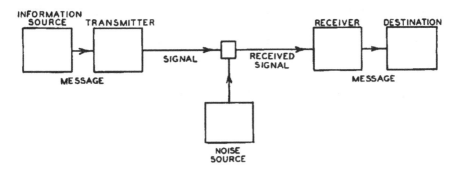

Fig. 5.1 Schematic diagram of the Shannon-Weaver communication model

those used by Stibitz and von Neumann to describe computer operations in human terms. Shannon's model divorced the terms *information* and *meaning*, finding the latter to be irrelevant to the statistical manipulation of language that was his goal. In extending Shannon's work, Warren Weaver foresaw that "utilizing the powerful body of theory concerning Markoff processes[6] seems particularly promising for semantic studies, since this theory is specifically adapted to handle one of the most significant but difficult aspects of meaning namely the influence of context" [37, p. 12]. In order to analytically separate communication from meaning and context, Weaver set out three levels of communication problems in the order of their complexity:

Level A. How accurately can the symbols of communication be transmitted? (The technical problem)
Level B. How precisely do the transmitted symbols convey the desired meaning? (The semantic problem)
Level C. How effectively does the received meaning affect conduct in the desired way? (The effectiveness problem) [37, p. 2]

Weaver found that the "*technical problems* are concerned with the accurate trans-ference from sender to receiver of sets of symbols" [37, p. 2]. This was the topic of Shannon's mathematical theory of communication. Further, "*semantic problems* are concerned with the identity, or satisfactorily close approximation, in the interpreta-tion of meaning by the receiver, as compared with the intended meaning of the sender" [37, p. 2]. This interpretive function was not covered in Shannon's theory but would take place between human receivers and senders. In Weaver's classification of problems, defining terms would be a Level B semantic problem. He implied the importance of a communication's context on its meaning in saying, "The semantic problem has wide ramifications if one thinks of communication in general. Consider,

---

[6]Weaver defined Markoff process as it relates to Shannon's theory of communication: "A system which produces a sequence of symbols (which may, of course, be letters or musical notes, say, rather than words) according to certain probabilities is called a *stochastic process*, and the special case of a stochastic process in which the probabilities depend on the previous events, is called a *Markoff process* or a Markoff chain" [37, p. 5].

for example, the meaning to a Russian of a U.S. newsreel picture" [37, p. 2]. Here Weaver pointed to the importance of meaning to communication as sent by people and received by other people. In Shannon's communication model, the only location of a possible person would be in the destination position, despite the implied need for a person to initiate the message that was initially transmitted from the information source [37, p. 2]. In order for a person to interpret the meaning of a message in the destination position in Shannon's communication model, some meaning had to be written into the message at the information source position, which would have been beyond the ability of a machine such as a computer, whether relay or electronic design, using a mathematical model of language divorced from meaning. In machines that operate automatically through programming, the person who wrote the program would have encoded some kind of meaning into the machine instructions.[7]

In Weaver's Level C of problem complexity, "effectiveness problems are concerned with the success with which the meaning conveyed to the receiver leads to the desired conduct on his part. … [W]ith any reasonably broad definition of conduct, it is clear that communication either affects conduct or is without any discernible and probable effect at all" [37, p. 2]. In considering that Shannon's communication model did not account for either meaning or impact of a message, Weaver suggested that a "real theory of meaning" [37, p. 12] was needed. He concluded, "It is almost certainly true that a consideration of communication on levels B and C will require additions to the schematic diagram … but it seems equally likely that what is required are minor additions, and no real revision" [37, p. 11]. He suggested the addition of "another box labeled 'Semantic Receiver' interposed between the engineering receiver … and the destination" to give the message "a second decoding." He also suggested adding a box for "semantic noise" and relabeling the existing "noise" box as "engineering noise" [37, p. 11]. Weaver suggested that in measuring the semantic meaning of a message, that a "general theory at all levels will surely have to take into account not only the capacity of the channel, but also (even the words are right!) the capacity of the audience. … [B]y direct analogy, if you overcrowd the capacity of the audience you force a general and inescapable error and confusion" [37, p. 12].[8] Here Weaver is using the machine

---

[7] See further discussion of politics and bias in technology design in Bijker [6], Ferrell [11], and Winner [39].

[8] Also consider the definition of rhetoric that Aristotle introduced over 2000 years ago as a human-centered approach to decreasing the probability of confusion in an audience's understanding of a message: An effective rhetorician has "the ability to see what is possibly persuasive in every given case" (*Rhet.* I.2, 1355b26f.) And further: "The systematical core of Aristotle's *Rhetoric* is the doctrine that there are three technical means of persuasion. The attribute 'technical' implies two characteristics: (i) Technical persuasion must rest on a method, and this, in turn, is to say that we must know the reason why some things are persuasive and some are not. Further, methodical persuasion must rest on a complete analysis of what it means to be persuasive. (ii) Technical means of persuasion must be provided by the speaker himself, whereas preexisting facts, such as oaths, witnesses, testimonies, etc. are non-technical, since they cannot be prepared by the speaker. … Technical means of persuasion are either (a) in the character of the speaker, or (b) in the emotional state of the hearer, or (c) in the argument (*logos*) itself" [26].

model as the standard into which human intelligence must be incorporated. Whereas Stibitz and von Neumann had used the human nervous system against which to measure machine operation, Weaver substituted machine operation as the standard against which to measure human language understanding. The computer was becoming the standard for measuring human intelligence in a new field called *information theory.*

This new understanding of human-computer relations was becoming common knowledge in communities of computer developers, who were familiar with the "computer is like human" analogy. In many instances, developers had been introduced to computer logic through von Neumann's use of this analogy in the *First Draft of a Report on the EDVAC*. The "computer is like human" idea was a foundational concept in computer design. Norbert Wiener at MIT had been discussing this analogy and neurophysiology with von Neumann in 1944 [18, p. 182], but Wiener's subsequent work on cybernetics took this communication model in a more sociological direction than von Neumann's work. In introducing his cybernetic theory of communication and control, Wiener pointed out that in the half-century of war and chaos that the world had just experienced, Newtonian physics had given way to a more "incomplete determinism, almost an irrationality in the world, [which] is in a certain way parallel to Freud's admission of a deep irrational component in human conduct and thought" [38, p. 11]. Citing Willard Gibbs' theory of entropy, also employed in Shannon's mathematical theory of communication, Wiener set out his "theory of messages" in a larger context than was possible in von Neumann's or Shannon's analogic models: "Besides the electrical engineering theory of the transmission of messages, there is a larger field which includes not only the study of language but the study of messages as a means of controlling machinery and society, ... [and] certain reflections upon psychology and the nervous system" [38, p. 15]. He defined this wider view of message theory as *cybernetics* [38, p. 15], which included a feedback loop as modeled below (Fig. 5.2):

While acknowledging the utility of the "computer is like human" analogy for understanding computer design, Wiener insisted on conserving a human element in the consideration of message theory. For example, *information* in his model is defined as "a name for the content of what is exchanged with the outer world as we

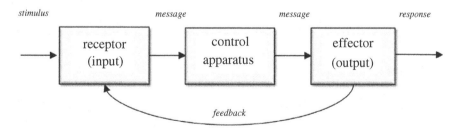

Fig. 5.2 The cybernetic model [34, p.42]

adjust to it and make our adjustment felt upon it. The process of receiving and of using information is the process of our adjusting to the contingencies of the outer environment and of our living effectively within that environment" [38, p. 17–18]. In this definition, Wiener used the first person *we* as the perspective from which to understand the use and impact of information within a social network. Unlike the purely mathematical communication models put forward by von Neumann and Shannon, Wiener's cybernetic model retained human communication as the standard against which to measure machine communication, thus reflecting his focus on *The Human Use of Human Beings* [38].[9]

In 1949 the concept of a computer as a human-like machine was introduced to the general public through the publication of Edmund Berkeley's book *Giant Brains or Machines that Think*. Berkeley felt that the average American should know about these machines, which he described as coming "closer to being a brain that thinks than any machine ever did before 1940" [5, p. vii]. For the first time, Berkeley's book explained the workings of automatic computing devices to people who were not familiar with computers, using Rudolf Flesch's "scientific rhetoric" [12]. By 1947, Flesch was widely acknowledged as "the undisputed high priest of a … cult of 'readability'" [1, p. 22]. Berkeley sent Flesch draft chapters of *Giant Brains* for review to ensure that Berkeley's writing style would make the technical information about this unfamiliar topic clear to his intended readers in the general public. Flesch responded with two pages of recommendations, summed up with this comment: "I think you have concentrated 100% on the logic of the subject and neglected the psychology of the reader. What he needs is the whys and wherefores, the drama of the thing, the human element in the development of these machines" [13]. He suggested that Berkeley omit all references to symbolic logic and foreground the human "story" about "the men who worked on these giant brains and a picture of what it's like to watch them in operation" [13]. In other words, foreground the human element so the reader could relate to the technical information about these unfamiliar machines.

Berkeley began *Giant Brains* with a discussion of the similarities between computers and human brains, arguing that "mechanical brains" can do some kinds of "thinking" better than humans [5, p. 5]. Despite these thinking capabilities, he found that there were still four kinds of thinking that machines could not perform: think intuitively, make bright guesses and leap to conclusions, determine all necessary instructions, and perceive and interpret complex situations outside itself [5, p. 8]. For the purposes of comparing human and machine thinking, Berkeley defined four important terms:

- *Thinking* is "computing, reasoning, and other handling of information."

---

[9] See Heims for background on this book: "After World War II Wiener took on the role of the independent, technologically knowledgeable, humane intellectual" [18, p. 331]. This "new role brought him a new and large audience: the educated public. His first book for this audience, *Cybernetics* (1948), turned out to be a best seller in spite of its partly technical and mathematical content. *The Human Use of Human Beings* (1950), with technical and mathematical language eliminated, was even more popular" [18, p. 335].

- *Information* is "collections of ideas – physically, collections of marks that have meaning."
- *Handling* is "proceeding logically from some ideas to other ideas – physically, changing from some marks to other marks in ways that have meaning."
- *Languages* are "systems for handling information" [5, p. 10].

Berkeley argued that languages were both a *"scheme for expressing meanings and physical equipment* that can be handled" [5, p. 11, italics in original]. Using spoken English as an example, Berkeley specified that meanings are expressed through 150,000 words and rules for combining them, while sound waves and people's ears are the physical equipment. Mathematics using Arabic numerals is another example of a language, with ten digits and rules for combining them, using the physical equipment of a pencil and paper, or a mechanical desk calculator. Berkeley pointed out that it would not be possible for someone to exchange the physical equipment of spoken English and mathematics to express meanings. This contrasted with Weaver's concept of language expressed in terms that Eddington used to explain *entropy* in "The Nature of the Physical World:" "Entropy is only found when the parts are viewed in association, and it is by viewing or hearing the parts in association that beauty and melody are discerned. All three are features of arrangement" [37, p. 12]. Equating the terms entropy, beauty, melody, and meaning, Weaver concluded, "I suspect [Eddington] would have been thrilled to see, in this theory, that entropy not only speaks the language of arithmetic; it also speaks the language of language" [37, p. 12]. Unlike Berkeley, Weaver did think that it would be possible to exchange the physical equipment of English and mathematical languages.

In the last chapter of *Giant Brains,* "Social Control: Machines that Think and How Society May Control Them," Berkeley argued that people needed to establish systems of control over intelligent machines to ensure that they would be "of true benefit to all of humanity" [5, p. 196]. He argued that responsibility for implementing these controls should be shared by people everywhere:

> Now the problem of rational control over robot machines and other parts of the new technology is no respecter of national boundaries. To be solved it requires a worldwide point of view, a loyalty to human society and its best interests, a social point of view. ... It is not easy to think of any yet organized group of people anywhere that would have both the strength and the vision needed to solve this problem through its own efforts. For example, a part of the United Nations might have some of the vision needed, but it does not have the power. ... [W]e need a public body responsible for study, education, advice, and some measure of control. It might be something like an Atomic Energy Commission, Bacterial Defense Commission, Mental Health Commission, and Robot Machine Commission, all rolled into one." [5, p. 208]

Berkeley's emphasis on teaching people to work with "machines that handle information automatically" reflected a belief in science that characterized the post-World War II and Cold War years in the United States. Because technological progress and national security were central concerns of this postwar culture, Berkeley's work helped to educate civilians in the United States about the high-speed computers that would become important components in aircraft defense systems for national security. As Paul Edwards (1996) noted, "The military organization of science during and after World War II played a crucial role in creating conditions under which fruitful encounters among psychology, computer science, mathematics, and linguistics could occur" [9, p. 176]. The writings of mathematicians and early computer engineers took place under these conditions at a time before computer science was recognized as a separate profession. Their work served an important cultural and political function that helped to establish electronic computing as a legitimate profession separate from mathematics or engineering.

References

1. Anonymous. 1947, April 12. Apostle of plain talk. *Business Week*: 22–25.
2. ———. 1953, October. National Bureau of Standards western automatic computer: Recent developments and operating experience. *National Bureau of Standards Technical News Bulletin* 37(10): 143–150.
3. Axelrod, Robert. 1973, December. Schema theory: An information processing model of perception and cognition. *The American Political Science Review* 67(4): 1248–1266.
4. Bartha, Paul. 2019, Spring. Analogy and analogical reasoning. In *The Stanford encyclopedia of philosophy*. Edward N. Zalta, ed. https://plato.stanford.edu/entries/reasoning-analogy/#AriThe. Accessed 4 Nov 2020.
5. Berkeley, Edmund C. 1949. *Giant brains or machines that think*. New York: Wiley.
6. Bijker, Wiebe E. 2017. Constructing worlds: Reflections on science, technology, and democracy (and a plea for bold modesty). *Engaging Science, Technology, and Society* 3: 315–331.
7. Burks, Arthur W., and Harry D. Huskey. Report on the ENIAC. *Smithsonian Libraries*. https://library.si.edu/digital-library/author/burks-arthur-w. Accessed 4 Nov 2020.
8. Curtiss, John H. 1951, June 29. Foreword. In *Problems for the numerical analysis of the future*, Applied Mathematics Series, 15: iv. Washington, DC: National Bureau of Standards.
9. Edwards, Paul N. 1996. *The closed world: Computers and the politics of discourse in Cold War America*. Cambridge, MA: MIT Press.
10. Entwistle, F. I. 1949/1951, September 13. Opening address. *Proceedings of a second symposium on large-scale digital calculating machinery*. Cambridge, MA: Harvard University Press: 5–6.
11. Ferrell, Patricia. 2019, August 30. Bias, racist robots, and AI: The problems that coders fail to see. *Better Programming*. https://medium.com/better-programming/bias-racist-robots-and-ai-the-problems-in-the-coding-that-coders-fail-to-see-305f6f324793. Accessed 4 Nov 2020.
12. Flesch, Rudolf. 1947, May 29. Letter to Edmund Berkeley. Edmund C. Berkeley Papers [CBI50] Charles Babbage Institute, University of Minnesota, Minneapolis.
13. ———. 1947, June 27. Letter to Edmund Berkeley. Edmund C. Berkeley Papers [CBI50] Charles Babbage Institute, University of Minnesota, Minneapolis.
14. Goldman, Stuart D. 2012, August 28. The forgotten Soviet-Japanese war of 1939. *The Diplomat*. https://thediplomat.com/2012/08/the-forgotten-soviet-japanese-war-of-1939/. Accessed 3 Nov 2020.
15. Goldstine, Herman H. 1972. *The computer from Pascal to von Neumann*. Princeton: Princeton University Press.
16. Grier, David A. 2005. *When computers were human*. Princeton: Princeton University Press.
17. Gruenberger, Fred J. 1980, July. A short history of digital computing in Southern California. *IEEE Annals of the History of Computing* 2(3): 246–250.
18. Heims, Steve J. 1982. *John von Neumann and Norbert Wiener: From mathematics to the technologies of life and death*. Cambridge, MA: MIT Press.

19. Hofstadter, Douglas R. 2001. Analogy as the core of cognition. In *The analogical mind: Perspectives from cognitive science*, ed. Dedre Gentner et al., 499–538. Cambridge, MA: MIT Press.

20. Huskey, Harry D. 1980/August 1991. The SWAC: The National Bureau of Standards Western Automatic Computer. *NBS-INA – The Institute for Numerical Analysis – UCLA 1947-1954*. NIST Special Publication 730. Washington, DC: U.S. Department of Commerce, National Institute of Standards and Technology. Appendix C.

21. ———. 2006, February 7. Oral history interview. William Aspray, interviewer. Computer History Museum, Reference number: X3455.2006. https://www.computerhistory.org/collections/oralhistories/?s=Huskey. Accessed 30 Dec 2020.

22. Leitgeb, Hannes, and Andre Carus. 2020, Fall. Rudolf Carnap. In *The Stanford Encyclopedia Of Philosophy*. Edward N. Zalta, ed. https://plato.stanford.edu/entries/carnap/index.html#RoadSynt. Accessed 4 Nov 2020.

23. McCulloch, Warren S., and Walter Pitts. 1990. A logical calculus of the ideas immanent in nervous activity. *Bulletin of Mathematical Biology* 52 (1/2): 99–115.

24. Nickles, Thomas. 2000, September. Kuhnian puzzle solving and schema theory. *Philosophy of Science* 67, Supplement. Proceedings of the 1998 Biennial Meeting of the Philosophy of Science Association: S242–S255.

25. Oppenheimer, Robert. 1958. Analogy in science. *The Centennial Review of Arts & Science* 2: 351–373.

26. Rapp, Christof. 2010, Spring. Aristotle's rhetoric. In *The Stanford encyclopedia of philosophy*. Edward N. Zalta, ed. https://plato.stanford.edu/entries/aristotle-rhetoric/#agenda. Accessed 4 Nov 2020.

27. Rees, Mina. 1980, October. The mathematical sciences and World War II. *American Mathematics Monthly* 87: 607–621.

28. Rosen, Saul. 1968, July. *Electronic computers – A historical survey in print*. Paper 184. Purdue University Department of Computer Science Technical Reports. https://docs.lib.purdue.edu/cstech/184. Accessed 4 Nov 2020.

29. Rutland, David. 1995. *Why computers are computers: The SWAC and the PC*. Philomath: Wren Publishers.

30. ———. 1997. Memories of the SWAC. *IEEE Annals of the History of Computing* 19 (2): 63–69.

31. Shannon, Claude E. 1948, July. A mathematical theory of communication. *The Bell System Technical Journal* 27(3): 379–423.

32. Stibitz, George R. 1945, February. *Relay computers*. OSRD Report 4996; AMP Report 171.1R. Washington, DC: National Defense Research Committee, Applied Mathematics Panel.

33. Stibitz, George R., and Jules A. Larrivee. 1957. *Mathematics and computers*. New York: McGraw-Hill Book Company.

34. von Bertalanffy, Ludwig. 1968. *General system theory: Foundations, development, applications*. New York: George Braziller.

35. von Neumann, John. 1946/1993. First draft of a report on the EDVAC. *IEEE Annals of the History of Computing* 15 (4): 27–43.

36. Ware, Willis H. 1976, November. *Project RAND and Air Force decisionmaking*. The Rand Paper Series, P-5737. Santa Monica: The Rand Corporation. https://www.rand.org/pubs/papers/P5737.html. Accessed 5 Nov 2020.

37. Weaver, Warren. 1949/1963. Some recent contributions to the mathematical theory of communication. In *The mathematical theory of communication*, 1–28. Urbana/Chicago: The University of Illinois Press.

38. Wiener, Norbert. 1950. *The human use of human beings*. Boston: Houghton Mifflin Company.

39. Winner, Langdon. 1980, Winter. Do artifacts have politics? *Daedalus* 109(1): 121–136.

Chapter 6
Technology Development Strains Standardization of Human Communication

Abstract This chapter places efforts to standardize computer terminology within a historical context of language standardizing efforts for earlier technologies of electricity and radio. It describes nationalistic concerns in assigning names to electrical concepts at the turn of the twentieth century. It also describes how standardization of radio terminology was considered to be important to concerns with safety and secure transportation systems. Language standardization efforts from the Institute of Radio Engineers (IRE) and American Institute of Electrical Engineers (AIEE) began to focus on creating glossaries of terms relating to automatic computing devices in the late 1940s, reflecting the growing importance and specialization of this emerging professional field. The glossaries developed in these organizations reflected the priorities of committee members with backgrounds in military, academic, and industry projects.

> *"As a matter of fact, when I just joined the staff [at the Institute for Numerical Analysis], I really could not help but notice that one mathematician of a very senior rank always went into the computer room with a stick in his hand. And, if the computer problem that he was working on blew up, he would go around the computer and bang on it. He would go back to the console and test it, and, you know what? Sometimes it worked." Ragnar Thorensen, "Pioneer Day Remarks," 1978* [49]

> *"Information is a commodity rather than a concept. Calculation, control, and communication are significant because they allow the economic exploitation of information." Paul N. Edwards, "The Closed World," 1996* [21]

> *"Language forms a kind of wealth ..." Pierre Bourdieu, "Language and Symbolic Power," 1991* [16]

In 1947 when participants in the Harvard Symposium on Large-Scale Calculating Machinery expressed concern about the lack of standardized terminology impeding postwar computer development, they voiced a concern that was common to previous eras of rapid technology development. At the turn of the twentieth century, for example, mining engineer and journal editor Thomas A. Rickard wrote what can be considered the first book on technical writing to provide guidance for writers of scientific papers. He began his 1908 book by claiming, "It has been said that in this age the man of science appears to be the only one who has anything to say, and he

© Springer Nature Switzerland AG 2021
B. Longo, *Words and Power*, History of Computing,
https://doi.org/10.1007/978-3-030-70373-8_6

is the one that least knows how to say it" [45, p. 7]. During what Samuel Florman has called "the Golden Age of Engineering" [22], Rickard expressed the urgency of scientists and technicians knowing how to communicate their ideas clearly through the written word. He urged technical writers to employ the efficiency and precision of an engineer when crafting their writing. Without this attention to detail, Rickard said "the scientific man is unscientific in his writing" [45, p. 10]. On the contrary, when scientists and engineers employed the right words in the right places, they created texts that could contribute to a general fund of scientific knowledge for the good of humankind: "Let us have a mintage that will pass current at full value throughout the English-speaking world; let it be the refined gold of human speech" [45, p. 19]. Rickard expressed the belief that when writers expressed technical ideas efficiently using a precise, standardized terminology, the knowledge they communicated could be translated into economic and political value. It is this connection between standardized technical terminology and societal value that underpins the importance of efforts to define technical terms, especially in periods of rapid technology development.

6.1 Electrical Engineering Defines Terms for Power and Communication

One such period of rapid technology development took place in the late nineteenth century around the application of electric power generation, telegraphy, and electrical devices. In 1884, interest in this new field of electricity had grown to the extent that electrical engineer and inventor Nathaniel S. Keith sent out a call for participation to 73 people working in this field to organize what would become the American Institute of Electrical Engineers [32]. Thomas Edison was among the small group of people who joined the meeting organized by Keith in New York City on 15 April 1884 to form the American Institute of Electrical Engineers (AIEE) [12]. This group's first technical meeting was held at the International Electrical Exhibition at the Franklin Institute in Philadelphia in October 1884, which provided a venue for scientists and technicians working in this new field to meet and exchange information that would help to shape this new profession. In the nineteenth century, "exhibitions were a major means of transferring technical knowledge," and the Franklin Institute which sponsored the exhibition had a "tradition of promoting the technical arts" [23, p. 170]. This exhibition, which ran from 2 September through 11 October, was the site of many demonstrations of new technologies and meetings of people working with electricity. It was the first such exposition in the United States to deal only with electricity. According to *Electrical World* magazine at that time, the exposition's classification of exhibits provided a "perfect nomenclatory survey of the whole field of electrical science" [23, p. 170], thus suggesting some standard terminology for this new field that would be especially useful for the practical engineers and operators who were among the 7000 attendees over the exhibit's run.

One piece of business during the meetings at the exhibit was to define the *watt* as a unit of electrical power. On 11 September 1884, the fourth day of the National Conference of Electricians, members heard the report from a committee which was "appointed to consider the subject of the watt" [48, p. 67], which had been defined by Sir William Siemens in 1882 at the British Association for the Advancement of Science as "the amount of work per second which is done when an ampere current is maintained against the resistance of an ohm" [48, p. 68]. Siemens had named this unit of work after the Scottish inventor James Watt and there was discussion about the appropriateness of this name at the 1884 conference in Philadelphia. Electrical engineer William Henry Preece noted in his committee's report, "I have not the slightest doubt that the term 'watt' will be introduced all over the world. I tried to bring it before the Paris Conference last year, and the reason why it was not accepted was twofold: first the Germans objected to the introduction of any more English names, and, secondly, the French objected to it because they have no 'w' in the French language. … [W]e should be proud to apply his name to the unit which is connected with his measure" [48, p. 68]. At question here was not the definition of this unit of electrical power but the naming of this unit in honor of the Scottish scientist. National pride underpinned these contested discussions over whose group would be recognized and remembered as the legitimate progenitor of this fundamental concept in electrical power. The discussion was political as much as lexicographical.

When the committee report was put forward for approval on the sixth day of the meeting, the question of naming arose again. This time, Civil War veteran and Captain of Ordnance at Philadelphia's Frankford Arsenal O. E. Michaelis make a case for the United States:

> I feel impelled to make a suggestion as an American citizen … I find that in naming these units very many of the great names of those connected with the advancement of science have been applied. But I have yet failed to find that a single American name has been applied to a unit … I think the new horse-power which the committee proposes to establish, namely, a thousand watts, might very properly without interfering with the established symbol be called a "henry." … We have now more horse-power in operation than any other nation in the world, and I think in giving the name to that unit our country deserves consideration [48, p. 160–161].

Canadian civil engineer Charles Herschel Koyl suggested that the term "kilowatt" would be simpler than assigning names to various quantities of standard units: "The addition of another name would be, for example, as if some one should endeavor to give a name to a kilometer and call it a franklin" [48, p. 161]. President of the United States Electrical Commission and physicist Henry A. Rowland exercised his prerogative as conference chair to bring the discussion back to the business at hand: "The committee does not recommend anything with respect to [the term kilo-watt], but refers to it for further consideration. It only commends with reference to legalizing the term 'watt.' But I may say here that the definitions of these units must be very carefully prepared before any laws are made upon them" [48, p. 161]. During this period of rapid development of electrical knowledge and innovation, Rowland recognized that the terminology they helped to standardize at the

1884 conference would become the building blocks of future innovations. It was important that people attending the conference recognized their obligation to future engineers who would build on their knowledge. It was also important that people attending the conference not get bogged down in self-interest as they built the foundation for a new profession.

6.2   Radio Engineers Define Terms for Transportation Safety

Another period of rapid technology development took place in the early twentieth century, with the advent of radio transmitters and receivers. From 1899 to 1912, about 30 radio companies were started in the United States, and the number of radio stations grew from 50 to 700 [11, 36]. In May 1912, the Institute of Radio Engineers (IRE) was founded with 46 charter members [37]; the next year its six-member Committee on Standardization published a report for its members entitled "Definition of Terms, Graphical and Literal Symbols." In its first 16 months of existence, the IRE Committee on Standardization held more than 50 meetings and discussions to develop 22 pages of definitions of terms associated with the nascent profession of radio engineering, which included 125 definitions of terms, 60 literal symbols, and 35 graphical symbols [40, p. 47]. In issuing their preliminary report on definitions in September 1913, the committee prefaced their report by explaining the importance of standardizing terms:

> The early history of new branches of engineering always shows the discouraging spectacle of a confused and ill-defined nomenclature, together with widely different connotations assigned to the literal symbols by the various investigators and authors. Such a state of affairs gives rise to unfortunate misunderstandings, or, at best, to a considerable amount of unnecessary labor on the part of the practicing engineer and students of engineering [41, p. 3].

IRE leadership felt that this situation of misunderstanding and unnecessary labor existed among radio engineers internationally in the early 1900s. They, therefore, created the Committee on Standardization with "the express purpose of studying the terms and symbols used in the art, selecting and defining the suitable terms, and eliminating the remainder" [41, p. 3].

The IRE Committee on Standardization was chaired by Robert H. Marriott, who in 1913 was a Radio Inspector for the US Department of Commerce in New York City. Beyond that role, Marriott was also the founder and first president of the IRE [7], which suggests the importance that the young association placed on establishing a standardized vocabulary for this rapidly growing technology and profession. Marriott himself had been convinced of the need for a professional association of radio people as early as 1906, when he initially had the idea to form a "wireless society":[1] "By 1906, a wireless society was on my list of things I would like to see come about to help in developing wireless. But there were not enough people engaged in radio for a starter, in any one place ... where I was building and maintaining stations" [40, p. 7]. Marriott himself was working as an engineer at the United Wireless Telegraph Company but found that "the officers of the wireless companies of that time thought their employees should not even know the employees of another wireless company and certainly they should not associate with them. Being secretive between companies and even between employees in the same company was generally considered to be the only right and sensible policy" [40, p. 7]. In recalling this situation in 1952, IRE founders Alfred Goldsmith and John Hogan also stated that "there was an enormous amount of secrecy in those days. It was very difficult for an engineer ... to get any information on which he could depend." They differentiated between "competition, which is healthy ... [and] secrecy which is not, and opposition, which certainly wasn't" [22, p. 5].

This corporate impulse for protecting proprietary information about their operations worked well enough when the demand for radio equipment and installations was low. But when new devices were developed and new services started to be available, development of radio technologies was hampered by this secrecy. Within any one company, efficiency might be achieved by standardizing radio equipment at a static state to maximize profits [24, p. 8]. But for the industry as a whole, competing standards stymied overall development of radio technology and operations. Marriott, who advocated for experimentation and professional cooperation among radio engineers, sought to facilitate this cooperation by soliciting interest in a new professional association. In May 1908, he sent a letter to a number of "wireless people" asking for their interest in establishing an Institute of Wireless Engineers. The letter began, "You have often thought no doubt that wireless telegraphy would be developed faster if those engaged in it would work together more" [24, p. 9]. He concluded, "I believe an organization ... would materially improve wireless, increase the knowledge and ability of members, avoid friction between employees, between employees and employers, and to some extent between wireless companies" [24, p. 10]. The Institute of Wireless Engineers (IWE) was formed in March 1910, with Marriott elected as president.

At a June IWE meeting, Jack R. Binns read a paper entitled "How Business Can Best Be Handled in Case of Distress" and the group discussed the paper at length. In January 1909, Binns had been a 24-year-old wireless operator aboard the White Star ocean liner Republic when it was rammed by a cargo ship off the Nantucket

---

[1] In the early 1900s, the distinction between the terms *radio* and *wireless* was not well defined. The term *wireless* was most prominently used to describe what would later be known as *radio*. As late as 1925, this distinction was still being clarified: "If you think that there's any difference between a radio receiver and a wireless receiver then how do you explain hearing code signals on your so-called 'radio'? No, there's no difference; the same circuits that the ships and amateurs use for reception of radio telegraph or wireless telegraph signals will be found in a so-called 'radio.' ... If this is the radio age let us learn the correct classification of the various branches, instead of making one or two words put on various disguises for the many parts they are supposed to play" [28].

coast in the northeastern United States. "The collision killed two passengers and flooded the cabin that contained his radio equipment, but Mr. Binns found some spare batteries, and transmitted a distress signal for 36 hours, even as he suffered from hunger and cold. Finally, he managed to make contact with another White Star liner, the Baltic, which arrived to save the Republic" [18]. Binns became a hero in the United States and England for his work as a radio operator who saved lives in this emergency only six months before presenting his paper at the IWE meeting. His presence at the meeting was a testament to the importance of this new technology for the safety of society at large beyond the walls of any one company. After a lengthy discussion of the paper, the IWE members appointed a Committee on Standardization [40, p. 13], suggesting that this group believed there to be an association between standardized operations and safe operations, especially in emergencies.

On 24 June 1910, Congress passed the Wireless Ship Act which required all ships departing US ports with more than 50 passengers and traveling over 200 miles to have radio equipment and a skilled operator onboard to improve transportation safety. "Additionally, to prevent a global monopoly in radio communications and to promote efficiency in radio transmissions, the law mandated that the equipment and operators be capable of exchanging messages regardless of the communication system employed" [53]. According to US National Institute of Standards and Technology (NIST) history, this "legislation was prompted by a shipping accident in 1909, where a single wireless operator [Jack R. Binns] saved the lives of 1,200 people" [37]. Prior to this legislation, private companies and amateur radio operators competed for use of unregulated airwaves. "Additionally, the British and American Marconi companies, the largest wireless conglomerate in the industry, were increasingly reluctant to enable communications with ships or stations that used their competitors' equipment" [53]. This state of unregulated competition for airwaves was brought to a climax with the sinking of the passenger ship Titanic off of Greenland on 15 April 1912 [38]. Although the distress signals from the ship were received by a Marconi telegraph station in Newfoundland, the lack of a designated frequency for emergency signals meant that the Titanic's message was lost in radio chatter instead of being relayed to rescuers. Congress passed the Radio Act of 1912 to correct an oversight of the earlier Wireless Ship Act, to license radio operators, and to standardize who could use designated radio frequencies in order to improve shipping safety. As Marriott later recalled, "Demand for radio had arrived. ... The number of US commercial ships equipped increased over one hundred and twenty-five per cent between 1912 and 1914" [40, p. 45]. Early in the twentieth century, radio was the rapidly developing technology that promised to improve safety and efficiency, as long as producers and users of this technology could cooperate, as well as compete.

In May 1912, the Institute of Wireless Engineers merged with the Society of Wireless Telegraph Engineers to form the Institute of Radio Engineers (IRE), with Marriott as its first president. The purpose of this consolidation was to further "scientific and commercial development of radio communication" [40, p. 35], especially as this growing profession came under federal regulation. Engineers working with radio technology routinely found it difficult to share reliable information with others in that field. "There was considerable secrecy in the industry about this new technology of the time. The spirit of the time was driven by competition and not one of cooperation" [13]. This lack of cooperation meant that companies needlessly duplicated efforts as they developed new technologies in isolation from their peers. And worse than that, companies intentionally shielded their operations from view by prohibiting engineers from publishing or even talking with colleagues about their work. Goldsmith and Hogan recalled that in the early twentieth century, it was "an open secret that there were some very major organizations in the [radio] field at that time who were much opposed to any publicity of their engineering work. ... An engineer, if you met him in those days and said 'What are you working at,' wouldn't even mention the field of activity, much less a particular project" [22, p. 11]. Some engineers in that budding field felt stymied within this secretive environment.

The second issue of the *IRE Proceedings* in April 1913 included a paper by Marriott entitled "Radio Operations by Steamship Companies," in which he argued for the importance of radio operations to public welfare: "Radio communication is valuable to the public in general. It is particularly valuable to the ocean-going public, steamship companies, marine underwriters, newspapers, shippers, armies, navies, and weather bureaus. For all this service the public probably pays in the end, but the most apparent ... payment is that made by the steamship companies" [39, p. 4]. Citing the recent failure of radio communication in the sinking of the Titanic, Marriott stated that radio communication in the steamship industry was a "disgrace" [39, p. 5] in large part because steamship companies saw radio equipment and operators as an unprofitable expense. He contrasted this state of affairs to that within government and military agencies where knowledgeable experts worked with radio manufacturers to build "high class" equipment to their specifications and at "the most reasonable cost" [39, p. 5]. Rather than operating in secrecy, these government and military agencies shared information to develop specifications that could result in standardized manufacturing and operations, thus cutting costs. Marriott believed that the IRE could provide a platform for sharing information more widely within the radio profession to streamline technology development in this growing field that would soon become so important in the US Navy operations during World War I [17].

In forming the IRE, a six-member standing Committee on Standardization and Publicity was one of the three initial committees established within the association bylaws. The mandate of this committee was to "lead in any movements toward the standardization of wireless apparatus or its ratings, to inform the public correctly ... [on] necessary concerning wireless matters ... as shall be regarded the duty of the Society to publish for the benefit of the public and the wireless industry" [40, p. 38]. In the first monthly meeting of the IRE, Marriott "spoke on the need of standard terms, units, and symbols," other members discussed "provisions for the safety of life at sea," and resolutions were passed "regarding the death of Mr. John Phillips the chief operator of the steamer 'Titanic'" [40, p. 41].

Despite some concern for standardizing operations and terminology among radio engineers and operators as a matter of public safety, Marriott found "inertia and opposition," even in making *radio* the standard term for their profession versus the more commonly used *wireless* [40, p. 46]. He later recalled:

> Trying to name anything or define anything stirred up hornets. The Wireless Institute had a Standards Committee. It did not produce. The Institute of Radio Engineers Committee duplicated that nonproductiveness in 1912. I appointed those committees and was disappointed at not getting any standards. ... In 1913 I asked [IRE] President Pickard to appoint me as chairman of the Standards Committee. Then I found that influential people wanted to make the radio standards but they did not want to make them until sometime, maybe within a few years. However, our Committee on Standards went ahead [40, p. 46].

Marriott does not elaborate on who the "influential people" were that were objecting to establishing standardized terminology and ratings as a first order of business for the new Institute for Radio Engineers. But evidently these "influential people" had the potential to derail what Marriott and others considered to be an important project for both developing radio engineering as a profession and protecting public safety: "Being so conscious of the influential opposition caused us to go over and over the work, shrinking long definitions and throwing out doubtful definitions and symbols. Because of the opposition we called our report a preliminary report" [40, p. 47]. When the preliminary report was distributed to IRE membership, it included a three-question feedback form that members could use to send comments to the Committee on Standards as they revised this report into its final version in order to accommodate any objections by "influential people." Marriott reported that the preliminary report of May 1912 was "favorably received" and the final version of this report was released in September of that year in Volume 1 of the *IRE Proceedings* [40, p. 47]. The IRE list of definitions for radio professionals was revised and updated five times between 1915 and 1931 [39, p. 47]. In 1936, the IRE Technical Committee on Electronics prepared an unpublished glossary of terms relating to vacuum tubes for the Standards Committee [30], reflecting the importance that this emerging technology had for what would become the electronics field and computer development. These glossaries of technical definitions represented contests over knowledge production that were brought to consensus through strong leadership. They also represented technological and professional developments as new fields broke off, requiring more specialized glossaries.

6.3   Computer Engineers Start to Professionalize

By the 1940s – and especially in relation to World War II – interest in computing technologies grew in importance among members of the American Institute of Electrical Engineers (AIEE) and Institute of Radio Engineers (IRE). In 1946, AIEE members of the Basic Sciences Committee established a Subcommittee on Large-Scale Computing Devices to accommodate growing interest in digital computers like the ENIAC being developed at the University of Pennsylvania, largely to meet wartime applications. Electrical engineer Charles Concordia was named chairman of this subcommittee. Before the war Concordia worked for General Electric, focusing on systems engineering and public utilities operations. During the war he worked on generators and turbines for naval destroyer propulsion, researched super-chargers for airplanes, and helped develop ships' electrical drives [1]. Concordia later recalled the challenges in recruiting members to this subcommittee: "Despite the very great development of, and interest in, large digital computers during and following World War II, I had some difficulty in assembling a subcommittee, for there were not then a great many AIEE members familiar with the field" [19]. In October 1946 there were seven members of the committee: Charles Concordia (General Electric), John G. Brainerd (University of Pennsylvania), Samuel H. Caldwell (Massachusetts Institute of Technology), Edwin L. Harder (Westinghouse Electric Company), Walter C. Johnson (Princeton University), Gilbert D. McCann (California State Polytechnic Institute), and Julian D. Tebo (Bell Laboratories). This group organized a general session at the AIEE Winter Meeting in January 1947, where 350 attendees discussed papers presented by Howard Aiken (Harvard University), Julian Bigelow (Princeton University), Jay Forrester (Massachusetts Institute of Technology), John McPherson (International Business Machines), T. Kite Sharpless (University of Pennsylvania), and Samuel Williams (Bell Laboratories) representing the "six leading centers of digital-computer development" at that time [18]. At the AIEE Summer Meeting in June 1947, 70 attendees discussed papers on applications of digital computers presented by A. W. Rankin (General Electric Company) and Henrik W. Bode and Ernest G. Andrews (Bell Laboratories) [19].

In addition to sharing information on digital computer development at AIEE meetings, the Subcommittee on Large-Scale Computing Devices subsequently set to work developing standard definitions of terms relating to this nascent profes-sional field in coordination with the IRE and the Association for Computing Machinery (ACM), which was established in 1947. Concordia later stated that "it seemed not only desirable but necessary to coordinate the nomenclature of the three societies primarily concerned" with digital computers [14, p. 44]. Members of this coordinating committee were Walter H. MacWilliams (Bell Laboratories, AIEE), Robert Serrell (Radio Corporation of America, IRE), and Ernest G. Andrews (Bell Laboratories, ACM).

After World War II, rapid development of electronic computers in the context of national security required that open communication channels be established among private businesses, government agencies, and university laboratories. These chan-nels needed standardized terminology to facilitate collaboration. In explaining how the IRE came to develop its first glossary of computer definitions, Nathaniel Rochester (IBM) and Willis Ware (RAND Corporation) provided this rationale for the project: "In a rapidly changing field like computer engineering today, there is a rapid growth of language. One source of new terminology is the naming of newly invented devices. Even more new terms arise as laboratory slang gradually becomes acceptable for formal use. In only a few years the language changes so much that one would need an interpreter if he did not keep up to date" [46]. As Samuel Caldwell had noted at the 1947 Harvard Symposium on Large-Scale Calculating Machinery, Rochester and Ware went on to describe how the lack of a standardized vocabulary impeded computer development: "This growth of language tends to produce confusion because inconsistent or even contradictory usages arise as local dialects. The same developments take place independently in different laboratories and different names are used for similar things. This makes it difficult to write a technical paper or a specification so that everyone can understand it" [46]. Within the context of deteriorating relations and an accelerating weapons race between the United States and Soviet Union, these impediments to rapid computer development because of idiosyncratic language usage could result in national security threats. Coming up with a standardized vocabulary for computer development took on an urgency in the Cold War United States.

In 1948, the IRE created a decentralized structure around professional groups, allowing the organization to more easily incorporate new fields such as electronic computers and information theory [11]. Under these professional groups, the IRE formed technical committees "which, among other things, produce glossaries indicating conventional usage of terms" [46]. In the following 3 years, IRE Technical Committees produced glossaries of terms for antennas (1948), electroacoustics (1949/1951), radio aids to navigation (1949), electron tubes (1950), wave propagation (1950), pulses (1951/1952), circuits (1951), and traducers (1951) in addition to electronic computers (1951). By 1957, IRE Technical Committees had published 27 glossaries of terms in their fields [4]. In discussing the importance for precise definitions of technical terms in electrical engineering, AIEE Fellow and Harvard professor C. L. Dawes stated, "Precise and authentic definitions of electrical terms are highly essential in the art and practice of electrical engineering, in scientific publications and textbooks, specifications, contracts, and other legal documents, as well as in litigation. Such a glossary fulfills for electrical engineering the function of an authentic English dictionary and it is intended to be the ultimate authority in the definition of any electrical or related quantity" [20, p. 416–417]. He further emphasized the importance of defining terms for rapidly changing technologies: "In view of the rapid and extensive developments in science and technology … which were greatly accelerated by the war effort, it became apparent … the many new terms which had come into being and the many new developments had so changed the scope and meaning of many of the existing terms that their definitions were either inadequate or no longer valid. Hence, almost immediately after the end of the war, in 1946, the AIEE Standards Committee authorized the revision of the 'Definitions'" [20, p. 417]. This terminology definition work that Dawes described as being so important in the established field of electrical engineering was especially important in the emerging field of electronic computers after the rapid development of these calculating machines during World War II.

In early 1948, the IRE Electronic Computers Committee began compiling a glossary of computer definitions through the work of a subcommittee for this project. This Subcommittee on Definitions of Electronic Computer Terms was comprised of members who had been active in electronic computer development during the war years and were now working in industry and academia, often continuing their military work through government contracts. Subcommittee Chair Robert Serrell "spent about three years (1942 to 1945) as Group Leader and Consulting Engineer at the

Radio Research Laboratory of Harvard University, Cambridge, Massachusetts. From 1944 to 1947, he was in charge of television operations at Columbia Broadcasting System (CBS). Serrell worked, from 1947 to 1953, at the Princeton Laboratories of Radio Corporation of America (RCA), engaged in research in applied mathematics and in electronic computer theory" [9]. Other members of the committee brought their wartime experiences to the project as well:

- Charles H. Doersam, Jr. "was in the Combined Research Group of the Naval Research Laboratory ... with IFF [Identification, Friend or Foe] Mark V development and the Special Devices Center of the USN, where [he] was project engineer on Whirlwind and Hurricane computers and related devices." He later worked at "Sperry Gyroscope Co., where [he] computerized Loran C for tactical aircraft bombing" and "Fairchild Camera and Instrument, innovating electronic scanning aerial cameras" [26, p. 39].
- Robert D. Elbourn worked at the US Naval Ordinance Laboratory from 1941 to 1947 where his work was "chiefly concerned with the development of mines and torpedoes ... In 1947, he became a member of the professional staff of the Electronic Computers Section of the National Bureau of Standards, Boulder, Colorado. ... Here he continued work on digital magnetic recording, participated in the design of SEAC [Standards Eastern Automatic Computer], and was engaged in research and development for improving circuits and components for high-speed electronic digital computers" [8].
- Herbert R. Grosch was a physicist for US Navy Ordnance in 1942 and an optical engineer at Sperry Gyroscope Company in 1943. He "joined the [IBM] Watson Lab at Columbia in 1945 to do backup calculations for the Manhattan Project, becoming the second scientist ever hired by IBM as Wallace Eckert recruited his lab team" [3]. He worked with IBM until 1951.
- Francis J. Murray "joined the faculty of Columbia in 1936 and was promoted to professor in 1949. He is best known for his series of papers with John von Neumann, from 1936 to 1943, on rings of operators, and for his proof of the complex version of the Hahn-Banach theorem of functional analysis." He was also a mathematics consultant with the United States Navy, United States Army, United States Air Force and defense firms from 1947 to 1970 [54].
- Nathaniel Rochester "worked on radar at the MIT Radiation Laboratory from 1941 to 1943 and for Sylvania Electric Products until he joined IBM in 1948. After being chief architect of IBM's first scientific computer and of the prototype of its first commercial computer (IBM-701, Defense Calculator), and in 1953 having developed symbolic assembly language programming, in 1954 he was appointed engineering manager of the 700 series, which included both" [35].
- Willis Ware was employed at Hazeltine Electronics Corporation from 1942 to 1946, where he worked on classified research and development for radar and Identification, Friend or Foe (IFF) command and control systems. He moved to Princeton in 1946, where he worked for John von Neumann to build the Institute for Advanced Study (IAS) large scale, general purpose electronic computer. "He then worked at North American Aviation in Los Angeles before joining the Rand

Corporation [in 1952], where he worked for over 40 years" [35]. Ware "headed the computer science work" at RAND and became "one of the American experts on the Soviet computer industry" [25, p. 253].

The seven-member Subcommittee on Definitions of Electronic Computer Terms worked under the Electronic Computers Committee, chaired by Jay W. Forrester, who was a member of the MIT Servomechanisms Laboratory from 1940 to 1946, working on gunnery control systems for the US Navy. He was then director of the MIT Digital Computer Laboratory from 1946 to 1951. "Forrester became interested in digital computing when a project to develop a Navy aircraft stability analyzer was determined to be too difficult for an analog computer. ... Perry Crawford, then with the Special Devices Center of the US Navy, suggested the use of a digital system. Forrester took charge of the design and construction of Whirlwind I ... Forrester developed the basic concept of random-access storage ... that became the standard internal memory for computers for nearly 30 years" [34].

Electronic Computers Committee Past Chair James R. Weiner was chief engineer at Eckert-Mauchly Computer Corporation, then Remington Rand, working on the BINAC for the Northrop Aircraft Company, which was interested in developing a computerized guidance system for the Snark long-range missile being developed for the Air Force [44, pp. 179, 270]. Committee Vice-Chair Nathaniel Rochester (IBM) served on the Subcommittee on Definitions.

This IRE group brought perspectives to the task of standardizing terminology from their various backgrounds and professional experiences in computer development for wartime applications. They now needed to come to a consensus on definitions that might differ according to their idiosyncratic usage in particular labs and workshops so that people from these different locations could work together efficiently. Looking back in 1954, definitions subcommittee co-chairs Rochester and Ware described the subcommittee's work in this way: "In the preparation of this glossary, there was no intention to dictate what language people should use. ... The intent was to record usage, considering both the extent of usage and just who uses certain terms in certain ways. ... The policy of recording usage appears to be the only way to aid in eliminating dialects without stifling progress" [46]. Rochester and Ware recounted how problems had arisen in the initial definition work, though, when use of a term differed among people in different locations. In these instances, the committee needed to decide which definition would prevail, which meant privileging one group's understanding over that of another group. Sometimes this meant deciding that one group's definition was correct and another group's was in error:

> There are also the problems of contradictory and erroneous usage. For an example of contradictory usage, consider 'Flip-Flop' which in [the US] refers to a device with two stable states and in at least some parts of England refers to a device with one stable state. Sometimes erroneous usage arises when a person will start using a term in a certain way because he actually does not understand the phenomenon of which he speaks. Definitions subcommittees deal with these questions as individual problems to be settled usually be some compromise but sometimes by recognizing only one side of the controversy [46].

Determining correctness and error is a necessary task when establishing standard terminology, but this act also results in privileging one (correct) group's understanding over that of another (erroneous) group. The people who make this inevitable value judgment exercise their power to set standards based on some cultural capital that they bring to bear on the situation and, in this case, their relationships with other computer developers. In the example of the definition of "flip-flop" highlighted in Rochester and Ware's description of the IRE definition process, the strength of US technology developers and the relative position of the United States versus England after WWII was reflected in the committee's decision to adopt US usage instead of that of their English colleagues, which was deemed to be in error despite it being effectively used in some locations there.

The IRE Subcommittee on Definitions of Electronic Computer Terms met once a month during the winter of 1949–1950 to come up with their initial glossary of definitions. Their seven-page glossary was reviewed and approved by both the Electronic Computers Committee and the Standards Committee; it was published in the *Proceedings of the IRE* in 1951. It included this definition for flip-flop: "An electronic circuit having two stable states and ordinarily two input terminals" [31, p. 273] that reflected the dominant US usage of this term.

Two years after completing the first glossary of computer definitions, the IRE Committee on Electronic Computers appointed another subcommittee to revise those original definitions. In this second iteration of the project, two subcommittees were formed based on geographical representation: an eastern subcommittee chaired by Nathaniel Rochester meeting in New York and a western subcommittee chaired by Willis Ware meeting in Los Angeles. The rationale for splitting the committees was "so as to be able to record the language on both side of the mountains" [46], indicating an awareness that rapid technology development in far-flung locations was resulting in conflicting terminologies that could impede cooperation on computer development projects for national security. This bifurcation of the committee also recognized the growth of the computer industry in the western United States in support of air defense and guided missile systems development. In order to address this need for a more standardized vocabulary, the two IRE subcommittees worked together on the revised glossary of computer terms. In recruiting membership for these subcommittees, chairs Rochester and Ware stated that members "were drawn from a variety of industrial, governmental and academic organizations" [46]. By including members from a range of economic sectors on their committees, these two groups sought to add diversity of perspective to their geographic diversity. In describing their work, subcommittee chairmen Rochester and Ware stated, "The members of these committees do not act as agents of their own organizations to argue for their own terminology. Instead they cooperate as members of the committee, and seek to do a good job of lexicography" [46]. As much as individual members sought to cooperate, it would be impossible to ask them to forget their own understandings of the terms they worked with, even as they sought consensus on definitions as a committee.

Nathaniel Rochester (IBM) continued on the definitions project as chair of the eight-member Eastern Definitions Subcommittee. Robert Elbourn (RAND) continued from the earlier subcommittee and James Weiner (Eckert-Mauchly Computer Corporation/Remington Rand) moved from the Electronic Computers Committee to the Subcommittee on Definitions Eastern Division. They were joined by five new members:

Linder Charlie Hobbs "earned a master's degree in electrical engineering from the University of Pennsylvania in 1952 and an MBA from the University of Pennsylvania in 1956. During his early career, Hobbs worked as an engineer at the Radio Corporation of America, [and] in the Univac division of Sperry Rand" [2] where he "held technical and supervisory positions" [27, p. 10] at least through 1956. He worked on mass memory storage devices and later worked in the Aeronutronic defense division of Ford Aerospace, owned by Ford Motor Company, in Newport Beach, California where he was "manager of Data Processing Engineering" [27, p. 10].

Jacob R. Johnson worked with Nathaniel Rochester at IBM in Poughkeepsie, New York. In 1955, Rochester and Johnson, along with IBM colleagues Gene M. Amdahl and Walter E. Mutter, submitted a patent application entitled "Recognition of Recorded Intelligence" [47]. This invention was an improved optical character recognition (OCR) system that would "provide a means for identifying two dimensional intelligence patterns by analyzing the white regions thereof" and that would store the results [47, sec. 1]. The patent was granted in 1959.

Rollin P. Mayer was in charge of the EPSCOM positioning system development for the Semi-automatic Ground Environment (SAGE) air defense system at the Lincoln Laboratory at Massachusetts Institute of Technology. This system was developed as an early warning network to locate and intercept incoming airplanes, using the Whirlwind computer at MIT. The EPSCOM project developers wrote the programming for SAGE that would analyze radar patterns and communicate with the Whirlwind (AN/FSQ-7) computer [42]. In May 1956, 39 people worked on the EPSCOM project from five organizations: Western Electric, Bell Telephone Labs, RAND, IBM, and MIT Lincoln Lab.

George W. Patterson "joined the staff of the Moore School of Electrical Engineering of the University of Pennsylvania [in 1946], where he designed the logic for EDVAC arithmetic circuits and coordinated the logic design for the entire machine. From 1950 to 1955, Patterson was with the Research Center of the Burroughs Corporation. … Patterson was active in computer standardization, as a member of the IRE Electronic Computers Committee beginning in 1949, and serving as Vice Chairman in 1962. He was also a member of the ACM committee that wrote the first programming glossary, and a member of the ASA Y32-14 task group that developed standards for computer logic systems" [10].

Louis D. Wilson was one of the small group of people who built the ENIAC at the Moore School. He also worked as an engineer on the Eckert-Mauchly Computer Corporation BINAC small computer for Northrop Aircraft Company. In 1952, Wilson, Herbert F. Welsh, and Presper Eckert representing the Sperry Rand Corporation submitted a patent application for an Information Translating Apparatus [55]. In 1953, Wilson was among another group from Sperry Rand that submitted a patent application for A Machine for Recording on Magnetic Tape [15].

Willis Ware continued on the Subcommittee on Definitions as the chair of the Western Division. Five members joined him on this effort from organizations in the western United States:

- Harry T. Larson joined the team at the University of California, Los Angeles (UCLA), in June 1949 as an engineer to work on the memory function of the National Bureau of Standards (NBS) Western Automatic Computer (SWAC) being built in conjunction with the NBS Applied Mathematics Division [25]. From there, he moved first to Hughes Aircraft and then to Aeronutronic Systems, Inc. [5], which later became a defense division of Ford Motor Company Aerospace, specializing in space and defense communications. In 1954, Larson was the chairman of the IRE Professional Group on Electronic Computers [33].
- William (Bill) S. Speer was employed by Computer Research Corporation (CRC) in Hawthorne, California in 1952. In 1953, CRC became the Electronics Division of by National Cash Register (NCR) when NRC acquired the company. CRC was formed in 1949 by five computer engineers who had been working at Northrop on programming for the Snark missile system. In the early 1950s, CRC was developing the CRC 102 general purpose, magnetic drum computer under contract with the Cambridge Air Force Research Laboratories [50, p. 689].
- William E. Smith worked to develop magnetic drum memory at Aeronutronic Systems, Inc. [49] which later became a defense division of Ford Motor Company Aerospace, specializing in space and defense communications.
- Louis D. Stevens "joined IBM in 1949 at the Poughkeepsie, New York, development laboratory, where he worked on early magnetic tape and drum devices and contributed to the design of the input/output system of the IBM 701 [Defense Calculator]. In 1952, he joined the newly established San Jose research and advanced development laboratory, where he managed the IBM 305 RAMAC and IBM 350-355 disk file development programs from 1953 to 1956. He served as the first manager of the [IBM] San Jose development laboratory from 1956 to 1959" [6].
- Ragnar Thorenson joined the Machine Engineering and Development Unit at the Institute for Numerical Analysis at the University of California, Los Angeles in 1952, where he worked as an electronic scientist. He worked on the design of magnetic drum memory for the Standards Western Automatic Computer (SWAC) [29, 42, 43]. He later joined Magnavox Research Company in Los Angeles, where he continued his work on magnetic memory [53].

The subcommittee began by sending copies of the 1950 IRE glossary to "all known English speaking computer organizations ... asking for comments" [46]. They then "considered" the comments they received when determining the definitions that would appear in the updated glossary. Subcommittee chairs Rochester and Ware described the committee's process being based on discussions among members with different viewpoints: "[I]t is nearly impossible for one individual to write a definition so well that a critical review by several others with differing backgrounds will not reveal some vital defect. Since no one person is familiar with enough different usages, the only safe procedure is group discussion ... It seems to be impossible to write any one definition of any one term which will be completely acceptable to everybody … The finished definition of the committee is phrased to meet, as nearly as possible, the requirements of all known users" [46]. In coming to a definition "for all known users," the committee's revised glossary, which was published in the *Proceedings of the IRE* in September 1956, was intended to set the definitive meanings of the computer terms it included. This standardized terminology would be one more step toward establishing computer science as a new professional discipline.

References

1. Anonymous. n.d. Charles Concordia. *IEEE Computer Society*. https://www.computer.org/profiles/charles-concordia. Accessed 9 Nov 2020.
2. ———. n.d. *Collection guide to the Linder Charlie Hobbs collection*. Online Archive of California. https://oac.cdlib.org/findaid/ark:/13030/c8js9xft/. Accessed 9 Nov 2020.
3. ———. n.d. *The first corporate pure science laboratory: Herb Grosch*. IBM. https://www.ibm.com/ibm/history/ibm100/us/en/icons/scientificresearch/team/. Accessed 9 Nov 2020.
4. ———. 1958, February. Index to IRE standards on definitions of terms 1942–1957 (58 IRE 20.S1). *Proceedings of the IRE* 46 (2): 449–476. https://doi.org/10.1109/JRPROC.1958.286918. Accessed 24 Apr 2021.
5. ———. 1958, May. Program announced for Western joint computer conference. *Electrical Engineering* 77 (5): 449–450.
6. ———. 1981, September. Authors: Louis D. Stevens. *IBM Journal of Research and Development* 25 (5): 833–846.
7. ———. 2017, June 9. Robert Marriott. *Engineering and Technology History Wiki*. https://ethw.org/Robert_H._Marriott. Accessed 9 Nov 2020.
8. ———. 2018, July 24. Robert Elbourn. https://ethw.org/Robert_Elbourn. Engineering and Technology History Wiki. Accessed 9 Nov 2020.
9. ———. 2018, July 27. Robert Serrell. Engineering and Technology History Wiki. https://ethw.org/Robert_Serrell. Accessed 9 Nov 2020.
10. ———. 2018, July 30. George W. Patterson. Engineering and Technology History Wiki. https://ethw.org/George_W._Patterson. Accessed 10 Nov 2020.
11. ———. 2019, September 11. *History of the Institute of Radio Engineers 1912–1963*. Engineering and Technology History Wiki. https://ethw.org/IRE_History_1912-1963. Accessed 9 Nov 2020.
12. ———. 2020, August 13. *History of the American Institute of Electrical Engineers 1884–1963*. Engineering and Technology History Wiki. https://ethw.org/AIEE_History_1884-1963. Accessed 9 Nov 2020.
13. ———. 2020, August 13. *History of the Institute of Electrical and Electronic Engineers (IEEE) Standards*. Engineering and Technology History Wiki. https://ethw.org/History_of_Institute_of_Electrical_and_Electronic_Engineers_(IEEE)_Standards#cite_ref-refnum13_13-0. Accessed 9 Nov 2020.
14. Astrahan, Morton M. 1976, December. In the beginning there was the IRE professional group on electronic computers. *Computer* 9 (12): 43–44.
15. Blain, Albert, et al. 1959, February 17. Patent 2,874,369: Machine for recording on magnetic tape. United States.
16. Bourdieu, Pierre. 1991. *Language and symbolic power*. Trans Gino Raymond and Matthew Adamson. Cambridge, MA: Harvard University Press.

17. Brady, Hillary. 2014, May. *The Golden Age of radio in the US*. Digital Public Library of America. https://dp.la/exhibitions/radio-golden-age. Accessed 28 Mar 2021.
18. Chan, Sewell. 2009, November 6. Remembering Jack Binns, heroic radio operator. *New York Times*. https://cityroom.blogs.nytimes.com/2009/11/06/remembering-jack-binns-heroic-radio-operator/. Accessed 9 Nov 2020.
19. Concordia, Charles. 1976, December. In the beginning there was the AIEE committee on computing devices. *Computer* 9 (12): 42.
20. Dawes, C.L. 1952, May. Revision status of American standard definitions of electrical terms. *Electrical Engineering* 71 (5): 416–418. https://doi.org/10.1109/EE.1952.6437475. Accessed 24 Apr 2021.
21. Edwards, Paul N. 1996. *The closed world: Computers and the politics of discourse in Cold War America*. Cambridge, MA: MIT Press.
22. Florman, Samuel C. 1996. *The existential pleasures of engineering*. New York: St. Martin's Press.
23. Gibson, Jane Mork. 1980, August. The international electrical exhibit of 1884: A landmark for the electrical engineer. *IEEE Transactions on Education* E-23.3: 169–176.
24. Goldsmith, Alfred N., and John V. L. Hogan. 1952, February 22. *The I.R.E.: From acorn to oak*. Engineering and Technology History Wiki. https://ethw.org/Archives:From_Acorn_to_Oak. Accessed 9 Nov 2020.
25. Goldstine, Herman H. 1972. *The computer from Pascal to von Neumann*. Princeton: Princeton University Press.
26. Graham, Arthur. 2010, Spring. Alumni notes: Charles H. Doersam. *Columbia Engineering* 39.
27. Hobbs, Linder Charlie. 1976, December. A look at the future: Guest editor's introduction. *Computer* 9 (12): 9–10.
28. Hubert, Edward C. 1925, January. Radio vs. wireless. *Radio News* 6 (7): 1165.
29. Huskey, Harry D. 1980/August 1991. The SWAC: The National Bureau of Standards Western Automatic Computer. *NBS-INA – The Institute for Numerical Analysis – UCLA 1947–1954*. NIST Special Publication 730. Washington, DC: U.S. Department of Commerce, National Institute of Standards and Technology. Appendix C.
30. Institute of Radio Engineers Technical Committee on Electronics. 1936, March 30. *Report on electronics definitions*. https://ethw.org/Archives:Electronics_Definitions,_Standards_Committee_(IRE),_1936. Engineering and Technology History Wiki. Accessed 9 Nov 2020.
31. Institute of Radio Engineers Subcommittee on Definitions of Electronic Computer Terms. 1951, March. Standards on Electronic Computers: Definitions of Terms, 1950. *Proceedings of the IRE* 39 (3): 271–277.
32. Keith, N.S. 1884, April 11. *Call for a meeting to organize the American Institute of Electrical Engineers*. The Thomas A. Edison papers digital edition. http://edison.rutgers.edu/digital/files/original/cs/cs0489.jpg. Accessed 9 Nov 2020.
33. Larson, Harry T. 1954, December. PGEC news: Message from Chairman Harry T. Larson. *Transactions of the I.R.E. Professional Group on Electronic Computers EC* 3 (4): 32.
34. Lee, J.A.N. 1995. Jay Wright Forrester. In *Computer pioneers*. Los Alamitos: IEEE Computer Society Press. https://history.computer.org/pioneers/forrester.html. Accessed 9 Nov 2020.
35. ———. 1995. Nathaniel Rochester. In *Computer pioneers*. Los Alamitos: IEEE Computer Society Press. https://history.computer.org/pioneers/rochester.html. Accessed 9 Nov 2020.
36. ———. 1995. Willis Howard Ware. In *Computer pioneers*. Los Alamitos: IEEE Computer Society Press. https://history.computer.org/pioneers/ware.html. Accessed 9 Nov 2020.
37. Lowe, John P. 2019, November 15. *The story of an old timer: Wireless Ship Act*. NIST Physical Measurement Laboratory. https://www.nist.gov/pml/nbsnist-radio-stations-story-old-timer/story-old-timer-navy/story-old-timer-wireless-ship-act. Accessed 9 Nov 2020.
38. Lucky, Robert W. 2012, April 27. 100 years of the Institute of Radio Engineers. *IEEE Spectrum*. https://spectrum.ieee.org/tech-history/dawn-of-electronics/100-years-of-the-institute-of-radio-engineers. Accessed 9 Nov 2020.

39. Marriott, Robert H. 1913, April. Radio operation by steamship companies. *Proceedings of the Institute of Radio Engineers* 1 (2): 3–7.

40. ———. 1937. *Notes on the history of the Institute of Radio Engineers*. Engineering and Technology History Wiki. https://ethw.org/Archives:History_of_the_IRE,_1937. Accessed 9 Nov 2020.

41. Marriott, Robert H., et al. 1913. Preliminary report of the committee on standardization of the Institute of Radio Engineers Inc.: Definitions of terms, graphical and literal symbols. *Proceedings of the Institute of Radio Engineers* 1 (4): 1–29.

42. Mayer, Rollin P. 1956, June 5. *EPSCOM biweekly report for 18 May 1956*. MIT ArchivesSpace: Project Whirlwind Collection. https://archivesspace.mit.edu/repositories/2/resources/1157. Accessed 10 Nov 2020.

43. National Bureau of Standards. 1953. *Report 2688: Projects and publications of the national applied mathematics laboratories, a quarterly report April through June 1953*. National Institute of Standards and Technology (NIST). https://pages.nist.gov/NIST-Tech-Pubs/RPT. html. Accessed 10 Nov 2020.

44. Norberg, Arthur L. 2005. *Computers and commerce: A study of technology and management at Eckert-Mauchly computer company, engineering research associates, and Remington Rand, 1946–1957*. Cambridge, MA: MIT Press.

45. Rickard, Thomas A. 1908. *A guide to technical writing*. San Francisco: Mining and Scientific Press.

46. Rochester, Nathaniel, and Willis H. Ware. 1953, December. Computer definitions (guest editorial). *Transactions of the IRE Professional Group on Electronic Computers* EC-2.4: 2.

47. Rochester, Nathaniel, et al. 1959, July 2. Patent 2,889,535: Recognition of recorded intelligence. United States.

48. Rowland, Henry Augustus. 1886. *Report of the electrical conference at Philadelphia, in September, 1884*. Washington, DC: Government Printing Office.

49. Smith, William E. 1957. *A digital system simulator. International workshop on managing requirements knowledge*. Los Angeles. https://doi.ieeecomputersociety.org/10.1109/ AFIPS.1957.1. Accessed 10 Nov 2020.

50. Sprague, Richard E. 1972, July. A western view of computer history. *Communications of the ACM* 15 (7): 686–692.

51. Thorensen, Ragnar. 1978. Pioneer day remarks. In Huskey, Harry D. 1997. SWAC – Standards Western automatic computer: The Pioneer day session at NCC July 1978. *IEEE Annals of the History of Computing* 19 (2): 51–61.

52. Thorensen, Ragnar, and W.R. Arsenault. 1955, March. A new nondestructive read for magnetic cores. In *Proceedings of the Western Joint Computer Conference*, 111–116. Los Angeles. https://doi.org/10.1145/1455292.1455314. Accessed 10 Nov 2020.

53. Tullai, Margaret. 2009. *Wireless Ship Act of 1910*. The First Amendment Encyclopedia. https://www.mtsu.edu/first-amendment/article/1052/wireless-ship-act-of-1910. Accessed 9 Nov 2020.

54. Warner, Seth L. 1996, May. In memory of Francis J. Murray. *Duke Math News*. https://web. archive.org/web/20060910222728/http:/www.math.duke.edu/math_news/May96/May96. html. Accessed 9 Nov 2020.

55. Wilson, Louis D., et al. 1958, November 18. Patent 2,860,756: Information translating apparatus. United States.

Chapter 7
Defining Terms and Establishing Priorities

Abstract This chapter describes the work of three computer terminology glossary projects: Edmund Berkeley's periodical publications in *Computers and Automation*, IRE committees' compilations of electronic computer terminology into "Definitions of Terms" glossaries, and the subsequent ACM committee compiling specialized terminology for computer programming as distinguished from computer machine design. These efforts illustrate the importance of institutional support for language standardization efforts, especially as computer developers were putting in place elements that were necessary for establishing computer science as a profession separate from mathematics, electrical engineering, and physics.

"During the war the Army, Army Air Forces, and the Navy have made unprecedented use of scientific and industrial resources. The conclusion is inescapable that we have not yet established the balance necessary to [ensure] the continuance of teamwork among the military, other government agencies, industry, and the universities." US Army Air Forces Commanding General H.H. (Hap) Arnold, Undated memo [6]

"If my first bête noir *in the semantics of our somewhat loose vocabulary is an adjectivally nude 'computer,' my biggest black beast is that deformed and shapeless (if that be semantically possible!) monster the random-access memory." Sir Robert Watson-Watt, "Are computers important?" 1956* [51]

"Comptologist ... A specialist in the systematic mathematical and/or logical solution or simulation of universal problems and systems by the utilization of digital and/or hybrid computers and techniques." Quentin Correll, "Letter to the editor," 1958 [20]

In a top secret memo dated 18 September 1945 to the US War Department, the Commander in Chief of the Army Forces in Japan began with a warning about the unstable situation in Korea: "The general situation in southern Korea at present is compared to a powder keg ready to explode upon application of a spark" [19]. A month earlier, the United States and Russia had divided Korea at the 38th parallel to demarcate zones of influence in the country ruled by the Japanese until their surrender to the allies. But Japanese forces remained in the country. According to the Commander in Chief of the Army Forces, Russian agents were working to disrupt the situation in the US sector: "Political ... agitators have begun parades, demonstrations and other propaganda to disrupt our work and to discredit the United States before Koreans" [19]. In the face of this unstable peace after World War II, people who had worked on technology development in the military and civilian sectors of

© Springer Nature Switzerland AG 2021
B. Longo, *Words and Power*, History of Computing,
https://doi.org/10.1007/978-3-030-70373-8_7

the United States during wartime now felt the need to establish defense systems for Cold War national security. Of special interest was the development of a nationwide air defense system to quickly detect incoming enemy aircraft that might pose a surprise attack threat of the kind that decimated the US Navy's fleet at Pearl Harbor in December 1941. Technology research and development during the war had resulted in radar and missile advances that helped the allies to prevail against the Axis powers in 1945. Looking forward, Army General Curtis LeMay argued that "the security of the United States of America will continue to rest in part in developments instituted by our educational and professional scientists" [39, p. 6]. One of these developments, air defense and weapons systems employing guided missiles would depend on computers to ensure the accuracy and effectiveness of those systems. "Discussions among people in what was then the war department, the Office of Scientific Research and Development, and industry focused on the need for a private organization to connect military planning and operations to relevant research and development" [50, p. 6]. Project RAND was established in October 1945 as a partnership between Douglas Aircraft Company in Santa Monica, California, and the US Army Air Forces. Army Air Forces Commanding General Hap Arnold was joined by Edward L. Bowles, who had worked on microwave technology at MIT and was a consultant to the Secretary of War during WWII; Donald Wills Douglas, president of Douglas Aircraft; Arthur Emmons Raymond, chief engineer at Douglas; and Frank Collbohm, Raymond's assistant. Both Raymond and Collbohm had worked at the Pentagon with Bowles on B-29 bombing effectiveness during the war.

7.1   Building Computer Power for Guided Missiles and Air Defense

In May 1946, RAND engineers from Douglas Aircraft delivered a report entitled *Preliminary Design of an Experimental World-Circling Spaceship* to the Air Force, proposing two designs for a multistage satellite with computer-guided trajectories. At the time this report was prepared, people working at RAND were working with punched card accounting machines, desktop mechanical calculators, and an analog computer that were all available at Douglas Aircraft. In 1948, Project RAND purchased a Reeves Electronic Analog Computer which "supported many of the early studies on missile trajectories, air-to-air combat maneuvers, and earth-to-moon orbits" [50, p. 10]. They also rented punched card machines and six IBM 604 calculators [22, p. 9]. By 1949 the RAND team needed more computing power, so John Williams, George Brown, and Bill Gunning were sent out to visit potential vendors where they might purchase a ready-made electronic computer. This team was interested in learning about future plans for new computer designs, as well as the capabilities of existing machines. They visited IBM in Poughkeepsie, New York, the University of Illinois, the Moore School at the University of Pennsylvania, and Eckert-Mauchly Computer Corporation in Philadelphia. Bill Gunning's assessment was discouraging: "They were doing all kinds of tweaky things to circuits to make them work. It was all too whimsical" [22, p. 10; 49, p. 53]. "As John Williams noted in a summary memo of the trip, 'It was a dismal scene.' There was no electronic-computer industry, nor were there plans anywhere for electronic machines" [50, p. 11]. The team also visited the Institute for Advanced Study in Princeton, New Jersey, where they were impressed with John von Neumann's computer design and where they met electrical engineer Willis Ware who was working at the IAS. By the early 1950s the RAND team had Air Force approval to begin building an electronic computer with the Princeton design, which they named the JOHNNIAC in honor of von Neumann. Bill Gunning, who had been a test flight engineer at Douglas Aircraft, was put in charge of the JOHNNIAC project. To help prepare for this project, he "spent three days a week working at UCLA on the Standards Western Automatic Computer (SWAC) machine being built there by [the US Bureau of Standards]" [50, p. 54] in late 1950. The JOHNNIAC went into operation in the first half of 1953, staffed by people who would become the core of a new profession called "computer science."

In 1954, Willis Ware had been at RAND for two years, where he compiled this inventory of seven electronic computers built in the Princeton design: "There is the original still at the Institute for Advanced Study; there is one at the Argonne National Laboratory and another at Oak Ridge National Laboratory. A fourth is at Los Alamos Scientific Laboratory, a fifth and sixth at Aberdeen Proving Grounds and at the University of Illinois; and the last at the RAND Corporation in Santa Monica" [49, p. 8].[1] Ware stated that there was "a total of nearly 50 big computers" in existence by the end of 1954. He forecast rapid growth of the computer field: "With further production of some of these types plus the introduction of new types in the next year or two, there will probably be at least 200 and perhaps as many as 500 digital computers of various sizes in operation by the 1956-57 period" [49, p. 8–9]. Despite this rapid growth of the computer field, there was still no established profession of people who designed and operated these electronic machines.

A profession is generally established with a defined body of knowledge and expertise that is differentiated from that of other fields. Members of a profession are certified through some form of higher education, usually a university degree in the professional discipline. Practicing professionals are regulated through standards most often set through collaborations of professional associations and government agencies. Professional services are controlled by groups of self-governing peers, which grant professionals some autonomy over their professional judgments and practices. Professions are guided by ethical codes, which are foundations for claims of altruistic professional practices. Because a group of professionals claims to serve the larger society, the profession is necessarily implicated in larger institutional power and knowledge relationships. The members of the profession can enjoy a

---

[1] In 1948 Project RAND was reorganized as RAND Corporation, a nonprofit California corporation separate from Douglas Aircraft Company. In the Articles of Incorporation, RAND's purpose was stated in this way: "To further and promote scientific, educational, and charitable purposes, all for the public welfare and security of the United States of America."

sheltered position within these institutional relationships with some market control over production and consumption decisions. Because of their societal positioning, members of a profession can benefit from cultural rewards, such as prestige, social standing, upward class mobility, work autonomy, decision-making authority, market dominance, and money. Therefore, the question of who qualifies as a member of a particular profession has important implications for the other members of that profession; boundaries around a profession are closely monitored by professional groups. All this activity rests on the ability of professionals to be trained and practice through a commonly understood, specialized language of technical terms relating to their field of knowledge and expertise [1, 21, 34]. Establishing that specialized language as a distinct body of professional knowledge is a process that rests on defining technical words. The people engaged in that work of defining terms are also defining boundaries around their fledgling profession, determining who will be admitted as one of these professionals and who will be outside this group [38]. Thus, the people who were engaged in defining computer terminology were also determining who would become a computer scientist – with all the societal rewards that came along with that professional position – and who would not be in this newly forming professional community.

When Samuel Caldwell called for a new professional association of computer developers to be established during his closing talk at the 1947 Harvard Symposium on Large-Scale Digital Calculating Machinery, he recognized a need for establishing communication channels to facilitate rapid development of computing technology as a specialized field apart from mathematics, physics, and electrical engineering. Edmund Berkeley, a mathematician who at that time directed an effort to integrate electronic computers into Prudential Insurance operations, took up this call to form a new professional association and was joined in this effort by John Curtiss (US Bureau of Standards), Franz Alt (Army Aberdeen Proving Grounds), and Mina Rees (US Office of Naval Research). They formed the Association for Computing Machinery (ACM) in the fall of 1947 with the stated purpose to "advance the science, design, construction, and application of the new machinery for computing, reasoning, and other handling of information. Anyone interested in this purpose may become a member" [8]. This statement of purpose began to narrow the scope of a computer field, while also opening it to anyone who was interested, without specifying any specialized knowledge or expertise. This statement was a first step in defining the field of computer science. But in its populist approach to accepting amateurs as well as professionals, it did not yet define the field by indicating the need for specialized knowledge, education, or certification.

7.2   Standardizing Terms in a Populist Model

By 1952, Edmund Berkeley had left Prudential Insurance under a cloud of suspicion from his work with the National Council of American-Soviet Friendship [30] and had started publishing a monthly journal called *The Computing Machinery Field* under the auspices of his consulting firm, Berkeley Enterprises, Inc. A year later he renamed this publication *Computers and Automation*, which was the first specialized journal for computer professionals. He gave the name "information engineers" to people working in this new field, whether in "research, construction, applications, or just the pure science" [9]. In a January 1953 position paper entitled "Brains: Electronic and Otherwise," Oak Ridge National Laboratory chair and mathematician Alston S. Householder argued that the need for "sound professional training" was essential "if our technological civilization is to thrive or even survive" [25, p. 8]. He called for strengthening local school systems to better prepare students for entering baccalaureate-level technical training programs. He noted that mathematical and engineering professional associations were also taking steps to train workers for the computing industry, indicating the importance of this growing profession. In this paper, Householder addressed specialized education as yet another step toward establishing what would become computer science as a profession separate from mathematics and engineering, even though it had some overlap with those fields.

In the early 1950s, Berkeley continued as ACM Secretary on the association's Executive Council. He maintained a list of computer professionals, which he initially distributed as stapled, mimeographed copies in 1951 under the title "A Roster of Organizations in the Computing Machinery Field." He also compiled a "Glossary of Computer Terms" with contributions from colleagues such as Grace Hopper, then working as senior mathematician at Eckert-Mauchly Computer Corporation. In 1953, Berkeley first made this glossary available to other people interested in computers by publishing it in *Computers and Automation*, thereby contributing to the work of standardizing technical terminology for this new field. His efforts in defining computer terms were not without controversy, however, based on his underlying philosophy of what he was doing. Was he reporting common usage or was he legislating proper usage? Berkeley believed that he was reporting how computer terms were commonly used in practice, which could differ in different locations. He wrote definitions for terms in his glossary and asked readers to discuss the definitions and contribute alternatives. This approach to defining and standardizing computer terminology met with pushback, though, from people who objected to defining terms in such an idiosyncratic way.

In the March 1953 issue of *Computers and Automation*, Berkeley published the first installment of his glossary, covering 24 words beginning with the letters A and B. He included these introductory remarks: "This is a glossary of terms used in the field of computers and automation. It is the purpose of this glossary to report the meaning of terms as used and not to legislate about them. Additions, comments, corrections, and criticisms will be appreciated" [10, p. 25]. The May 1953 issue included the next installment of the glossary, covering 50 terms beginning with the letters C, D, and E. It also included a critical letter from mathematics professor C. L. Perry at the US Naval Postgraduate School, an applied mathematician who was active with the Mathematical Association of America, Northern California Chapter. Prof. Perry began by cautioning Berkeley that "the value of such a glossary depends on the accuracy and completeness of the definitions included in the glossary. One way to assure accuracy would be to have the definitions reviewed by several competent reviewers. This, of course, should be accomplished before publication" [11, p. 21]. Perry noted that the ACM Committee on Terminology and the IRE Professional Group on Electronic Computers were developing glossaries, also that Harry Huskey at Wayne University had compiled a glossary. He noted that John Carr from the University of Michigan and Grace Hopper from Remington Rand were working with the ACM nomenclature effort and that Nathaniel Rochester from IBM was heading the IRE subcommittee. Perry suggested, "In order to avoid conflicting definitions as much as possible it would be desirable for you to compare definitions with these people." Stating that "[s]ome of your definitions appear (to me) to be misleading," such as the definition for the term *analog*, he also suggested that "a listing of sources and reviewers … would also be desirable for a glossary" [11, p. 21].

In Berkeley's 1953 glossary, the terms *analog* and *analog computer* appeared in this way:

> analog – using physical variables, such as distance or rotation or voltage, to represent and correspond with numerical variables that occur in a computation; contrasted with "digital".
>
> analog computer – a computer which calculates by using physical analogs of the variables. There is usually a one-to-one correspondence between each numerical variable occurring in the problem and a varying physical measurement in the computer. [10, p. 25]

Perry stated this objection to what he felt was "misleading" in these definitions: "In some mechanical counters rotation is used to represent a digital quantity. In a digital computer a given rotation represents one value from a finite set of values. In an analog computer a given rotation represents one value from an infinite set of values" [11, p. 21]. Berkeley published his own response to Perry directly under Perry's letter in that issue of *Computers and Automation*: "Mr. Perry's viewpoint is important and widely held, and does have some advantages, which his letter makes clear. We believe however that it is in some essential respects both impractical and undesirably authoritarian" [11, p. 22]. Berkeley argued that consulting existing professional committees that were working on glossaries was impractical "because it is extremely difficult for the several existing committees on terms in the computer field to get together and issue quickly a coordinated report on terms." He continued, "In any new field, terms with new meanings spring up all the time, with different expressions used in different laboratories. It will take some years of wear and tear, and competition, for good terms to be sifted out. Language grows and flowers by its own rules, and these do not often include the deliberations and decisions of committees." Berkeley felt that this committee approach was "authoritarian, in that the opinion of 'authorities' is 'sanctified.' It leads committees to think that they should establish by fiat the meaning of new terms, instead of simply reporting different usages in different places." He concluded, "The principle that it seems to us should guide the presentation of glossaries in this early stage of the computer field is simple reporting of the meanings attached to terms. … After all, the people who will refer to the glossary are mainly newcomers to the field; and as soon as they obtain a substantial part of the idea or ideas corresponding to a term, they will proceed to guess the rest of its meaning (and modify its meaning) from the way it is used in the context" [11, p. 22]. Here Berkeley expressed his view that the computer field should be open to all who were interested, amateur and trained professional alike. In these early years before there were established training programs or university curricula to certify that someone was indeed a professional computer scientist, this open viewpoint helped to encourage people to enter the field which needed more people to staff available positions. As the field of computer science coalesced and professionalized, however, boundaries would be drawn around the profession to identify professionals from nonprofessionals.

In the December 1953 issue of *Computers and Automation*, Berkeley published the last installment of his initial glossary, with 122 words beginning with the letters F through Z. Alston Householder continued the discussion about reporting vs. legislating definitions in a letter that Berkeley published in February 1954. Householder pointed out that "when a definition appears on a printed page, it becomes in some degree standardized; people will refer to it and tend to use the word in just that way" [26, p. 22]. He also pointed out that Berkeley's "reporting is at best partial, subject to the limitations of one's own experience, judgment, and understanding." He urged Berkeley to "think seriously, as you formulate your definitions, not only of how you think the terms are used, but also of how they might best be used." In addition to only reporting on how a term was used in general usage, Householder advised Berkeley to accept his role as legislating standard definitions in order to further enable clear and unambiguous scientific discourse. He recommended that Berkeley not wait for formal committee decisions but should encourage anyone who objects to one of his definitions to write to him and that he publish the objections and proposed alternatives for further discussion. He then added his own discussions of the terms *routine*, *subroutine*, *readaround*, *cell*, *infinity*, *rounding*, *truncating*, and *regenerating* [26, p. 22–23].

In responding to Householder, Berkeley stated that in order "to make a real success of this [glossary] endeavor, we need the help of many people." He specifically called on help from Ernest G. Andrews (Bell Labs), Grace Hopper (Sperry Rand), John W. Carr (University of Michigan), Samuel B. Williams (Bell Labs), and Charles V. L. Smith (Office of Naval Research) to work with him: "[W]henever he notices a new expression being used, or whenever he notices that an expression that he may have coined is coming into use in his vicinity, [he][2] might send us a note, mentioning the expression and telling the meaning which he gives to it" [26, p. 24]. Berkeley claimed that by publishing these contributions from experts in the computing field, they would not be "a 'legislated' new term, but … a report of a new term that has gone into use." The definition would only be the "meaning which is presently has." Berkeley also noted that a committee on nomenclature had been formed by the IRE chaired by Axel G. Jensen (Bell Labs). He continued, "But unfortunately most committees are clannish; they feel that they should not report their work until it is complete, and that it should then be reported first in the proceedings of the

---

[2]Author's note: I am using the archaic terminology of the universal "he" here to conform to Berkeley's usage of that term in 1954.

society which has sponsored that committee. Although we would of course be very glad to report their discussions of terms as and when occurring, it seems doubtful that any committee members will feel free to tell us." Instead of relying on established committees from professional associations, Berkeley suggested that anyone interested in being a correspondent for *Computers and Automation* should contact him to report on the terminology used "at various computing centers" [26, p. 24]. This open model of lexicography relied on input from interested readers of *Computers and Automation*, a journal published by Berkeley Enterprises without any institutional backing. Although this approach to defining technical terms might reflect common usage, its haphazard approach to consensus-building could not result in a common technical vocabulary upon which to build a professional discipline or even collaborate across working locations.

Berkeley advocated for computer professionals to be called *information engineers*; in his glossary he defined *information* as "basically, a set of marks or an arrangement of equipment that has meaning" [12, p. 16]. Householder identified this as a problematic definition and he referred to Shannon's use of the term *information* in his mathematical model of communication [36]. Householder also referred to Shannon's use of the term *bit* as a measure of *information*. Berkeley had defined *bit* as "a binary digit (colloquial)." Berkeley defined *binary digit* this way: "a digit in the binary scale of notation. This digit may be only 0 or 1. It is equivalent to an 'on' condition or an 'off' condition, a 'yes' or a 'no', etc." [10, p. 26]. Householder responded:

> It may be true, as you say that 'bit' is used colloquially for 'binary digit" (at Los Alamos they say 'bigit"), but if so it is by an extension of the meaning proposed by John Tukey and endorsed by Shannon. In binary machines, generally every state of a cell or register is meaningful; hence with n elements in a register there are 2^n possible messages. Hence using Shannon's measure, the amount of information is equal to the number of binary digits, which could account for the colloquial use of the word 'bit'. Nevertheless, it seems to me that the Los Alamos term 'bigit' should be encouraged, since in a decimal machine a decimal digit requires 4 bigits, but the information is only log 2^{10} bits. [26, p. 23]

Here Householder implies that Berkeley's definition of *information* is not adequate to underpin a sophisticated notion of information engineering. He instead suggests Shannon's use of the term *information*, which Shannon did not explicitly define in his ground-breaking paper from Bell Labs explaining a mathematical model for mechanical communication, such as telephony and television. Householder further proposed the use of the term *bigit* instead of Shannon and Tukey's term *bit*, based on the work being done at the Los Alamos lab, where they were running the Mathematical Analyzer Numerical Integrator and Computer (MANIAC), built with the Princeton architecture, to run calculations relating to thermonuclear processes. Although Berkeley's approach to rapid development of computer terminology enabled him to publish his definitions in *Computers and Automation* amid other efforts to standardize nomenclature, in the long run, this approach did not save time because it relied on extended discussions being written, sent through the mail, and published in his journal. It relied on people reading his journal and being motivated to respond to his definitions. Ultimately, this approach to language standardization was not successful because the definitions were not developed within a professional governing body that would lend them credibility and authority. By 1953, Berkeley was no longer ACM Secretary nor a member of the Executive Council, so his definitions were put forward as the work of an entrepreneur and consultant.

7.3   Standardizing Terms in an Institutional Model

In contract to Berkeley's work on computer terminology, the Institute of Radio Engineers Electronic Computers Committee Subcommittee on Definitions of Electronic Computer Terms, which was formed in 1948, initially included seven members with connections in businesses (RCA, IBM), universities (Columbia, Institute for Advanced Study in Princeton), and government agencies (US Navy, US Air Force, US Army, Bureau of Standards). Members of this IRE committee also claimed to be reporting usage of terms but did come to consensus on a preferred usage when definitions of a term differed from location to location [33]. As Householder pointed out in his reaction to Berkeley's glossary, once a definition is published, people tend to regard it as authoritative. This is especially true if the definition has been vetted by a group of people who are recognized experts on the topic and who have the backing of an established professional association, such as the IRE in this case. The glossary of computer terms that was published in the March 1951 *Proceedings of the IRE* put forward a standard for computer terminology, but other people continued to develop glossaries that reflected usage in particular locations or among particular groups of computer developers. This IRE glossary did not include the terms *information* or *bit* that were being used in another developing profession called *information theory* based on Shannon's mathematical communication model. It did include the term *binary digit*, though, which was used both electronic computer development and information theory, defining it as "A digit of a binary number" [27, p. 272]. The glossary also included this definition of the terms *analog* and *analog computer*:

> **Analog (in computer work).** A physical system on which the performance of measurements yields information concerning a class of mathematical problems.
> **Analog Computer.** A physical system together with means of control for the performance of measurements (upon the system) which yield information concerning a class of mathematical problems. In an analog computer quantities are represented without explicit use of language [27, p. 272].

By early 1952, the IRE Electronic Computers Committee decided to update the glossary of definitions for electronic computers. For this iteration they divided the work into two subcommittees, one for the eastern and one for the western United States. Nathaniel Rochester from IBM chaired the seven-member eastern subcommittee, and Willis Ware from Rand Corporation chaired the five-member western subcommittee. Rochester began the work of his committee by seeking input on the 1950 glossary: "In order to stimulate comments I am planning to mail reprints of our first glossary to each computer outfit in the East and ask for their complaints and ask for copies of their glossaries" [32]. Because the eastern subcommittee was supported by both the IRE and IBM, Rochester could take on the expense of sending copies of the IRE glossary to "each computer outfit in the East" with the expectation that he would get responses in return. In the western United States, Willis Ware also sent copies of the IRE glossary to 75 "companies active in the field" to ask for "comments, criticisms, and additions" [40]. Rochester and Ware could generate interest in this project from people at other locations because they were well connected among computer developers. By comparison, private entrepreneur Edmund Berkeley needed to charge US$1.00 for his October 1956 glossary published in *Computers and Automation*. He explained, "We have received a number of requests for permission to reprint the glossary free. We are reluctant to grant such permission, since the glossary represents a great deal of work done by members of the staff of 'Computers and Automation'" [13, p. 4]. Without strong institutional backing, Berkeley's commercial efforts could not have the authority for setting professional standards that Rochester and Ware's work with the IRE accomplished.

In preparing for the western subcommittee's work, Ware sent a memo to members on 6 August 1952, with some items for consideration. Among them were items that started to create boundaries around what would become the field of computer science, as differentiated from other fields:

> 2) When we get started with our actual definitions work … one thing we must consider is a group of terms … which were analog and servomechanical in nature, and some terms which were felt … to be too specialized. …
> 3b) Terms which are specifically servomechanical will be referred to Professor Pease's committee on Servo-Systems.
> 3c) Descriptions of large-scale computers which were formerly appended to the list of definitions will not be brought up-to-date.
> 3d) Programming terms will be taken up again in an attempt to extend the definitions and to clarify meanings of the terms now in use. …
> 3f) A new subcommittee on magnetic recording has been formed under Sam Alexander of BuStds [Bureau of Standards] in Washington. …
> 3g) A similar committee on computer diodes is being considered [42].

The minutes from the 15 January 1953 meeting of the western subcommittee show a further distinction being drawn between electronic computers and older technologies of analog machines and servomechanisms: "Servo terms and analog terms will be separately collected. The servo terms will be forwarded to Professor Pease and analog terms held for action by some local analog people" [43]. These older technologies would not be linguistically included in the field of computer science that was being formed through the IRE language standardization effort.

In a 16 July 1953 meeting, Willis Ware (RAND), Harry Larson (Institute for Numerical Analysis), Bill Speer (Computer Research Corp.), William Smith (Aeronutronic Systems), and Ragnar Thorensen (Institute for Numerical Analysis)[3]

---

[3] Louis D. Stevens from IBM was also a member of this western subcommittee, but did not attend this July 1953 meeting. Stevens was among a group of engineers who patented a magnetic disk storage device. In the 1954–1955 committee roster, Willis Ware continued at RAND, Harry Larson worked at Hughes Aircraft Company, William Speer worked at National Cash Register Computer

voiced a need to extend the field into programming terminology: "A list of programming-coding terms needing definition will be prepared and circulated to members of 8.5 [western subcommittee] who will in turn get their programmers to review these terms and do some advance thinking on said terms; some coder from each organization represented on the committee will then form a task group to battle through these terms" [45]. The subcommittee members noted that some other organization, such as the ACM, might already be working on these definitions. Nonetheless, they felt that their group should also extend their work into the area of programming, as well as hardware development and operations.

At that same meeting, the committee members pushed back on Berkeley's glossary: "Committee 8.5 is considerably alarmed to note the stand of 'Computers and Automation' (v2, no. 4, May 1953, p. 21) on the subject of how definitions should be written and who should write them. It seems to us that a certain well known gentleman is, by his irresponsible action, again doing more harm than good" [45]. By phrasing this objection as coming from the committee versus coming from individuals, this objection gained the authority of the IRE-sanctioned working group to distinguish its work from less structured efforts of Berkeley's publication. The committee continued, "Perhaps in an effort to counter this intrusion of a pulp magazine into the technical literature of the computer field, we should make available the work which 8.4 [Eastern Subcommittee] and 8.5 [Western Subcommittee] have agree on, to the Transactions or to the Newsletter for prompt publication" [45]. They also suggested that the IRE could make *the Transactions of the Professional Group on Electronic Computers* available to a wider audience of readers who might subscribe to the lower-cost *Computers and Automation*: "This might have a big appeal to people who are on the fringe of the field, and who are interested in getting an informative, relatively inexpensive journal. What has happened and is apparently continuing to do so, is that the pulp magazine is being passed out gratis at technical meetings, and is making a big appeal to these fringe people; hence the misinformation which is contained in it is getting wide circulation, and this goes in the direction of giving stature and status to the publication and its mistakes" [45]. The committee especially objected to three of the terms in Berkeley's glossary:

card feed – a punch card machine or mechanism which feeds cards.
card punch – a machine or mechanism which punches cards.
complement – in decimal notation, the number obtained by replacing each decimal digit by nine minus that digit; in binary notation, the number obtained by replacing each digit by one minus that digit. For example, the complement of 1101011 is 0010100. [11, p. 17–18]

The subcommittee stated that "his definition of 'complement' is out-and-out incorrect; the definitions of 'card-feed' and 'card-punch' are trivial, non-informative, and useless" [45]. The subcommittee sent its concerns to Nathaniel Rochester (chair of the eastern subcommittee, IBM), Robert Serrell (chair of the IRE Committee on Electronic Computers, RCA), and Larry Cumming (technical secretary, IRE). By

---

Division, William E. Smith worked at North American Aviation, Ragnar Thorensen worked at Magnavox Research, and Louis Stevens was no longer on the committee [47].

advancing this objection up the chain of command, the members of the western subcommittee brought their institutional weight to bear on this effort to establish authority in standardizing terminology for the computer field. The IRE 1950 glossary did not include the "card feeder" or "card punch" terms; it defined complement in this way:

> **Complement.** A number whose representation is derived from the finite positional notation of another by one of the following rules:

(a) True complement – Subtract each digit from the radix less 1, then add 1 to the least significant digit, executing any carries required.
(b) (Radix-1)'s complement – Subtract each digit from the radix less 1. [27, p. 272–273]

As computer programming became more essential to the field, the IRE definition of complement became more fully articulated in the 1956 revision of their glossary:

> **Complement.** 1) A number whose representation is derived from the finite Positional Notation of another by one of the following rules: a) True complement – Subtract each digit from one less than the base; then add 1 to the least significant digit, executing all carries required. b) Base minus one's complement – Subtract each digit from one less than the base (*e.g.,* "9's complement" in the base 10, "1's complement" in the base 2, etc.). 2) To form the complement of a number.
>	*Note:* In many machines, a negative number is represented as a complement of the corresponding positive number. [28, p. 1168]

## 7.4	Establishing the Field of Programming by Defining Terms

Ware recognized the need for developing specialized terminology for computer programming in July 1953, when he contacted John Carr, a mathematician at the University of Michigan, who was involved with an effort at the ACM to develop a glossary of programming terms. Ware stated that the IRE subcommittees had "accumulated a considerable number [of terms] which is restricted to the programming or coding part of the field. We had intended to gather a small task group of people actively engaged in programming and get their assistance in defining these terms. However, hearing of your committee, we wondered if there was a needless overlap of effort" [44]. John Carr was a member of the ACM Nomenclature Committee, established in January 1949 and chaired by Grace Hopper, to develop and publish glossaries of computer terminology [2, p. 304]. In 1953, that committee was working to complete their "First Glossary of Programming Terminology," which was sent as a Report to the Association for Computing Machinery in June 1954. Members of this committee included the following:

- Grace Hopper, chair of the ACM Nomenclature Committee, served as a mathematical officer in the US Navy Bureau of Ordnance and was on the team that built the Mark I and II computers with Howard Aiken at Harvard Computation Laboratory during World War II. In 1949, she joined the Eckert-Mauchly

Computer Corporation. In 1952 she became a systems analyst and director of Automatic Programming Development for the UNIVAC project at Sperry Corporation [29].

- Charles W. Adams was a faculty member in the MIT Department of Electrical Engineering, working in the Digital Computer Laboratory on the Office of Naval Research Whirlwind. He previously worked in the MIT Servomechanisms Lab, "which was established in 1940 to develop automatic control systems and military fire control" [31].

- John W. Backus joined IBM in 1950 and was the manager of the IBM Programming Department in 1954. "By 1953, he was leading a small team to create an easy-to-use programming language for scientific users. At the time, programming was exceedingly difficult – Backus once described it as 'doing hand-to-hand combat with the machine.' After four years of intense effort, Backus' team produced the FORTRAN programming language" [3].

- John W. Carr was a research mathematician at the University of Michigan since 1952. He had worked on Project Whirlwind at MIT where he developed automatic programming subroutines while earning his PhD in Mathematics there [16].

- Roddy F. Osborn directed the purchase and installation of the eighth UNIVAC at General Electric's Appliance Park in Louisville, Kentucky, in January 1954 [14], thus ushering in the use of electronic computers for business operations such as payroll. He "predicted that the UNIVAC would effect the same kind of changes on business as it had already begun to effect in science, engineering, and mathematics" [18, p. 32].

- George W. Patterson "joined the staff of the Moore School [in 1946], where he designed the logic for EDVAC arithmetic circuits and coordinated the logic design for the entire machine. From 1950 to 1955, Patterson was with the Research Center of the Burroughs Corporation. ... Patterson was active in computer standardization, as a member of the IRE Electronic Computers Committee beginning in 1949, and serving as Vice Chairman in 1962" [4].

- Jerry Svigals was one of the first programmers on the ENIAC at the Aberdeen Proving Ground. He later recalled how he learned programming there: "My teacher was a gal whose name was Ruth [M. Davis] ... who went on to be the Under Secretary of Defense. And she was one of the senior programmers. There were about a half-dozen women who ... sort of took you under their wing to get you educated" [37, p. 5]. In 1952, Svigals joined RCA "working on an ordnance connected computer called BIZMAC" [37, p. 5].

- Joseph H. Wegstein was the Acting Chief of the Office for Information Processing Standards, at the National Bureau of Standards. In 1959, he was active on the committee that first met at the Pentagon to develop a common business language, which became COBOL [35].

An introduction to the 2 June 1954 ACM glossary stated, "This 'programmer's glossary' had its inception in a glossary compiled by Dr. Grace Murray Hopper for the Workshops on Automatic Coding held in 1953 under the sponsorship of the Bureau of Census, the Office of the Air Comptroller and Remington Rand, Inc." [7,

p. 2]. It noted that this glossary "borrowed heavily" from the 1950 IRE glossary and the glossaries published in *Computers and Automation* [7, p. 2]. In providing an overview to the glossary, the committee narrowed the scope of their work to omit "common terms of business, mathematics, or logic unless they have acquired an added meaning. Neither are the words which are used in the design, construction or maintenance of computers given unless they are also terms used regularly by the programmers." Here the committee is differentiating the work of programmers from people who design and build computer hardware, thereby beginning to define terms for a new field of programming or software. Because this ACM glossary was targeted to programmers, its definition of the term *complement* was more detailed than that of the glossaries from the IRE or *Computers and Automation*:

> Complement – a quantity which is derived from a given quantity, expressed to the base n, by one of the following rules and which is frequently used to represent the negative of a given quantity.

> a) Complement on n: subtract each digit of the given quantity from n-1, add unity to the least significant digit, and perform all resultant carrys. For example, the twos complement of binary 11010 is 00110; the tens complement of decimal 456 is 544.

> b) Complement on n-1: subtract each digit of the given quantity from n-1. For example, the ones complement of binary 11010 is 00101; the nines complement of decimal 456 is 543. [7, p. 8]

7.5   Establishing Professional Boundaries Through Glossaries

The ACM committee further narrowed their scope to electronic computer programming: "Terminology used in the applications of punched card and analog systems is omitted" [7, p. 3]. This focus on electronic computer design to the exclusion of analog designs was also taking place in the IRE western subcommittee as recorded in the minutes of their two meetings in late January 1954: "We would like to state our suggestion that it's time to activate [Professional Group on Electronic Computers] subcommittee 8.X to do an analog computer glossary. We further propose that our flossary [sic] be then retitled – ...Computers; Definitions of Digital Terms" [46, p. 15]. This need to focus on electronic computer design indicates that the number of specialized terms in this field was growing, while people refined these digital computer designs as differentiated from other possible designs, such as analog or relay machines. This specialization was also going on in computer programming, as seen in the ACM committee's work. By using their own specialized vocabulary for the design and operation of electronic computers, people working in this field in the early 1950s were constructing the linguistic tools they would need for rapid communication of complex technical concepts.

In a 22 April 1954 letter to Willis Ware, David R. Brown [MIT Lincoln Lab, Project SAGE] reported on a discussion Brown had for Ware's proposal to publish the revised IRE glossary early with "tentative definitions" in response to the publication of Edmund Berkeley's glossary in *Computers and Automation*: "At the IRE

Standards Committee Meeting of April 8, 1954, I discussed your proposal for pub-lication of tentative definitions in the Professional Group [on Electronic Computers] Transactions with Dr. Ernst Weber [Director, Microwave Research Institute, Polytechnic Institute of Brooklyn]. The Standards Committee is firmly opposed to any such procedure. The Standards Committee sympathizes with our need for early publication but feels that any publication, even though it were labeled tentative, would tie the hands of the Standards Committee. The Standards Committee would rather assist us in expediting publication of a partially completed list of definitions through normal channels" [15]. Here Brown cautioned Ware to work within the established guidelines of the professional association rather than to adopt more entrepreneurial practices to compete with Berkeley's glossaries in *Computers and Automation*.

In a 2 June 1954 letter to Robert Serrell (RCA), chair of the IRE Committee on Electronic Computers, Willis Ware noted that he had "received Grace Hopper's glossary; it's a monumental work but I doubt if we will have much opportunity to work it into our almost completed new Glossary" [47]. Nonetheless, in mid-June 1954, the IRE eastern subcommittee considered how the language standardization efforts at the IRE and ACM might be coordinated: "[Linder Charlie] Hobbs has had a telephone conversation with Dr. Hopper and is making arrangements for a meeting with her to discuss the work of the two committees. [George W.] Patterson and Hobbs have both talked with Dr. [Samuel B.] Williams who feels that there is a fairly clear line between the interests of the ACM and the IRE and that hence there should be not be [sic] too much overlap. However Dr. Williams agrees that those terms that are defined by both committees should have a common definition wher-ever possible" [23]. Charlie Hobbs (RCA) sent a letter to Willis Ware (RAND) days after the eastern subcommittee's meeting in order to inform him of this contact with Grace Hopper (Sperry Rand) "as soon as possible" so that members of the two IRE subcommittees could coordinate their effort to collaborate with the ACM. Members of the IRE and ACM committees felt some urgency to make their glossaries avail-able to people working with electronic computers as soon as possible: "The tenta-tive ACM glossary prepared by Dr. Hopper was reviewed by her with Jack Backus of IBM and Charlie Adams of MIT and numerous revisions were made. This revised glossary will definitely be published at the ACM Ann Arbor meeting [23–25 June 1954] as a tentative glossary to solicit comments and suggestions. It will be clearly marked as tentative and unofficial and Dr. Williams will emphasize this in his address to the conference" [23].[4]

Not to be outdone by the ACM committee, the IRE eastern subcommittee pushed again for early publication of their revised IRE Standards on Electronic Computers: Definitions of Terms: "Hobbs reported on a discussion with Bob Serrell concerning the early publication of the work of 8.4 [Eastern Subcommittee] and 8.5 [Western Subcommittee]. It was decided that the best idea would be to complete as soon as possible the revision of all terms in the old glossary and to submit those terms

---

[4] Samuel B. Williams was ACM President from 1952 to 1954.

remaining from the old glossary plus any new terms already agreed upon to the main Computer Committee and the Standards Committee for their approval. This partial glossary would then be published in the [Professional Group on Electronic Computers] transactions after approval by the Standards Committee while the work on the remaining new terms was being completed. After completion of this work these new terms would then be submitted to the main Computer Committee and the Standards Committee. Following their approval of these additional terms the entire glossary would then be published in the IRE Proceedings" [23].

The IRE procedure for approving definitions was cumbersome and slow, compared to the ACM procedure for developing their glossary ("The tentative ACM glossary prepared by Dr. Hopper was reviewed by her with Jack Backus of IBM and Charlie Adams of MIT and numerous revisions were made." [23]) or Berkeley's procedure of publishing his definitions in *Computers and Automation* and then waiting for reader responses. However, the benefit of the slower IRE process was that the resulting definitions had the authority of many layers of review from noted professionals with expert knowledge of electronic computers. But when rapid development of electronic computers was tied to national security and air defense systems, there was pressure to speed up the institutional procedure represented by the IRE administration. Hobbs came up with a proposal for facilitating the development of approved electronic computer terminology: "Hobbs will extract from the old glossary all terms requiring action by 8.4 and 8.5 and send a list of these before the next meeting to all members with a recommendation to 'delete', 'leave as is', or 'revise' for each term. At the next meeting discussion will be started on those terms marked 'revise' and on those terms marked 'delete' or 'leave as is' where there is any disagreement. … This procedure was approved by the numbers [sic] of 8.4" [23]. The eastern subcommittee proposed a deadline of 1 October, or two months, for completing this glossary revision; Ware agreed to this proposal on behalf of the western subcommittee: "I think that this is the only way that we will make headway with the pulp paper definitions" [48].

Later in August 1954, Linder Charlie Hobbs noted in a letter to Robert Serrell that he was at "Remington Rand now … in a better position to work with Dr. Hopper concerning the ACM activities. … She wants to leave engineering terms alone and is willing to accept the IRE definitions of these. Since 8.4 wants to leave programming terms alone, this should work out quite well – if we can get 8.5 to go along with us on the programming question" [24]. Hobbs further reported that "Committee 8.4 felt that it would be a good idea to try to get the [Professional Group on Electronic Computers] Transactions to publish our new glossary, the ACM glossary, and the [British Standards Institute] definitions, one following the other in the same publication to provide a comprehensive dictionary of computer engineering and programming terms in both this country and England. … I would also appreciate your comments … concerning new computer terms introduced by business applications" [24]. Although Berkeley continued to make his glossary of computer terms available through *Computers and Automation* and through mail order, by the middle of 1954, a standard technical vocabulary was being developed with the institutional backing of the members of the IRE and the ACM who were connected with industry, academia, and governmental agencies. The IRE revised Definitions of Terms was approved by the Standards Committee in July 1956 and was published in the IRE Standards on Computers in September 1956.

At the Eastern Joint Computer Conference in New York City in December 1956, ACM President Dr. John W. Carr III gave the concluding Conference Summary. Carr had worked with Grace Hopper on the 1954 ACM "First Glossary of Programming Terminology." From 1953 to 1957 at the University of Michigan, he supervised programming and operations for the Michigan Digital Automatic Computer (MIDAC) at the university's Willow Run Research Center Digital Computation Department, where his research team worked on missile guidance problems for the US Air Force [5]. As an associate professor in University of Michigan's Department of Mathematics in 1952, Carr taught an undergraduate course in numerical methods and machine language programming. Undergraduate computer education expanded in 1956 when the university installed its first IBM 650 and received financial instructional support through IBM's Educational Contribution Program. As he presented his concluding summary at the Joint Computer Conference at the end of 1956, Carr began by noting that "major problems of our somewhat diffuse computer field began to raise their ugly heads" at the conference [17, p. 147]. The first problem he identified was "manpower, or how to continue to find personnel to satisfy the needs of an everexpanding [sic] computer research economy." The second problem he identified was "preservation and rehabilitation of the position of the universities in the area of computer circuits, design, and logic." The third problem dealt with "intercommunication across the artificial barriers, such as … that which separates the logical program designer from the logical hardware designer" [17, p. 147–148]. He argued that all these problems involved "university research and education programs" and required imagination more than money. These problems required stronger university educational programs to prepare graduate students to fill the needs for more computer developers. But when universities' computer research programs were underfunded, they could not fulfill their teaching mission with the imaginative new approaches that a rapidly changing computer field demanded: "When university research in computers disappears, university teaching in that area crumbles, and when the latter happens, not even a trickle of qualified graduate students educated in any depth will talk to … recruiting personnel" [17, p. 148]. Carr argued that in an era of rapid computer commercialization, universities continued to have an important societal role to play as places where people could "think out of the box," having freedom to use their imagination to explore innovation without the need to consider bottom-line profits that might result from their efforts.

Carr especially saw an important role for universities to play in the third problem he identified: communication. Noting that "no one put it more eruditely or wittily than Sir Watson-Witt" in his luncheon address to the conference, Carr asked, "How is the discipline organized so that it can intercommunicate?" [17, p. 148]. His work with the ACM Committee on Nomenclature served to help organize this intercommunication by establishing a standardized vocabulary to facilitate communication across locations. In his Eastern Joint Computer Conference Concluding Summary he expanded on this idea: "Who, in the final analysis, develops the glossaries and standard terminology? Committees of the professional and technical societies, nominally, yes, but the university teachers accept or reject them, mold them, in passing them on to the next generation" [17, p. 148]. In order to provide the foundation for training people to enter a fledgling computer profession equipped with the imagination that this profession and industry demanded, Carr argued for the important role that people in universities played in filling this need. But this education depended on intercommunication between people working in programming and hardware design at different locations, which required a standardized vocabulary. Carr saw this as a programming problem in matching "the human to the machine" that had been designed with the human in mind, so that the system could operate "more automatically and therefore more reliably" [17, p. 148]. He saw the need to educate students who would lead the country into this new world where machines and humans understood each other.

In reviewing the state of computer design in 1956, Carr pointed out "cracks in the armor of our historical patterns:" "We see systems in which there are several operations being performed concurrently. ... But our machines are still the same old combination of desk calculator, girl operator, and notebook, that was the model for the EDVAC and the Princeton series. Perhaps the girl now has two notebooks, or writes with both hands, or works two desk calculators at once, but the same structure is basically there" [17, p. 149]. He called for a new structure that would be developed only with the freedom for imagination that was possible in university labs: "Some day ... an engineer or a mathematician will come before an audience such as I am addressing and describe a device which will accept information from its environment, process it inductively, meet situations not specifically planned for by its designer ... and make decisions on the basis of 'studied reasoning'" [17, p. 149–150]. He called the development of such a machine the "'controlled thermonuclear reaction' of the computer world ... Such machines must automatically have the ability to accept one another's languages, the ability to accept problems which have not been formulated formally. ... Men are thinking about such machines now, sometimes in the large commercial laboratories, but more often in university departments or independent laboratories" [17, p. 150]. This imagined computer design would rely on a common language among people and machines that was being developed along with the computer designs themselves. Car concluded, "The job of intercommunication, as Sir Watson-Witt noted, is most important" [17, p. 150]. The development of a profession called computer science depended on this intercommunication. The stability of democracy depended on it.

References

1. Abbott, Andrew. 1988. *The system of professions: An essay on the division of expert labor.* Chicago: University of Chicago Press.
2. Alt, Franz. 1962. Fifteen years ACM. *Communications of the ACM* 5 (6): 300–307.

3. Anonymous. 1977. John Backus. Computer History Museum. https://computerhistory.org/profile/john-backus/. Accessed 12 Nov 2020.

4. ———. 2018, July 30. George W. Patterson. Engineering and Technology History Wiki. https://ethw.org/George_W._Patterson. Accessed 10 Nov 2020.

5. ———. 2020. *The history of CSE at Michigan.* University of Michigan Computer Science and Engineering. https://cse.engin.umich.edu/about/history/. Accessed 12 Nov 2020.

6. Arnold, H. H. (Hap). 1945. *Report to Secretary of War.* Rand Corporation. https://www.rand.org/about/history/a-brief-history-of-rand.html. Accessed 12 Nov 2020.

7. Association for Computing Machinery Nomenclature Committee. 1954, June. First Glossary of Programming Terminology. https://archive.org/details/bitsavers_mitsummerslossaryofProgrammingTerminologyJun54_1794300. Accessed 12 Nov 2020.

8. Berkeley, Edmund. 1947, June 25. Notice on organization of an Eastern Association for Computing Machinery. Edmund C. Berkeley Papers [CBI50] Charles Babbage Institute, University of Minnesota, Minneapolis.

9. ———. 1952, October. Communication and control in the computing machinery field. *The Computing Machinery Field* 1(4): 14–15. Edmund C. Berkeley Papers [CBI50] Charles Babbage Institute, University of Minnesota, Minneapolis.

10. ———. 1953, March. Glossary – Section 1: A, B (cumulative). *Computers and Automation* 2(2): 25–26.

11. ———. 1953, May. Glossary – Section 2: C, D, E (cumulative). *Computers and Automation* 2(4): 17–22.

12. ———. 1953, December. Glossary – Section 3: F to Z (cumulative). *Computers and Automation* 2(9): 16–22.

13. ———. 1956, December. The Editor's notes: The glossary reprinted. *Computers and Automation* 5(9): 4.

14. Betts, Mitch. 2008, May 16. GE's Appliance Park: Cradle of business computing in the U.S. *Computerworld.* https://www.computerworld.com/article/2478555/ge-s-appliance-park%2D%2Dcradle-of-business-computing-in-the-u-s-.html. Accessed 12 Nov 2020.

15. Brown, David R. 1954, April 22. Letter to Willis Ware. IEEE History Center Library Archives. Stevens Institute of Technology, Hoboken.

16. Carr, John W. 1952, May. Progress of the Whirlwind computer toward an automatic programming procedure. *Proceedings of the 1952 ACM National Meeting.* Pittsburgh: 237–241. https://doi.org/10.1145/609784.609817. Accessed 12 Nov 2020.

17. ———. 1956. Conference summary. *Papers and discussions presented at the 10–12 December 1956 Eastern Joint Computer Conference.* New York: 147–150.

18. Ceruzzi, Paul E. 2003. *A history of modern computing.* Cambridge, MA: MIT Press.

19. Commander in Chief, Army Forces Advance. 1945, September 18. Memorandum to War Department. Harry S. Truman Library. https://www.trumanlibrary.gov/library/research-files/war-department-incoming-classified-message. Accessed 11 Nov 2020.

20. Correll, Quentin. 1958, July. Letter to the editor. *Communications of the ACM* 1(7): 2. https://doi.org/10.1145/368873.368877. Accessed 11 Nov 2020.

21. Freidson, Eliot. 1988. *Professional powers: A Study of the Institutionalization of formal knowledge.* Chicago: University of Chicago Press.

22. Gruenberger, Fred J. 1968, October. *History of the JOHNNIAC: Rand memorandum RM-5654-PR.* Santa Monica: Rand Corporation.

23. Hobbs, Linder Charlie. 1954, June 18. Letter to Willis Ware. IEEE History Center Library Archives. Stevens Institute of Technology, Hoboken.

24. ———. 1954, August 26. Letter to Robert Serrell. IEEE History Center Library Archives. Stevens Institute of Technology, Hoboken.

25. Householder, Alston S. 1953, January. Brains: Electronic and otherwise. *The Computing Machinery Field* 2(1): 5–9.

26. Householder, Alston S., and Edmund Berkeley. 1954, February. Glossary of terms in computers and automation – Discussion. *Computers and Automation* 3(2): 22–24.

27. Institute of Radio Engineers Subcommittee on Definitions of Electronic Computer Terms. 1951, March. Standards on electronic computers: Definitions of terms, 1950. *Proceedings of the I.R.E.* 39(3): 271–277.

28. Institute of Radio Engineers Committee on Electronic Computers Subcommittee on Definitions. 1956, September. IRE standards on electronic computers: Definitions of terms. *Proceedings of the I.R.E.* 44(9): 1166–1173.

29. Lee, J. A. N. 1995. Grace Brewster Murray Hopper. In *Computer pioneers.* Los Alamitos: IEEE Computer Society Press. https://history.computer.org/pioneers/hopper.html. Accessed 12 Nov 2020.

30. Longo, Bernadette. 2015. *Edmund Berkeley and the social responsibility of computer professionals.* San Rafael: Morgan & Claypool Press – ACM.

31. MIT Digital Computer Laboratory Staff. 1953, October 1. The Digital Computer Laboratory of the Massachusetts Institute of Technology. https://dome.mit.edu/handle/1721.3/37455/bro wse?value=Digital+Computer+Laboratory+Staff&type=author. Accessed 12 Nov 2020.

32. Rochester, Nathaniel. 1952, April 11. Letter to Willis Ware. IEEE History Center Library Archives. Stevens Institute of Technology, Hoboken.

33. Rochester, Nathaniel, and Willis H. Ware. 1953, December. Computer definitions (guest editorial). *Transactions of the IRE Professional Group on Electronic Computers* EC-2.4: 2.

34. Saks, Mike. 2012. Defining a profession: The role of knowledge and expertise. *Professions & Professionalism* 2 (1): 1–10.

35. Sammet, Jean E. 1978, August. *The early history of COBOL.* ACM SIGPLAN Notices. https://doi.org/10.1145/960118.808378. Accessed 12 Nov 2020.

36. Shannon, Claude E. 1948/1963. A mathematical theory of communication. In *The mathematical theory of communication,* 29–107. Urbana/Chicago: The University of Illinois Press.

37. Spicer, Dag. 2007, June 19. Oral history of Jerome Svigals: CHM reference number X4067-2007. *Computer History Museum.* https://www.computerhistory.org/collections/catalog/102658148. Accessed 12 Nov 2020.

38. Swales, John. 1987, March. Approaching the concept of discourse community. *Paper presented at the Conference on College Composition and Communication.* https://eric.ed.gov/?id=ED286184. Accessed 11 Nov 2020.

39. von Karman, Theodore. 1945. *Toward new horizons: Science, the key to air supremacy.* Washington, DC: Army Air Forces Scientific Advisory Group.

40. Ware, Willis H. 1952, July 28. Letter to Larry Cumming. IEEE History Center Library Archives. Stevens Institute of Technology, Hoboken.

41. ———. 1952, August 5. Letter to Nathaniel Rochester. IEEE History Center Library Archives. Stevens Institute of Technology, Hoboken.

42. ———. 1952, August 6. Memorandum to Members of Committee 8.5. IEEE History Center Library Archives. Stevens Institute of Technology, Hoboken.

43. ———. 1953, January 20. Minutes of the meeting of Committee 8.5 I.R.E. 15 January 1953. IEEE History Center Library Archives. Stevens Institute of Technology, Hoboken.

44. ———. 1953, July 21. Letter to John W. Carr, III. IEEE History Center Library Archives. Stevens Institute of Technology, Hoboken.

45. ———. 1953, August 3. Minutes of the meeting of Committee 8.5 I.R.E. 16 July 1953. IEEE History Center Library Archives. Stevens Institute of Technology, Hoboken.

46. ———. 1954, January 28. Minutes of the meeting of Committee 8.5 I.R.E. 21 and 26 January 1954. IEEE History Center Library Archives. Stevens Institute of Technology, Hoboken.

47. ———. 1954, June 2. Letter to Robert Serrell. IEEE History Center Library Archives. Stevens Institute of Technology, Hoboken.

48. ———. 1954, August 5. Letter to Linder C. Hobbs. IEEE History Center Library Archives. Stevens Institute of Technology, Hoboken.

49. ———. 1954, October 5. The digital computer: Where does it go from here? *Paper presented before the Los Angeles section of the Institute of Radio Engineers.* Santa Monica: Rand Corporation.

50. ———. 2008. *Rand and the information evolution: A history in essays and vignettes.* Santa Monica: Rand Corporation.
51. Watson-Watt, Robert. 1956, December. Are computers important? *Proceedings of the Eastern Joint Computer Conference.* New York: 67–68. https://doi.org/10.1145/1455533.1455550. Accessed 11 Nov 2020.

Chapter 8
Establishing the Field of Computer Science

Abstract This chapter describes the importance of training people to work in the growing computer field as military and industry projects demanded more workers for their projects. The transition from university labs as sites for building one-off computers and businesses as sites for building standardized computer machinery created staffing needs for the growing computer industry. This need for people prepared in a specialized computer field prompted universities to consider developing curricula and departments in what would become known as computer science. But tensions between mathematics departments and computer scientists needed to be worked out in order for this new profession to be established.

"Ideally one would hope to establish a sharp dichotomy between the mathematical and engineering phases of the question. In point of fact this is not feasible. The practice of the coder must not only devote considerable attention to the mathematical aspects of a problem but also to their relationship to the engineering ones." Herman Goldstine, "Some experience in coding and programing with the Institute computer," 1953 [26]

"By 1958 several universities, through their numerical analysis centers, electrical engineering departments, or computer laboratories, were offering fellowships specifically earmarked for concentration in computer work, and many others routinely included one type of computer-related course or project in science, engineering, mathematics, and business curricula." Seymour V. Pollack, "The development of computer science," 1982 [43]

"Wherever there are phenomena, there can be a science to describe and explain those phenomena." Allen Newell, Alan J. Perlis, Herbert A. Simon, "What is computer science," 1967 [40]

In his opening remarks to the Second Symposium on Large-Scale Digital Calculating Machinery at Harvard University in September 1949, Navy Rear Admiral Frederick I. Entwistle remarked, "This science of computation … has grown up from the association of people requiring such machines and their results with other people willing to incorporate themselves into the effort to design and to build such machines" [19, p. 6]. He especially pointed to the ongoing collaboration between the US Navy and Harvard Computation Laboratory as being instrumental for supporting the Navy in its "work in national defense:" "In the installation of computers, the time factor and accuracy of the machine are certainly important. But more important … is the coordination of the university and the military. This is, in itself, a step forward in the university's aims of first teaching the individual and then going further to educate the

© Springer Nature Switzerland AG 2021   121
B. Longo, *Words and Power*, History of Computing,
https://doi.org/10.1007/978-3-030-70373-8_8

country" [19, p. 6]. Entwistle's remarks credited connections between the development of computation technologies and teaching the "science of computation" for building an educated public that would underpin national defense as the United States entered a new Cold War era in which the military was tasked with preventing war as much as preparing for it [19, p. 5]. In the partnership between the university and the military, Entwistle emphasized that the university's primary mission was teaching individuals and, by extension, the citizens of the country, even while the university also participated in technology development.

In his opening remarks at this symposium, Harvard Administrative Vice President Edward Reynolds credited the university's partnership with the US Navy, Air Force, and Atomic Energy Commission, and the generosity of those agencies, for "helping us to broaden the scope of the problems to which [the Mark I computer] has been applied and thus to broaden the field of interest and usefulness of this type of machinery" [44, p. 30]. Despite the fruitfulness of this collaboration, Reynolds remarked, "We feel that rather too much time has been devoted to the development of actual machinery growing out of this research, and have some hope that one of the by-products of this and other meetings may be to stimulate the interest of others in this phase of the application of our research and thus to eliminate the need for this activity on the part of our staff" [45, p. 4]. In other words, Harvard's vice president thought that the building of computers was best left to people in industry, rather than to academics, and he hoped that a computer industry would grow to translate the work of academic research into marketable products. This goal, however, would require trained people to work in such an industry built on what Entwistle called the "science of computation." Reynolds recognized this need, as well: "Increased awareness of the usefulness of these new tools in the field to activities in other branches of science inevitably increases the demand for the already inadequate number of men and women who are educated not only in the theories of design and operation of such machinery but in the understanding of their applicability" [45, p. 4]. Reynolds put the responsibility of preparing people to work in this new industry at the feet of the Harvard faculty members and staff working in their Computation Laboratory: "This emphasizes the other great responsibility of the staff of this Laboratory – meeting their obligations as teachers to provide the instruction required for the training and development of personnel interested in these lines. ... While we are endeavoring to develop support for this program from other sources and to obtain permanent endowment for the Laboratory, the understanding contractual support from these Government sources has been and continues to be invaluable" [45, p. 4]. In these remarks, Reynolds saw the need for a new industry to produce calculating machinery on a larger scale than the one-off approach to building computers that was taking place in 1949, when he could have counted all the existing computers on his ten fingers. He also saw a need for training people to work in this new industry and to lead development of this type of machinery for civilian — as well as military – applications. Reynolds and Entwistle shared this vision of a citizenry that was educated in the science of computation as a foundation for industrial development and national defense.

In his opening remarks at the symposium, Director of the Harvard Computation Laboratory Howard Aiken added his voice to the earlier remarks by Reynolds and

Entwistle on the importance of computer development for industry and national security:

> There is an ever-increasing number of industries interested in constructing computing machines outside the universities. ... On the technical side, machines have been proposed involving automatic computers in connection with air-traffic control, airport control and almost every other manufacturing operation up to and including the automatic factory. But until our universities are able to offer well-rounded programs in numerical methods and the application of computing machinery to prepare men to operate these machines, the success of many of the proposed industrial programs will not be realized. [2, p. 7]

Aiken also agreed with Reynolds and Entwistle on the importance of educating people to develop, build, and operate these automatic computing machines but saw this as a gaping hole in university curricula: "I have often remarked that if all the computing machines under construction were to be completed, there would not be staff enough to operate them. Instruction in computing machinery represents one of the more aggravated aspects of a generally recognized problem in technical education" [2, p. 7]. Like Reynolds, Aiken foresaw that universities would get out of the business of building computers and instead support what would become the computer industry by training people to work in this new industry: "We feel that the further development of mathematical methods and the extended use of computing machines in the various fields represented by speakers here are those points at which levers should be placed to make the greatest possible advance in computer research. Only by completing computing machines and then operating them can the operating experience and experimental results be obtained that are so essential as a point of departure in passing from one design to another" [2, p. 7]. Instead of building one-off computers, Aiken stated that the focus of the Harvard Computation Laboratory would be computer research. "Therefore, at our laboratory we have decided not to undertake the construction of any more large-scale computing machines with the exception of one, which we hope to build for our own use and keep at Harvard" [2, p. 7]. In the future, universities would provide education for people working with computing machines built by companies in a new industry. Many of these universities had developed close ties with military and federal government agencies during World War II. These ties, which were "buttressed by a massive influx of federal dollars," "reflected the important place of higher education in the nation's life and especially the crucial role that universities played in the Cold War struggle with the Soviet Union" [35, p. 7]. In the postwar United States, universities became "a central component of America's national security apparatus" [35, p. 27].

8.1 Compiling the Elements of Computer Science

Despite these important societal needs voiced by Entwistle, Reynolds, and Aiken at the second Harvard symposium in 1949, the necessary elements for building a profession on the science of computation did not yet exist. There were no formal degree programs or textbooks to support such programs. There was not yet a standardized language or established communication channels to facilitate collaboration among people in different locations. But one of these necessary elements – professional associations – was coming into place. The Association for Computing Machinery (ACM) had been established in 1947 and held its first national meeting at the US Army Aberdeen Proving Grounds in December of that year. During their second ACM national meeting at Oak Ridge National Laboratory in April 1949, Mina Rees (Office of Naval Research) and John Mauchly (Remington Rand) suggested to Howard Aiken (Harvard Computation Laboratory) that a Second Symposium on Large-Scale Digital Calculating Machinery be held at Harvard to bring together computer developers from disparate locations so they could share information. The first Harvard symposium in 1947 had 300 participants; the second symposium in 1949 had 700 participants, which "clearly indicated the rapidity with which the field of automatic computation [was] growing" [3, p. v]. These symposia and meetings of the ACM served as starting points for building the professional associations that could develop standards of conduct and expert knowledge for what would become the computer science profession. In 1951, the Institute of Radio Engineers (IRE) established a Professional Group on Electronic Computers, which provided another forum for creating and disseminating information for people working in that fledgling profession. The work of the IRE to develop the 1950 Standards on Electronic Computers: Definition of Terms as a project of their Standards Committee, begun in 1947, also served to help develop a standard terminology for people working on computer technologies across locations. This standardized vocabulary meant that computer developers could share information about their work through participation in professional associations, as well as through face-to-face visits and document sharing based on personal relationships.

In his "Foreword" to the 1951 US National Bureau of Standards Applied Mathematics Division (AMD) publication *Problems for the Numerical Analysis of the Future*, AMD chief John Curtiss noted that a "new computational science, founded partly on the older hand-machine techniques and partly on theories radically new in numerical analysis, is now taking shape at the Institute [for Numerical Analysis at the University of California, Los Angeles] and elsewhere" [16, p. iv]. He foresaw that "skill in the analysis, formulation, and programming of problems will become the controlling factor in the proper use of the computing machines of the future" [16, p. iv]. Although he pointed to the need for what would become a scientific approach to computing, his vision of the future was yet to be fully articulated. Mathematicians in the early 1950s who used numerical analysis to prepare problems for electronic computers considered their work to fall under the discipline of applied mathematics, not a separate discipline called computational science.

Along with a standard terminology and professional associations, another of the necessary components for establishing computer science as a profession was the development of academic programs that would certify a graduate's knowledge about the computer field – what would become the discipline of computer science. As Howard Aiken and Edward Reynolds had both stated in their opening remarks to the 1949 Second Symposium on Large-Scale Digital Calculating Machinery, Harvard University wanted to get out of the computer building business and concentrate on the core mission of the university, which is educating students. But in the absence of a coherent profession, creating an academic discipline for the computer field was difficult. At the same time, in the absence of a discipline, establishing a functioning profession was difficult. People in the computer field needed to break this stalemate in order to create a disciplinary and professional structure for ensuring the sustained development of electronic computing technology and the training of people to operate these machines. Michel Foucault put forward the concept of a discipline as an engine with the power to accomplish such goals within a knowledge economy: "Discipline may be defined neither with an institution nor with an apparatus; it is a type of power, a modality for its exercise, comprising a whole set of instruments, techniques, procedures, levels of application, targets; it is a 'physics' or an 'anatomy' of power, a technology" [24, p. 215]. In this sense, establishing an academic discipline called computer science would give the profession a knowledge technology with which computer people could accomplish their collective professional and societal goals. The discipline would serve as a technology for communicating standardized professional knowledge from person to person in order to prepare a workforce to carry out professional practices within society. Until the profession of computer science had academic programs at prestigious, accredited universities, it would not have enough people trained to design, build, and operate computer systems. Establishing these academic programs would depend on textbooks, which in turn depended on a standardized terminology.

When the Second Symposium on Large-Scale Digital Calculating Machinery was held at Harvard University in 1949, there was no profession called computer science and there were no university programs or textbooks in what would become that field. Yet only 30 years later, the Association for Computing Machinery (ACM) listed 207 US computer science departments "granting bachelor's degrees, 127 granting master's degrees, and 73 offering Ph.D. or D.Sc. degrees," as well as "computer science programs at all levels embedded in 163 mathematics departments, 56 business schools, 29 electrical engineering departments, and 40 other schools or departments" [43, p. vii]. In the Cold War years after World War II, people who worked to design, develop, and operate automatic calculating machines also built the necessary elements to establish a profession and academic discipline that would be called computer science.

In these early postwar years, people developing automatic calculating machines largely worked in isolation from each other, with only a few of "the prominent people" [36, p. 62] participating in professional associations and sharing information among themselves. This period in the development of computer science as a discipline – separate from mathematics, electrical engineering, and physics –resembles what Thomas Kuhn (1970) characterized as a pre-paradigmatic phase before a community of scientists shared enough common concepts to practice "normal science" [33, p. 10]. In this early phase of a developing science, people working in that field need to agree on foundational theoretical concepts to underpin their discipline. Kuhn argued that people in this phase look to related technological developments for these foundational concepts: "Because the crafts are òne readily accessible source of facts that could not have been casually discovered, technology has often played a vital role in the emergence of new sciences" [33, p. 15–16]. In the development of computer science as a discipline, would-be computer scientists looked to the design and building of electronic computing machinery as the source for these early foundational concepts. In this early phase, Kuhn argued that practitioners share their information primarily in books that can be understood by a general readership, such as Edmund Berkeley's (1949) *Giant Brains or Machines that Think* [7]. But as the scientific discipline becomes more organized, concepts become more widely agreed-upon, and terminology becomes more specialized. In other words, people in that field come to a consensus about the foundational principles of their science, that then become the paradigm through which people can carry on "normal science" [33, p. 19–20]. In this phase, practitioners begin to publish their research findings in articles rather than books. In periods of normal science, "textbooks expound the body of accepted theory, illustrate many or all of its successful applications, and compare these applications with exemplary observations and experiments" [33, p. 10]. When a scientific field has gained sufficient theoretical consensus to practice "normal science" and publish "accepted theory" in textbooks, it can then build an academic discipline on these foundational concepts. This theoretical consensus had not yet been reached for people working in the computer field in the 1950s.

In the case of computer science, practitioners worked with competing designs at the end of World War II without a clear determination of which design would become predominant. George Stibitz advocated for the relay switch design he had developed at Bell Laboratories. Jay Forrester and the people at the MIT Servomechanism Laboratory continued working with an analog computer design for military aircraft development until they saw the ENIAC electronic computer during the summer of 1946 when they attended the Moore School Lectures at the University of Pennsylvania. At that time, Presper Eckert and John Mauchly's electronic computer design was the newest among the competing designs, but it was not clear which of the computer designs would become the paradigm upon which a discipline of computer science would be built. In Kuhn's model of scientific development, these three competing computer designs would coexist until "an individual or group first produces a synthesis able to attract most of the next generation's practitioners," at which time "older schools gradually disappear" [33, p. 18]. For computer science, this moment of synthesis occurred when John von Neumann's *First Draft of a Report on the EDVAC* was made available to the participants of the Moore School Lectures in that summer of 1946. Herman Goldstine (1972), the Army's representative to the Ballistics Research Laboratory at the Moore School, later remarked that the *First Draft of a Report on the EDVAC* was "the most important document ever written on computing and computers. … Von Neumann was the first person … who understood explicitly that a computer essentially performed logical functions, and that the electrical aspects were ancillary" [27, p. 191–192]. When von Neumann put forward his new concept that automatic calculating machines had the potential to carry out functions that were more logically complex than simple arithmetic calculations, he introduced a new way of thinking about computers that was based in rhetoric and logic rather than in engineering. His new conceptualization of the computer as a logic machine enabled the building of theoretical principles required for establishing a discipline that would become computer science. When other people in this new field found von Neumann's concepts to be a more persuasive foundation for innovation than earlier computer designs could support, they adopted these electronic computer design principles. This new approach to computer design with von Neumann's logic became the paradigm for the new scientific field.

Kuhn (1970) explained that when a paradigm gains consensus in a field, "there are always some [people] who cling to one or another of the older views, and they are simply read out of the profession, which thereafter ignores their work. The new paradigm implies a new and more rigid definition of the field. Those unwilling or unable to accommodate their work to it must proceed in isolation or attach themselves to some other group" [33, p. 19]. In the case of the development of computer science as a discipline, the debates on terminology within the Institute of Radio Engineers (IRE) Electronic Computers Committee, Subcommittee on Definitions of Electronic Computer Terms illustrate how this group decided to draw a distinction between terms that dealt with electronic computers and those that dealt with analog computers. When this group was tasked in 1952 with revising their glossary of definitions, the subcommittee agreed not to include terms from the original 1951 glossary that dealt with servomechanisms: "[O]ne thing we must consider is a group of terms … which were analog and servomechanical in nature, and some terms which were felt … to be too specialized" [54]. Instead of including analog computer terms in their revised glossary, the subcommittee sent these terms to another IRE committee on servomechanisms, thus implicitly arguing that analog computer design would not be included in the field of computer science. This move to exclude analog computer terminology from their revised glossary of computer terminology reflected a determination that this older, mechanical approach to computer design was not within the field that would become computer science. This older design would not support the logical functions that von Neumann had set out in the *First Draft of a Report on the EDVAC* 6 years earlier [53]. In the intervening years, computer people had recognized that electronic computer designs with von Neumann's logic opened up possibilities for computers that exceeded the capabilities of automatic calculating machines based on mechanical designs. As Morris Rubinoff from the Moore School noted in his 1953 article in *the Proceedings of the IRE* special issue on computers, "The probability of marked improvements in analogue computers is rather low" [47, p. 1262]. Terminology related to these older designs was "read out" of the canon of computer science so that the field could be solidified into a discipline and a profession.

8.2   Establishing Computer Science as an Academic Discipline

In defining a discipline, Michel Foucault (1979) emphasized that the function of a discipline was to enable people to get things done: "'Discipline' ... is a type of power ... an 'anatomy' of power, a technology. And it may be taken over ... by institutions that use it as an essential instrument for a particular end (schools, hospitals)" [24, p. 215]. Pierre Bourdieu (1991) argued that the establishment of a standardized language and an educational discipline was necessary for constituting a community of interest: "In the process which leads to the construction, legitimation and imposition of an official language, the educational system plays a decisive role" [9, p. 48]. Bourdieu further argued that people organized in professional associations – in collaboration with educational institutions – can create a specialized language that confers cultural value to those who can use this specialized language correctly. Through the correct use of this specialized language, groups of professionals can cause a "dispossession" or reordering of social classes, providing opportunities for people to rise in social status: "The fact remains that this dispossession is inseparable from the existence of a body of professionals, objectively invested with the monopoly of the legitimate use of the legitimate language, who produce for their own use a special language predisposed to produce, as a *by-product*, a social function of distinction in the relations between the classes and in the struggles they wage on the terrain of language" [9, p. 59, italics in original]. Creating a standardized terminology for what would become computer science was the foundational "terrain of language" on which people working with early computers waged struggles for disciplinary and professional independence. Looking at a specialized language and a discipline as organizing structures for accomplishing a social goal in a knowledge economy, establishing computer science as an academic discipline was an important step toward organizing and training sufficient numbers of people for a growing computer industry that was critical to US national security in a Cold War world. As a byproduct, professionals in this new field could elevate their social, political, and economic status. To establish these education and training functions, publishing textbooks as "retrospective codifications of dominant professional practices" [37, p. 168] was another necessary step in establishing computer science as an academic discipline. These textbooks would rely on established definitions of terminology that were specialized for this field and practices that were considered to be best practices based on experience in the field. In the early 1950s, these prerequisites for forming an academic discipline were starting to come together, but people working with computers continued to be affiliated with departments of mathematics, electrical engineering, or business in US universities.

By 1954, the need for people to work with computers in industry had become so apparent that The First Conference on Training Personnel for the Computing Machine Field was held at Wayne University in Detroit, Michigan. "The Wayne Computation Laboratory was one of the first large scale computer laboratories in the United States. The Laboratory was organized in 1949 through the Industrial

Mathematics Society (IMS) as a joint effort between the University and local industry," such as automobile manufacturers [55]. In the mid-1950s, university computer laboratories were engaged in research and design activities, application development, and "instruction in computing and programming ... While much of this instruction was informal, intended to support internal users, many universities were quick to recognize an intrinsic educational responsibility to the rapidly growing population involved with computers" [43, p. 26]. "At many institutions ... academic computing centers served as an important catalyst for new interdisciplinary programs in computer science" [4, p. 279]. Thus, university computer laboratories were sites of theoretical research into automatic computing, development of applications for electronic computers in university operations, and instruction for students in courses that would form a basis for computer science curricula.

The 1954 conference at the Wayne University Computation Laboratory was held with cooperation from the Association for Computing Machinery (ACM), the Industrial Mathematics Society, and the Professional Group on Electronic Computer of the Institute of Radio Engineers (IRE). It was organized "with a focus on educating mathematicians and on scientific rather than business applications of computing. Participants in this NSF-funded meeting identified a large but unspecified demand for people highly skilled in computation" [25, p. 13]. It was at this meeting that "Leon W. Cohen, the [NSF] program director for Mathematical Sciences, made the first public announcement of NSF's support for computing infrastructure" [25, p. 13], which was an early institutional recognition of computational studies as a science.

In covering the Wayne University conference for a 1955 issue of *The Accounting Review*, University of California, Los Angeles accounting professor Paul Kircher described the need for the conference in this way: "The Wayne conference was held because present education for the use of the computer is inadequate. ... Skilled personnel for the development of the new systems are scarce. Programs to train more personnel are not adequate to meet the growing demand" [31, p. 725]. In his coverage of the conference for *The American Mathematical Monthly*, mathematics professor at the University of Illinois Franz Hohn echoed Kircher's assessment: "That such a conference was opportune hardly needs emphasis, for the shortage of competent candidates for positions in the computer field is becoming increasingly critical as the demand for computers grows. Not too widely recognized is the fact that this is a problem of importance to the entire mathematical fraternity" [29, p. 9]. After considering the educational roles that businesses could play in training people to work in the computer field, Hohn stated, "Clearly, the greatest responsibility for meeting this manpower need falls on the educational institutions" [29, p. 11]. Yet mathematicians in educational institutions were largely uninterested in the computing field in 1954: "Considerable regret was expressed by a number of speakers that many mathematicians view the whole science of computation as being somewhat beneath their consideration. Indeed, this attitude was felt to have constituted a serious impediment to progress" [29, p. 12]. In looking forward to consequences of mathematicians' disinterest in the growing field of automatic computing, Hohn predicted a future that ultimately came to pass: "Whether or not we as *mathematicians* exercise any significant influence thereon depends on the extent to which we are willing to cooperate in the education of workers in this field. If we are unwilling to recognize the rising importance of applied mathematics and computation, much of our present responsibility will of necessity be taken over by other departments of our universities and by industrial training programs" [29, p. 15, italics in original]. As Hohn foretold, the reluctance of university mathematics departments to incorporate studies of electronic computing into their curricula created conflicts as growth in the need for these courses outpaced university department structures. These discussions at universities played out within a larger societal context where "demands for computing education for all ... started to become louder. The more important a role computing started to play in work life, in society, and in people's lives, the stronger the feeling it needs to be taught in schools at an early age" [51, p. 4]. Computers were on the way to becoming ubiquitous in people's lives, but education programs were not keeping up with these societal changes.

At the 1954 Wayne University conference Howard Aiken, director of the Harvard University Computation Laboratory, noted the widespread integration of computers into scientific and general applications: "The salient point is that computing machines as functional installations are showing themselves to be of broad versatility, cutting a wide swath across traditional lines of scientific and industrial activity" [31, p. 726]. In an editorial for the *Proceedings of the IRE* special issue on computers, Werner Buchholz (IBM) further summarized the state of the computing field in 1953: "The urgent expansion of the electronic computer industry can be gauged by the many personnel advertisements appearing in the professional journals and the daily newspapers. The current situation is comparable to the rapid development of radar during World War II. Another sign of growth is the development of the IRE Professional Group on Electronic Computers: it has grown in just two years to be the third largest Professional Group in the IRE, having 2,000 members" [11, p. 1220]. Although Buchholtz acknowledged the role of earlier computer design – such as the analog Bush Differential Analyzer at MIT, punched card machines like those marketed at IBM, and the Harvard Mark I/IBM Automatic Sequence Controlled Calculator – he credited the growth of the computer industry to the development of electronic computing machines:

> Still, the present growth of the computer industry did not start until the results of the enormous development of electronic technology during World War II were brought into the field. It is interesting to note that many computer projects started around the nucleus of wartime radar experts. Electronics not only provided the technological means for greatly increased speed and capacity, and thereby enhanced the usefulness of computers many times, but the availability of cheap, mass produced components and of engineers trained to use them made it possible to experiment on a greater scale and at a lower capital investment than ever before." [11, p. 1220]

Buchholtz credited experiences gained in the years between World War II and 1953 as having a "maturing effect of several years of actual operation" on the computer industry, calling it a "period of sober adjustment" [11, p. 1221]. Despite any setbacks in production, staffing, and operations, the computer industry continued to grow, and electronic computers were "in commercial quantity production" [11,

p. 1221]. In summing up the state of computer production and operation in 1953, Buchholtz stated, "Computers have become indispensable for engineering calculations in defense industries, particularly in the aircraft industry. Even more are being built for accounting applications to cope with the problems of an economy of ever-growing complexity. Thus electronic computing may soon affect the average person as much, if not as obviously, as radio and television" [11, p. 1221].

Despite the growing importance of electronic computers for national defense and economic growth, even people working in the computer field – or people who wanted to work in the field – were not necessarily trained for this work. Buchholtz noted in the 1953 *Proceedings of the IRE* special issue on computers that "many readers may not be familiar with the technical language used by the computer engineer, particularly in the field of digital computing" [12, p. 1223]. To address this need for educating engineers about electronic computing, Buchholtz asked Arthur Samuel from the IBM Laboratory to write an article on terminology for the IRE special issue. Samuel stated his purpose in writing the article to give "the non-specialist reader a feeling that he [or she] has an understanding of the logical principles on which digital computers are constructed and that he [or she] is beginning to be acquainted with the specialized nomenclature which beclouds the issue" [48, p. 1230]. Samuel encouraged people who were interested in digital computers to pursue this interest despite their unfamiliarity with the terminology and principles of what he called computer engineering: "Regardless of what the reader may conclude regarding the long-range future of digital computers, the scientifically trained individual who is mildly interested in these devices and who does not follow up on this interest is missing some of the more exciting technical experiences of the present time" [48, p. 1230]. As Brent Jesiek (2013) explained in his delineation of the term "computer engineer" during the mid-1940s to the mid-1950s, the use of this term by the IRE to describe people working with digital computers was an extension earlier naming conventions for new technologies: "'[C]omputer engineering' had much in common with other appellations referencing specific domains of technology, including 'radio engineering,' 'broadcast engineering,' and 'power engineering'" [30, p. 13]. Jesiek noted the importance of these naming conventions within a scientific knowledge economy: "Such titles endowed engineers to swiftly claim jurisdiction over large swaths of technology and technical expertise, and use the 'engineering' moniker implied suitable disciplinary and professional stature and infrastructures" [30, p. 13].

Although claiming the name of computer engineer might have provided a veneer of professionalism, Nathan Ensmenger (2001) described the situation for computer people in the mid-twentieth century this way: "In the early 1950s, the disciplines that we know today as computer science and software engineering existed only as a loose association of institutions, individuals, and techniques. Although computers were increasingly used in this period as instruments of scientific production, their status as legitimate objects of scientific study and professional scrutiny has not yet been established" [18, p. 56]. In looking more closely at the state of computer science as a distinct profession in the mid-1950s, Ensmenger concluded that "computing had managed to acquire many trappings of a profession: research laboratories

and institutes, professional conferences, professional societies, and technical journals. ... But the existence of professional institutions did not necessarily translate
readily into widely recognized professional status" [18, p. 56]. The problem for the
computing field, however, was that it did not yet have all the elements of a suitable
disciplinary or professional stature. In particular, it did not yet have an academic
discipline to train people in a field called computer engineering.

Louis Fein's work as a consultant Stanford University the 1950s is illustrative of
the situation that computer people faced in universities at that time. From 1948 to
1951, Fein was chief engineer at Raytheon Manufacturing Company in Waltham,
Massachusetts, where he worked on the Raytheon digital automatic computer
(RAYDAC) along with Richard Bloch and Robert Campbell [21, p. 3; 8, p. 20]. In
1952, the RAYDAC was accepted for installation at the US Naval Air Missile Test
Center at Point Mugu in Southern California, where it would be used "in support of
the Lark missile program" [38, p. 48] for "real-time telemetry data reduction" [49,
p. 38]. Raytheon sent Fein and other engineers across the country from Massachusetts
to California in order to install and operate the computer for the Navy, where it was
operational until 1955. Paul Ceruzzi (1989) recounted that the RAYDAC had "a
number of advanced design features. It used a sophisticated method of storing data
on magnetic tape. Its designers also pioneered a method of error checking ... called
parity checking ... But RAYDAC was simply not fast enough" [14, p. 58].
Nevertheless, the RAYDAC "taught personnel at [the Naval Test Center] a great
deal about real-time data handling and digital processing" [48, p. 38]. "It advanced
the state of the art of both computer technology and missile tracking. It helped tip
the balance away from manned bombers toward long-range ballistic missiles as the
primary strategic weapon of the United States" [14, p. 58].

When Fein moved to Southern California in early 1954, he and the other
Raytheon staff started "the first computing center on the west coast" [20, p. 3] at the
Naval Testing Center at Point Mugu. In August 1955, Fein left the RAYDAC project
and decided that he would "write, consult, and teach perhaps" [20, p. 3]. By the end
of that month, he was "consulting for five or six computer outfits" [21, p. 3], including the Stanford Research Institute which was building the Electronic Recording
Machine, Accounting ERMA) computer for the Bank of America in Menlo Park,
California. Fein made his home in nearby Palo Alto, where he became acquainted
with people at Stanford University. By the fall of 1956, Fein had been hired by
Albert Bowker in the Department of Statistics at Stanford to investigate the "question of whether or not computer science ... was a discipline worthy of study by the
university [which] was not yet settled" [21, p. 4]. The purpose of his study was
threefold:

1) To study and evaluate the organization, curriculum, research program, computing equipment,
   financing and facilities of universities in the United States having computer and/or data processing and/or related programs.
2) To identify those fields of study (some already accepted and identified as disciplines as well as
   those not yet so designated) that are unambiguously part of the computer and data processing
   fields and those closely related fields that might legitimately be part of a university program.

3) To appraise the role of the universities in these fields and to determine what universities might do to build distinguished programs in these fields. [20, p. 119]

Fein began his year-long study by first determining more of the details of what was needed for a comprehensive curriculum to train people to work with computers. In answering the fundamental question "What makes a discipline worthy of pursuit at a university" [34, p. 5], he came up with six characteristics:

1) The terminology has been established, a glossary of terms exists.
2) Workers in the field do nonroutine intellectual work.
3) The field has sometimes been axiomatized.
4) The field is open, *i.e.*, problems are self-regenerating.
5) There is an established body of literature, textbooks, sometimes treatises … and professional journals.
6) University courses, sometimes departments … are devoted to the field. [20, p. 123]

With these characteristics in mind, Fein felt that he could develop a curriculum for a new discipline called computer science that reflected postwar US culture, with its "increasingly large and complex problems" that required "new techniques" and training people in "new fields" that were "guided by rationalistic and scientific rules of evidence" [20, p. 120].

Fein saw this new social complexity as a result of the overlapping activities among universities, government, and business sectors that had been praised by Truman in 1945 for rapid development of technologies to win World War II [52]. But this blurring of operational boundaries also led to the need for rational and scientific approaches, such as information processing and mathematical modeling, to be incorporated into industry, business, and government. The success of these scientific approaches would rely on the ability of trained people working with computers to process large amounts of data. Fein found, though, that "each of these three important segments of the community has been unprepared by virtue of its traditional organization, philosophy, responsibilities, and procedures to incorporate and cope with these new situations … Thus, the government has set up RAND Corporation(s) for research and project work; it has set up and supported institutes at universities for research and project work; it has indirectly supported development … [in] these fields as byproducts of government contracts to industry" [20, p. 120]. In addition to government agencies being involved in research and development, businesses such as IBM were involved in educating people to design, manufacture, and operate automatic computing machines. This left "scholars and practitioners in these new fields … uncertain both as to the nature and structure of the fields and their relation to each other" [20, p. 120]. Fein suggested that, within universities, the field of "computer, data processing, and closely related fields (let us call them the 'computer sciences') … may well select as their role" the following traditional activities that could be applied to a new discipline [20, p. 120]:

1. Training of professionals in these fields of "computer sciences" of interest and competence in the university.
2. Training scholars in these fields.
3. Doing exploratory research in these fields.
4. Developing the subject fields into new disciplines.

Fein recommended that these four activities form the core mission of a Graduate School of Computer Sciences within any university willing to consider and adopt his recommendations. The focus of faculty and students in such a discipline would be to develop "a competent theory of computing machines, a competent theory of models, and a competent theory relating the two" [20, p. 126].

When Louis Fein put forward his proposal for a Graduate School of Computer Sciences in the mid-1950s, the field of automatic computing was on its way to forming a discipline, but it did not yet have that status. People in the Institute of Radio Engineers (IRE), Association for Computing Machinery (ACM), and private businesses were establishing a standardized terminology and a body of professional literature. But fundamental axioms for the field and textbooks to formalize disciplinary knowledge were not yet developed. Knowledge about computers was being made in engineering laboratories, with interdisciplinary teams working largely with military funding and business partners to build one-off machines. In order to build machines that could use standardized, mass-produced "computer modules," as Fein had developed with Raytheon's RAYDAC digital computer at the Naval Air Missile Test Center at Point Mugu, California in 1955 [21, p. 3], a larger workforce of people trained to work with computers was needed. In his 1959 report on research done on the feasibility of creating a Graduate School to teach about computers at Stanford University, Fein proposed that a field called "computer sciences" be created to include "computers, data processing, and closely related fields" [20, p. 123]. In that same year, Roy Nutt left IBM and founded Computer Sciences Corporation with Fletcher Jones in Segundo, California, where they developed programming languages and systems software. The idea that computers could be studied as a science was in the zeitgeist; it was taking shape. But there was not yet a coherent curriculum to formalize that study as a discipline.

In 1956, "well over a dozen American universities had computation laboratories equipped with electronic digital computers … [T]here was great diversity in people's perception of the nature and extent of the educational needs" [42, p. 26]. Some schools offered computer courses as part of mathematics or engineering curricula, but the computer laboratory was the center for training students for computer-related careers in business and industry. Businesses, such as IBM, became interested in partnering with universities to help train workers for this growing industry. Government agencies supported these efforts through grants to university computing laboratories. At the same time, computer education continued to be offered through seminars and specialty training, as was offered at the Moore School summer lectures in 1946 on "Theory and Techniques for Design of Electronic Digital Computers," sponsored by the US Army Ordnance Department and the US Office of Naval Research. This early training for 28 participants focused largely on the construction of an electronic computer in the ENIAC model.

IBM also offered training in computer sales as early as 1916 when it graduated its first class of 20 men [5]. In 1932, IBM's educational programs expanded to include computer training through its Education Department, which was formally established by Thomas Watson "to manage the company's many educational activities for employees and customers" [6]. In their Schoolhouse built in 1933, IBM provided formal engineering education for its employees, replacing the company's earlier apprenticeship model of education. Watson, who notably said, "A businessman must be a teacher first," saw the educational programs at IBM as "a business tool for growing his company" [6]. In 1945, IBM partnered with Columbia University in New York City to establish the Watson Lab there for offering computer research and development to people outside IBM. The news release announcing the opening of the lab stated its purpose: "The research and instructional resources of the laboratory will be made available to scientists, universities, and research organizations in this country and abroad. … [T]he laboratory is designed not only to increase the already notable contribution of high efficiency calculating machines to the war effort, but by a broad interest in the computational problems of all branches of the physical and social sciences to strengthen the scientific and educational foundations of our national security and the welfare and peace of the world" [10, p. 13; 38, p. 129]. Columbia faculty member Wallace Eckert and IBM staff members taught courses through the Watson Lab on topics such as mathematics, physics, and astronomy. From its inception, the lab had as its "major mission the exploration of the use of applied mathematics and mechanical calculation to solve scientific problems of all kinds. Beyond that, it was to assist visiting scientists and others in the mastery of machine methods and techniques, design new machines, and instruct students in computational science" [10, p. 13]. This emphasis on scientific computation was strengthened at the end of the war when lab director Wallace Eckert recruited specialists in applied mathematics and computational theory to work in the Pure Science Department at the Watson Lab. In 1947 lab staff instructor Eric Hankam began teaching the Watson Laboratory Three-Week Course on Computing, which was offered to people working with computers, as well as to "high school mathematics and science teachers and to high school students in the New York metropolitan area" [11, p. 13]. The course was taught 11 times each year until 1957, when instruction was moved to IBM education centers around the United States. Nearly 1,600 people from over 20 countries participated in these IBM computing courses offered at the Watson Lab [11, p. 13].

IBM began offering Scientific Computation Forums in 1940 as another opportunity for people to discuss methods for solving scientific problems, originally using IBM punched card equipment. In 1948, the Forum changed focus: "Earlier meetings in this series … were devoted largely to statistical procedures. In the 1948 Forum, for the first time, an attempt was made to cover many of the fields in which large-scale computing methods have proved important … in fields as diverse as aerodynamics and physical chemistry" [28, p. 3]. These Scientific Computation Forums were held into the 1950s, with participants from IBM, aircraft industries, computer industry manufacturers, military installations, and universities. The need for people to work in the growing computer field was outstripping the number of people who were trained for this work. The training that IBM offered addressed this manpower need to some degree, while also conditioning people to adopt IBM equipment for their computing needs.

The connection between IBM and education grew stronger through a program for supplying their Model 650 computers to universities with the agreement that the universities would teach courses in data processing and numerical analysis using the machines [20, p. 121]. Computer scientist and Stanford University professor Donald Knuth (1972) credited IBM with a significant impact on shaping university computer curricula: "Apparently computer courses got started in universities largely because IBM donated about 100 'free' computers during the 1950s, with the stipulation that programming courses must be taught. This strategy made it possible for computing to get its foot in the academic door" [32, p. 722]. By 1958, Louis Fein estimated that 65 IBM 650s were installed in universities around the United States, compared to 12 Bendix G-15 machines, 7 Burroughs 205 machines, and 4 Sperry Rand Univac 1 machines [20, p. 126]. By far, IBM was outpacing the competition in universities that were interested in buying computers rather than building them. The standardization of IBM machines and their library of reusable programming modules provided a basis for developing courses that could train people to work with, develop, and sell these mass-produced electronic computers.

By 1960, "about 200 colleges and universities were equipped with digital computers, and the general infusion of computer usage into the educational process was well established" [43, p. 27]. Three years earlier, the National Science Foundation (NSF) began "providing support for training experienced mathematicians on the faculties of colleges and universities to prepare them to develop courses of instruction in the use and operation of modern computing machines" [25, p. 13]. The stage was set for establishing computer science as a profession. Terminology in this field was being standardized through the work of the IRE, ACM, *Computers and Automation*, and internal glossaries of terms developed at businesses such as Sperry Rand and IBM. Since 1947, the Association for Computing Machinery (ACM) served as a professional association devoted only to the computing field, while the Institute of Radio Engineers (IRE) and American Institute of Electrical Engineers (AIEE) established separate professional groups for electronic computing. These associations published journals to share knowledge among people in this growing field, as well as to encourage new research. They also held regular meetings where people in the field could learn about the latest developments in electronic computing and opportunities for career advancement. The last professionalizing component that was missing was a recognized credentialing program, but when computer science departments were established at universities, this missing piece was provided. Computer science was becoming a profession.

8.3   Computer Science Stands Alone

The name computer science continued to be contested throughout the 1960s, as this discipline distinguished itself from mathematics. In 1957, when computer education consultant Louis Fein presented the results of his year-long study on the state of computing science to Al Bowker, statistics professor in the Mathematics Department at Stanford University, Fein recommended that the university create a Computer Science Department with graduate-level coursework in this field. He later recalled that there was "very, very strong opposition in the mathematics department" from Bowker, department chair John Herriot, and George Forsythe, who worked with the SWAC electronic computer at the Institute for Numerical Analysis at UCLA and at that time was a consultant to Herriot on this topic. "So the opposition came from insiders not outsiders" [21, p. 11]. This initial disagreement stemmed from the fact that what was then called scientific computation was taught most often through mathematics departments and published most often in mathematics journals. People in universities did not consider scientific computation to have a distinct body of knowledge and expertise, even though it had been taught through IBM-sponsored courses around the United States. Fein's proposal was initially met with disapproval among Stanford administrators and faculty members. It was not until this idea gained institutional backing that computer science could become its own separate discipline.

One source of institutional support was the National Science Foundation (NSF), which lent credibility to the idea of the study of computing as a science when it recognized projects in that field as eligible for funding in 1957. In her study of ACM's contributions to the creation of computer science as a discipline, Janet Abbate (2017) pointed to the influence of Philip M. Morse, director of MIT's Operations Research Center, in persuading the NSF to recognize this new discipline: "Morse had founded MIT's Computation Center in 1956 with a donated IBM 704 and had persuaded NSF to support the facility as a shared computer center for forty colleges in the region" [1, p. 37]. IBM had made an expensive investment in the Massachusetts Institute of Technology (MIT) lab through the donation of its 704 model machine, which was the newer and more powerful model of the early 701, also known as the IBM Defense Calculator. MIT and IBM staff worked at the MIT lab to calculate satellite orbits and other astronomical problems.

In June 1960, Morse chaired a Conference of University Computing Center Directors, supported by the American Mathematical Society and funded by the NSF. In his report on this conference, Morse stated, "Computer science is a new scientific field ... This was the first conference to discuss in detail curricula related to computer science" [39, p. 520]. He also reported the "agreed-on conclusions" of "a majority of the directors of computing centers in this country," which included this call for creating separate computer science departments in universities: "The problems associated with exploiting fully the potentialities of present and projected computers are difficult and intellectually challenging ... Experts in the field of computing science are in very short supply; the shortage will remain acute until more colleges train more of them. ... Knowledge already gained justifies the creation of several undergraduate and graduate courses of instruction and the granting of degrees for studies in computer science" [39, p. 520]. Morse concluded, "Computer science is a discipline in its own right" and encouraged conference participants to continue sharing information on computer science curricula. The headquarters of the American Mathematical Society would provide staff to coordinate these curricula clearinghouse activities, thus asserting its disciplinary oversight of this new effort [39, p. 521].

In 1957, George Forsythe joined the faculty of Stanford University as a professor in its Mathematics Department. In 1961, Forsythe established the Division of Computer Science within that Mathematics Department to study topics such as programming, data processing, game theory, information theory, and computer linguistics [42, p. 51]. In that same year, he gave a talk at Brown University on "Educational Implications of the Computer Revolution" in which he provided a rationale for establishing a separate discipline for computer science: "Enough is known already of the diverse applications of computing for us to recognize the birth of a coherent body of technique, which I call *computer science*. ... We are extremely short of talented people in this field, and so we need departments, curricula, and research and degree programs in computer science. ... Universities must respond [to the computer revolution] with far-reaching changes in the educational structure" [32, p. 722; italics in original]. In January 1965, Stanford established a separate Computer Science Department within its School of Humanities and Sciences [23, p. 6]. By the spring of that year, Stanford mathematics professor and ACM President George Forsythe reported that he was "swamped with Stanford problems, mostly associated with the growth of computer education" [22, p. 143]. The number of students who wanted to take qualifying examinations for a Ph.D. in Computer Science was overwhelming the department faculty.

In October 1962, Purdue University established the first Computer Science Department in the United States with Samuel Conte as its department head. The department had five faculty members teaching "enough graduate courses for the M.S. and Ph.D. degrees and an undergraduate service course in programming" [46]. The department was located in the Division of Mathematical Sciences, along with the Departments of Mathematics and Statistics. A large number of US universities subsequently adopted the name *computer science* for their departments and programs, "while institutions in many other countries adopted variants of 'informatics'" for their programs [50, p. 146]. In the early 1960s, the naming of this new discipline was still contested. Influential computer programmer Edsger Dijkstra (1986) observed that these early computer science departments "predated computer science itself" [17, p. 3]. In addition to a contested name for the discipline, the legitimate topics of study were not settled either. Rather than working with recognizable, disciplinary curricula, Dijkstra described these early departments as being a hodge-podge of available courses: "[T]hey were no more than ill-considered cocktails of presumably computer-related topics that happened to be available on campus, e.g. some electronics, some numerical analysis, some statistics and economics, some business administration ... Forging coherence was one of the first tasks for those that were responsible for carving a niche in which a budding computing science would be viable" [17, p. 4; 41, p. 73]. Bringing together concepts and terminologies from a variety of disciplines would be necessary before computer science could develop paradigmatic knowledge.

At the Purdue University Computer Science Department, the "undergraduate program evolved initially from very sparse courses offerings in programming to a computer science option in the mathematics department to a separate B.S. degree approved in 1967. [Department head] Conte was an active member of the Association for Computing Machinery committee that recommended the model B.S. degree program known as Curriculum `68" [46]. Janet Abbate (2017) described this challenge for computer scientists in the 1960s: "But since computer science did not fit the canonical model of science – having neither a codified body of theory nor a domain of the natural world associated with it – its advocates were forced to explain and justify their claims to scientific identity" [1, p. 36]. One step toward claiming this identity was to separate computer science from mathematics. If mathematicians after the 1954 Conference for Training Personnel for the Computing Machine Field at Wayne University were not overly interested in embracing computer science, as University of Illinois mathematics professor Franz Hohn (1955) noted [29], people working in the computer field were equally reluctant to embrace their mathematics colleagues. Matti Tedre (2015) described the disciplinary breakup: "But if many computer scientists were wary of the abstractness of mathematics, many abstractly oriented mathematicians lacked respect for the pragmatic orientation of computer, too. The separation of computing and mathematics was not just a process of growing apart; many computer scientists were actively divorcing their field from mathematics" [50, p, 34]. This disciplinary separation was necessary for computer science to establish itself as a legitimate academic field of study and a profession.

In 1963, the ACM established a nine-member Curriculum Committee on Computer Science (C3S), chaired by William F. Atchison [18] from Georgia Institute of Technology, to study curricula in universities offering degrees in this new discipline, in order to "give some guidance to such schools and … serve as a coordinating force for the various diverse efforts" [15, p. 544]. This professional organization asserted that computer science (CS) had "become a distinct field of study" in its own right, as evidenced by its recognition from the US National Academy of Sciences. Yet the rapid growth of this field required "considerable modification in the educational offerings in our colleges and universities" [15, p. 543]. In their initial 1965 recommendations for a baccalaureate CS curriculum, the C3S found that this new discipline was "concerned with *information* in much the same sense that physics is concerned with energy" [15, p. 544; italics in original]. This included "all forms of information – numeric, alphabetic, pictorial, verbal, tactile, olfactory, results of experimental measurement, etc. … discovering the pragmatic means by which information can be transformed to model and analyze the information transformations in the real world" [15, p. 544]. This and subsequent curriculum work done by the ACM served to define the body of knowledge and expertise that would be claimed by the new profession called computer science. Looking forward, George Forsythe (1965) predicted that the "now common recognition of our field as a separate one will bring a great deal of new and important research, with concomitant publication, and there will be a large byproduct of valuable applications to all fields of technology" [22, p. 143]. Disagreements about whether computers were a tool [13] or a distinct theoretical field would continue throughout the decade. But by the early 1960s, computer science had all the elements – including a standardized terminology for information sharing – to become a profession in its own right.

In addition to a disciplinary separation from mathematics, computer scientists also had to establish themselves as having an academic field of study and application that was independent from industry and the capitalist marketplace. Establishing a standardized disciplinary nomenclature was an early step in this process, as were establishing professional associations and journals. Edsger Dijkstra (1986) described this process of professionalization as computer science claimed its independence from industry:

> In summary, the niche was carved, away from specific applications and away from specific machines. And, as time went on, in the same vein away from specific programming languages and operating systems. In the beginning this was done in order to protect the budding science from the volatility of the products from the market place, and when some of these products turned into de facto standards it was done to protect the flourishing science from the stagnation in the market place. Independent of the question whether to regret or applaud this separation, I want you to understand that for the emergence of computing science as a viable discipline this separation was and still is a condition sine quo non. [17, p. 4]

It might have been possible, as Dijkstra described, for computer science largely to separate its academic curricula from market forces, such as the influence of IBM's donated computers on early university computer services laboratories and courses. But Dijkstra further suggested why computer science will necessarily be a product of its Cold War history: "By an unfortunate accident of history, computing emerged during just those decades of unbounded faith in the wholesomeness and power of science and technology. Whereas the more established sciences had their roots and traditions soberer times, we embarked on computing with our expectations unbridled. From a historical perspective, the naïve optimism is quite understandable" [17, p. 3]. The culture of unbridled optimism in science and technology that gave birth to electronic computers continues to imbue their progeny and the people who engage them with the Cold War values of their inception. These values are carried forward through the language we use to describe computers, their superhuman intelligence, and the relations between humans and computers that we think are (im)possible.

References

1. Abbate, Janet. 2017. From handmaiden to "proper intellectual discipline": Creating a scientific identity for computer science in 1960s America. In *Communities of Computing: Computer Science and Society in the ACM*, ed. Thomas J. Misa, 25–46. San Rafael: Morgan & Claypool Press – ACM.
2. Aiken, Howard. 1949, September 13. Opening address. *Proceedings of a second symposium on large-scale digital calculating machinery*. The Annals of the Computation Laboratory of Harvard University, vol. XXVI. 1951. Cambridge, MA: Harvard University Press: 7–8.
3. ———. 1950, May. Preface. *Proceedings of a second symposium on large-scale digital calculating machinery*. The Annals of the Computation Laboratory of Harvard University, vol. XXVI. 1951. Cambridge, MA: Harvard University Press: v–vi.
4. Akera, Atsushi. 2007. *Calculating a natural world: Scientists, engineers, and computers during the rise of the U.S. Cold War research*. Cambridge, MA: MIT Press.

5. Anonymous. No date. Endicott schoolhouse. IBM Archives. https://www.ibm.com/ibm/history/exhibits/vintage/vintage_4506VV2034.html. Accessed 20 Feb 2021.

6. ———. 2011. A commitment to employee education. IBM 100. https://www.ibm.com/ibm/history/ibm100/us/en/icons/employeeedu/. Accessed 20 Feb 2021.

7. Berkeley, Edmund C. 1949. *Giant brains or machines that think*. New York: Wiley.

8. Bloch, Richard M. 1984, February 22. Oral history interview with Richard M. Bloch. Interviewed by William Aspray. Charles Babbage Institute OH 66. https://conservancy.umn.edu/handle/11299/107123. Accessed 15 Mar 2021.

9. Bourdieu, Pierre. 1991. *Language and symbolic power*. Trans. Gino Raymond and Matthew Adamson. Cambridge, MA: Harvard University Press.

10. Brennan, Jean Ford. 1971. *The IBM Watson Laboratory at Columbia University: A history*. New York: International Business Machines Corporation. http://www.columbia.edu/cu/computinghistory/brennan/index.html#[-13-. Accessed 14 Nov 2020.

11. Buchholtz, Werner. 1953, October. The computer issue. *Proceedings of the I.R.E* 41.10: 1220–1222.

12. ———. 1953, October. Editor's remarks. *Proceedings of the I.R.E.* 41 (10): 1223.

13. Carlson, Jack W. 1966, March. Letter to the editor: On determining C.S. education programs. *Communications of the ACM* 9.3: 135.

14. Ceruzzi, Paul E. 1989. *Beyond the limits: Flight enters the computer age*. Cambridge, MA: MIT Press.

15. Conte, Samuel D., et al. 1965, September. An undergraduate program in computer science – Preliminary recommendations. *Communications of the ACM* 8 (9): 543–552. https://doi.org/10.1145/365559.366069. Accessed 13 Nov 2020.

16. Curtiss, John. 1951, June 29. Foreword. *Problems for the numerical analysis of the future: Papers presented at the Symposia on Modern Calculating Machinery and Numerical Methods, 29–30 July 1948*. Washington, DC: National Bureau of Standards, Applied Mathematics Series 15: iv.

17. Dijkstra, Edsger. 1986. Science fiction and science reality in computing. University of Texas, Austin Libraries, Edsger W. Dijkstra archives. Document EWD952.html. Accessed 1 May 2021.

18. Ensmenger, Nathan L. 2001. The "question of professionalism" in the computer fields. *IEEE Annals of the History of Computing* 23 (4): 56–74.

19. Entwistle, Frederick I. 1949, September 13. Opening address. *Proceedings of a second symposium on large-scale digital calculating machinery*. The Annals of the Computation Laboratory of Harvard University, vol. XXVI. 1951. Cambridge, MA: Harvard University Press: 5–6.

20. Fein, Louis. 1959. The role of the university in computers, data processing, and related fields. Papers presented at the 3–5 March 1959 Western Joint Computer Conference: 119–126. https://doi.org/10.1145/1457838.1457859. Accessed 14 Nov 2020.

21. ———. 1979, May 9. Oral history interview with Louis Fein. Interviewed by Pamela McCorduck. Charles Babbage Institute OH 15. https://conservancy.umn.edu/handle/11299/107284. Accessed 15 Mar 2021.

22. Forsythe, George E. 1965, March. President's letter to the ACM membership: Why ACM? *Communications of the ACM* 8.3: 143-144. https://doi.org/10.1145/363791.363792. Accessed 13 Nov 2020.

23. ———. 1965, June 25. *Stanford University's program in computer science: Technical report CS26*. Palo Alto: Stanford University Computer Science Department.

24. Foucault, Michel. 1977. *Discipline and punish: The birth of the Prison*. Trans. Alan Sheridan. New York: Vintage Books. 1979.

25. Freeman, Peter A., W. Richards Adrion, and William Aspray. 2019. *Computing and the National Science Foundation, 1950–2016: Building a foundation for modern computing*. San Rafael: Morgan & Claypool Press – ACM.

26. Goldstine, Herman. 1953. Some experience in coding and programing with the Institute computer. *Proceedings of a Symposium on Large Scale Digital Computing Machinery*. Argonne National Laboratory, August 3–5: 273–278.

27. Goldstine, Herman H. 1972. *The computer from Pascal to von Neumann*. Princeton: Princeton University Press.

28. Grosch, Herbert R.J. 1950. Foreword. In *Proceedings: Scientific computation forum, 1948*. New York: International Business Machines Corporation.

29. Hohn, Franz. 1955. The First conference on training personnel for the computing machine field. *The American Mathematical Monthly* 62 (1): 8–15.

30. Jesiek, Brent K. 2013, July–September. The origins and early history of computer engineering in the United States. *IEEE Annals of the History of Computing* 35 (3): 6–18.

31. Kircher, Paul. *The Accounting Review* 30, no. 4 (1955): 725-26. http://www.jstor.org/stable/241074. Accessed 26 Apr 2021.

32. Knuth, Donald E. August 1972. George Forsythe and the development of computer science. *Communications of the ACM* 15 (8): 721–726.

33. Kuhn, Thomas S. 1970. *The structure of scientific revolutions*. 2nd ed. Chicago: University of Chicago Press.

34. Lee, J.A.N. 1995. William Atchison. In *Computer pioneers*. Los Alamitos: IEEE Computer Society Press. https://history.computer.org/pioneers/atchison.html. Accessed 14 Nov 2020.

35. Levin, Matthew. 2013. *Cold War university: Madison and the new left in the Sixties*. Madison: The University of Wisconsin Press.

36. Longo, Bernadette. 2015. *Edmund Berkeley and the social responsibility of computer professionals*. San Rafael: Morgan & Claypool Press – ACM.

37. ———. 2000. *Spurious coin: A history of science, management, and technical writing*. Albany: State University of New York Press.

38. McMurran, Marshall W. 2008. *Achieving accuracy: A legacy of computers and missiles*. Bloomington: Xlibris Corporation.

39. Morse, Philip M. 1960, October. Report on a conference of university computing center directors, 2–4 June 1960. *Communications of the ACM* 3 (10): 519–521. https://doi.org/10.1145/367415.993448. Accessed 14 Nov 2020.

40. Newell, Allen, Alan J. Perlis, and Herbert A. Simon. 1967, September 22. Letter to the editor: What is computer science. *Science* 157: 1373–1374.

41. Nikivincze, Irina. Solving a career equation: The first doctoral women in computer science. In *Communities of computing: Computer science and society in the ACM*, ed. Thomas J. Misa, 71–90. San Rafael: Morgan & Claypool Press – ACM.

42. November, Joseph. 2017. George Forsythe and the creation of computer science as we know it. In *Communities of computing: Computer science and society in the ACM*, ed. Thomas J. Misa, 47–70. San Rafael: Morgan & Claypool Press – ACM.

43. Pollack, Seymour V. 1982. The development of computer science. In *Studies in computer science*, ed. S.V. Pollack, vol. 22, 1–51. Washington, DC: The Mathematical Association of America Press.

44. Pugh, Emerson W. 1995. *Building IBM: Shaping an industry and its technology*. Cambridge, MA: MIT Press.

45. Reynolds, Edward. 1949, September 13. Opening address. In *Proceedings of a second symposium on large-scale digital calculating machinery*. The Annals of the Computation Laboratory of Harvard University, vol. XXVI. 1951. Cambridge, MA: Harvard University Press: 3–4.

46. Rice, John R. and Saul Rosen. 2017, March 15. History of the Computer Science Department. https://www.cs.purdue.edu/history/. Accessed 1 May 2021.

47. Rubinoff, Morris. 1953, October. Analogue vs. digital computers – A comparison. *Proceedings of the I.R.E.* 41.10: 1254–1262.

48. Samuel, Arthur L. 1953, October. Computing bit by bit or digital computers made easy. *Proceedings of the I.R.E.* 41.10: 1223–1230.

49. Scientific Advisory Board Editorial Committee (Pacific Missile Test Center). 1990. *Years of Challenge, Years of Change: A Technical History of the Pacific Missile Test Center.* Washington, DC: Department of the Navy.

50. Tedre, Matti. 2015. *The science of computing: Shaping a discipline.* Boca Raton: CRC Press.

51. Tedre, M. (2020). From a Black Art to a School Subject: Computing Education's Search for Status. *Proceedings of the 2020 ACM Conference on Innovation and Technology in Computer Science Education,* 3–4. https://doi.org/10.1145/3341525.3394983. Accessed 28 Apr 2021.

52. Truman, Harry S. 1945, August 6. Press release by the White House. Harry S. Truman Library. https://www.trumanlibrary.gov/library/research-files/press-release-white-house?documentid=NA&pagenumber=1. Accessed 29 Oct 2020.

53. von Neumann, John. 1946/1993. First draft of a report on the EDVAC. *IEEE Annals of the History of Computing* 15 (4): 27–43.

54. Ware, Willis H. 1952, August 5. *Letter to Nathaniel Rochester.* Hoboken: IEEE History Center Library Archives. Stevens Institute of Technology.

55. Wayne State University Computation Laboratory. No date. Computation Laboratory records. Wayne State University Library System. http://as.reuther.wayne.edu/repositories/2/resources/345. Accessed 1 May 2021.

Printed in the United States
by Baker & Taylor Publisher Services